INSPIRE / PLAN / DISCOVER / EXPERIENCE

# ROME

# ROME

# CONTENTS

# DISCOVER 6

# EXPERIENCE 60

# NEED TO KNOW 328

This page: The Spanish Steps
Previous: Skyline from the Victor Emmanuel Monument
Front cover: View of Rome from Castel Sant`Angelo

# DISCOVER

St Peter's Square and colonnade

# WELCOME TO
# ROME

With its spectacular piazzas, cascading fountains and exuberant street life, Rome is a Baroque extravaganza begging to be explored. Linger over a Campari Spritz, marvel at world-famous art, immerse yourself in ancient history: whatever your dream trip to Rome includes, this DK Eyewitness Travel Guide is the perfect companion.

1 Detail of *The Coronation of the Virgin* mosaic in Santa Maria Maggiore

2 The Roman Forum

3 Fontana dei Quattro Fiumi on Piazza Navona

Rome brings history to life like no other city. Whether visiting the Colosseum, the temples and basilicas of the Forum, or the Pantheon, you're transported back in time to ancient Rome. At the Baths of Caracalla and Palazzo Valentini digital technology restores ancient ruins to their former glory. Rome's second heyday is evident when you immerse yourself in the Baroque euphoria of Piazza Navona, float down the Spanish Steps, or throw a coin in the Trevi Fountain.

It's not just the city centre that is home to architectural and Roman delights. First, there's the archaeological park and the well-preserved Roman villa of Hadrian in Tivoli. Nearby, Villa d'Este and its gardens are a great example of Renaissance architecture. Then, there are the ancient ruins of Ostia Antica, a prime exemplar of Roman architecture near Pompeii.

However, this city is not just stuck in the past. Explore Rome's cosmopolitan side as you dive into the food markets of Campo de' Fiori and Testaccio and experience the hipster bars and restaurants of Monti and Trastevere.For dramatic modern architecture and art visit Zaha Hadid's MAXXI or MACRO's site in a converted beer factory.

So, with a huge number of ancient sites, museums, churches and galleries, where do you start? We've broken the city down into easily navigable chapters, with detailed itineraries, expert local knowledge and comprehensive maps to help you plan the perfect visit. Whether you're staying for a weekend, a week or longer, this DK Eyewitness Travel Guide will ensure that you see the very best this iconic city has to offer. Enjoy the book, and enjoy Rome.

# REASONS TO LOVE
# ROME

Ancient ruins, Renaissance palaces, Baroque churches, world-famous art, elegant shops and culinary delights: there are so many reasons to love Rome. Here are a few of our favourites.

## 1 MAGNIFICENT SQUARES AND FOUNTAINS

Rome is full of gloriously cinematographic piazzas with cascading fountains, great for people-watching over a coffee.

## ANCIENT MONUMENTS 2

Let your imagination run riot as you explore the myriad ruins of one of the world's most ancient cities - splendid palaces, amphi-theatres and triumphal arches, as well as baths and markets.

## 3 THE APERITIVO

The *aperitivo*, a pre-prandial drink with snacks, is an Italian tradition. Romans love to unwind over a wine, Aperol or Campari Spritz with olives, canapés or a buffet while watching the world go by from a pavement café.

## 4 PIAZZA SAN PIETRO AT DAWN

Designed by Bernini, Piazza San Pietro *(p286)* is one of the most magnificent public spaces in the world. To see it at its best, get up at the crack of dawn.

## DESIGNER SHOPPING 5

Romans would never shop for serious clothes in jeans and trainers, so to truly relish the experience, don your glad rags for an indulgent few hours drifting in and out of boutiques.

## EXCEPTIONAL GELATO 6

On a steamy afternoon or balmy night, strolling the cobbled streets of the *centro storico* with a *coppetta* or *cono* of ice cream is a time-honoured Roman tradition.

### 21ST-CENTURY ROME *7*

Leave history behind for a few hours for contemporary art at the ultra-modern MAXXI, or a jazz or classical concert at Auditorium Parco della Musica *(p318)*.

### THE SISTINE CHAPEL *8*

Standing in the Sistine Chapel, looking up at Michelangelo's immense, iconic frescoes on the ceiling, is one of the most awe-inspiring experiences Rome has to offer *(p294)*.

### *9* SUNSET OVER ROME

Famously built over seven hills, with a skyline defined by the distinctive domes of over 900 churches, Rome has no shortage of viewpoints. The city is most photogenic at sunset.

## ROMAN STREET FOOD 10

Don't leave Rome without trying *pizza bianca* (sprinkled with olive oil and salt). *Supplì* (fried rice balls with fillings) and *polpette di bollito* (meat croquettes) are other staples, best sampled at Testaccio Market *(p51)*.

## UNDERGROUND ROME 11

Head underground through layers of history to discover a hidden city of crypts and catacombs featuring spooky mummies, bone sculptures and sites of pagan sacrifice.

## VILLA BORGHESE 12

The lush expanse of Villa Borghese is Rome's green lung. Great for picnicking, boating on the lake or going for a bike ride, the large park also has several fascinating museums *(p144)*.

Tevere

Villa
Giulia

Villa
Ruffo

VITTORIA

Santa Maria
del Popolo

PRATI

CAMPO
MARZIO

**VATICAN**
*p282*

Vatican
Museums

Castel
Sant'Angelo

BORGO

**PIAZZA
DELLA
ROTONDA**
*p102*

VATICAN
CITY

Piazza
S. Pietro

PONTE

**PIAZZA
NAVONA**
*p120*

St Peters

PARIONE

Piazza
Navona

Pantheon

PIGNA

Campo
de' Fiori

Gesù

**JANICULUM**
*p270*

Villa
Farnesina

Palazzo
Farnese

**CAMPO DE' FIORI**
*p160*

ANGELO

Tevere

Gianicolo

Piazza S.
Apollonia

Villa
Abamelek

Santa Maria
in Trastevere

TRASTEVERE

**TRASTEVERE**
*p256*

Santa
Sabina

Villa
Sciarra

AVENTINE

**AVENTINE**
*p242*

TESTACCIO

# EXPLORE
ROME

This guide divides Rome into
15 colour-coded sightseeing
areas, as shown on this map.
Find out more about each area
on the following pages.

## ITALY

GREAT BRITAIN
NETHER-LANDS
POLAND
BELGIUM
GERMANY
CZECH REPUBLIC
Atlantic Ocean
FRANCE
SWITZ.
AUSTRIA
HUNGARY
Milan •
• Venice
Florence •
ITALY
SPAIN
**ROME**
Sardinia
• Naples
Mediterranean Sea
Sicily

Galleria Nazionale d'Arte Moderna
Galleria Borghese
*Villa Borghese*

**PIAZZA DI SPAGNA AND VILLA BORGHESE**
*p136*

LUDOVISI

SALLUSTIANO

Trinità dei Monti

**VIA VENETO**
*p306*

CASTRO PRETORIO

*Piazza di Spagna*

*Piazza Barberini*

*Piazza della Repubblica*

TREVI

Trevi Fountain

**QUIRINAL AND MONTI**
*p180*

MONTI

Santa Maria Maggiore

**ESQUILINE**
*p200*

SAN LORENZO

*Cimitero Monumentale del Verano*

**CAPITOL**
*p62*

Mercati Traianei

Palazzo Nuovo
Capitoline Museums

Roman Forum

*Parco di Traiano*

ESQUILINO

Palazzo dei Conservatori

*Domus Aurea*

Colosseum

**FORUM AND PALATINE**
*p76*

*Piazza Bocca d. Verità*

San Clemente

**LATERAN**
*p212*

*Parco del Celio*

LATERAN

*Pza. S. Giovanni in Laterano*

PALATINE

*Parco del Circo Massimo*

Santo Stefano Rotondo

San Giovanni in Laterano

RIPA

*Villa Celimontana*

CELIO

*Parco di Porta Capena*

*Piazza Albania*

**CARACALLA**
*p228*

*Parco Egerio*

*Piazzale Ostiense*

*Parco San Sebastiano*

GARBATELLA

| 0 metres | | 800 |
| 0 yards | | 800 |

N

# GETTING TO KNOW
# ROME

Rome's *centro storico*, cradled within a great loop of the Tiber river, is a maze of cobbled streets and piazzas studded with fountains, palaces and churches. It is interrupted by green swathes in which umbrella pines shade the toothy remains of the ancient city. Across the river, the dome of St Peter's dominates the horizon, rising high above Vatican City and the mellow façades and intimate piazzas of Trastevere.

## CAPITOL

PAGE 62

This is the monumental heart of ancient and modern Rome. The white marble behemoth of the Victor Emmanuel Monument, the focus of patriotic ceremonies and political demonstrations, dominates heavily trafficked Piazza Venezia. Behind it, Capitol Hill has been the seat of municipal government since ancient times. Civic marriages still take place in the registry office of the Palazzo del Senatorio, which, together with the Palazzo dei Conservatori and Palazzo Nuovo housing the Capitoline Museums, frame the elegant Piazza del Campidoglio.

**Best for**
Seeing iconic Roman sculptures

**Home to**
The Capitoline Museums

**Experience**
Views of the Roman Forum from the window in the Tabularium of the Capitoline Museums and across the city from the terrace of the Caffetteria dei Musei Capitolini

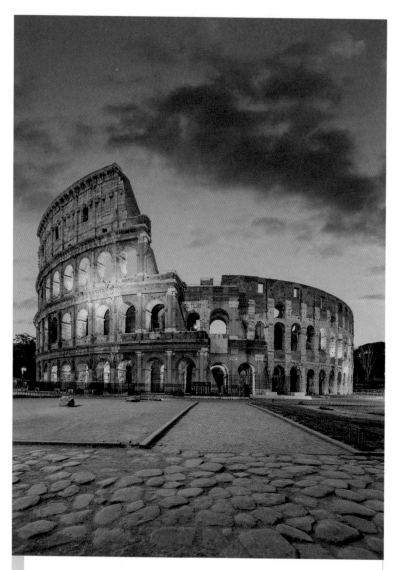

# FORUM AND PALATINE

Mussolini's Via dei Fori Imperiali slices above the ruins of the temples and basilicas that once formed the centre of political, commercial and judicial life in ancient Rome. By day it is peppered with souvenir stands and filled with crocodiles of tourists following umbrella-toting guides around the Roman Forum and Colosseum. Some of the Forum ruins are illuminated at night after the tour groups have left and can be viewed from Via dei Fori Imperiali. Crowds are easier to avoid at all times in the green, pine-shaded expanses of the Palatine Hill.

**Best for**
*Exploring the ruins of ancient Rome*

**Home to**
*Roman Forum; Palatine; Colosseum*

**Experience**
*The Colosseum floodlit at night*

$\rightarrow$

PAGE 102

# PIAZZA DELLA ROTONDA

The compact core of cobbled streets and piazza around the Pantheon is crammed with churches and palaces, restaurants, cafés and enticing *gelaterias*. Businessmen remonstrate into their phones, chauffeurs leap into action as paparazzi pounce on politicians, ice-cream eaters and tourists jam the streets. Hidden in the back streets are fragments from a temple of Isis, shops selling ecclesiastical paraphernalia and the ancient Temple of Hadrian, while the church of Sant'Ignazio di Loyola holds magnificent *trompe l'oeil* frescoes.

**Best for**
*Atmospheric strolling*

**Home to**
*The Pantheon; the Gesù*

**Experience**
*The ice creams of Giolitti or Crema Monteforte gelaterias*

PAGE 120

# PIAZZA NAVONA

An exuberantly Baroque oval dominated by the towering obelisk and cascading waters of Bernini's Fontana dei Quattro Fiumi, Piazza Navona is the social heart of Rome. An outdoor salon fringed with pricey pavement cafés, it is full from morning to night with tourists, Romans, buskers, mime-artists and itinerant street vendors. The picturesque cobbled streets around it are home to places to sleep, eat and drink that run the gamut from super-chic to super-cheap. Antiques shops, vintage clothes stores and some extremely stylish fashion, shoe and design boutiques are found here too.

**Best for**
*Baroque architecture and vibrant streetlife*

**Home to**
*Fontana dei Quattro Fiumi*

**Experience**
*The beauty of Piazza Navona at dawn*

PAGE 136

## PIAZZA DI SPAGNA AND VILLA BORGHESE

The triangle of streets between Piazza del Popolo and Piazza di Spagna are studded with designer boutiques, bijou cosmetics shops, art galleries, antiques shops and upmarket delicatessens. It's an area in which to wander, window-shop and people-watch in between a little leisurely sightseeing. Via del Corso is full of chain shops, transforming into a human river at peak times. For respite, head to the Villa Borghese park, with its green lawns, shady pines, boating lake, museums and cafés.

**Best for**
*Shopping; relaxing in a green space; art treasures*

**Home to**
*Piazza di Spagna; Santa Maria del Popolo; Villa Borghese park and the museums of Galleria Borghese and Villa Giulia*

**Experience**
*An aperitivo on Piazza del Popolo*

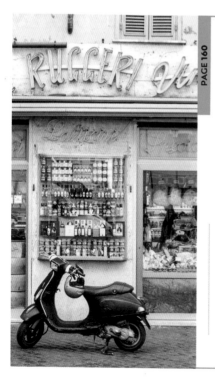

PAGE 160

## CAMPO DE' FIORI

The area between Corso Vittorio Emanuele and the Tiber river, Campo de' Fiori is dominated by the morning food market in Campo de' Fiori itself. In and around the square the neighbourhood's culinary traditions have spawned some of the city's most authentic places to eat Roman food – some long-established and some contemporary. The area gets very lively at sundown, with students, locals and tourists flooding its eateries and bars.

**Best for**
*Soaking up the market atmosphere; strolling along medieval streets lined with artisan shops*

**Home to**
*Campo de' Fiori piazza; frescoes in Palazzo Farnese*

**Experience**
*Crisp pizza bianca fresh from the oven from Antico Forno Roscioli*

$\rightarrow$

PAGE 180

# QUIRINAL AND MONTI

A sprawling zone cut through by traffic-clogged Via Nazionale, Quirinal stretches downhill, encompassing the slopes of the Viminal – dominated by the august façade and sombre denizens of the Ministry of the Interior – and across to the Quirinal Hill. Here the Palazzo del Quirinale, residence of the Italian president, dominates a rather desolate piazza. Rome's most famous fountain, the Trevi, is nearby. For coffee, lunch, shopping or an *aperitivo*, head to the livelier, fashionable Monti district.

**Best for**
*Exploring the streets, shops and cafés of Monti*

**Home to**
*Trevi Fountain; Palazzo Massimo alle Terme (Museo Nazionale Romano); Galleria Colonna*

**Experience**
*Lunch or a drink on Piazza Madonna dei Monti*

PAGE 200

# ESQUILINE

Central Rome's most multicultural quarter and one of the poorer areas of the city, the Esquiline's traffic-filled streets evoke gritty urban shabbiness interspersed with 19th-century elegance. Its most famous sights are the churches, whose interiors are mosaicked like jewellery boxes. This is the place for multi-ethnic dining options – take your pick of Eritrean, Chinese, Indian and Thai eateries. The huge, loud Nuovo Mercato Esquilino market represents all the different cultures here, and is full of the smells and colours of exotic spices and a vast array of international foods.

**Best for**
*International eateries; churches with glittering mosaics*

**Home to**
*Santa Maria Maggiore; Santa Pudenziana; Santa Prassede*

**Experience**
*Eritrean food; multicultural atmosphere*

# LATERAN

PAGE 212

Traditionally a working-class area, the Lateran retains an unpretentious feel, its left-wing traditions and loyalties still evident in the huge free May Day concert organized every year by the trades unions in the central large Piazza di San Giovanni. Modern avenues open out onto beautiful churches – the Lateran is the site of Rome's oldest basilica, San Giovanni. The area is also home to the huge Via Sannio clothes and shoes market.

**Best for**
*Travelling back through three layers of history in San Clemente*

**Home to**
*San Giovanni in Laterano; San Clemente*

**Experience**
*The spooky Mithraeum hidden below San Clemente*

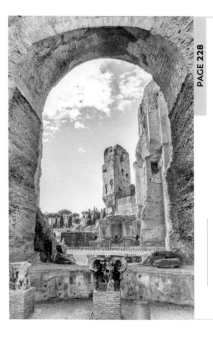

# CARACALLA

PAGE 228

Largely undeveloped except for an immense military hospital and a handful of beguiling churches, the Celian Hill rises, green and tranquil, from the busy thoroughfares that now cut along the valleys at its foot. It's a lovely place to stroll from one little church to the next along quiet roads. The Villa Celimontana park, at its heart, is perfect for a picnic, while anyone who really loves to walk can carry right on beyond the ancient city walls to the Via Appia Antica *(p323)*.

**Best for**
*A quiet stroll on the Celian Hill*

**Home to**
*Baths of Caracalla*

**Experience**
*A summer jazz concert in Villa Celimontana park*

$\rightarrow$

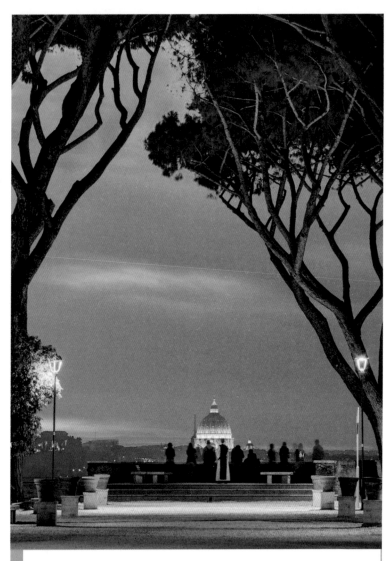

# AVENTINE

Rising above the Tiber river to the southwest of the Palatine, the twin-peaked Aventine Hill is a lush, leafy residential area with a handful of early Christian churches scattered among its secluded villas, gardens and convents. Although in the centre of Rome, it is remarkably peaceful, and for once the sound of birdsong is louder than the roar of traffic. On the far side of the hill, Testaccio, a working-class neighbourhood defined by the huge market at its heart, is one of Rome's trendiest areas and the best place in the city for anyone seriously interested in food.

**Best for**
*Niche fashion and food shops*

**Home to**
*Il Mattatoio; the Pyramid of Caius Cestius; Santa Maria in Cosmedin*

**Experience**
*The takeaway food stalls at the Mercato di Testaccio*

# TRASTEVERE

PAGE 256

With its picturesque, higgledy-piggledy cobbled streets, mellow rose and ochre façades and intimate piazzas, bohemian Trastevere epitomizes a stranger's romantic notion of Rome. Shrines to the Madonna still protect tiny piazzas housing chic bars, restaurants and boutiques. In the evening this district becomes the centre of Rome's liveliest nightlife, with most of the action concentrated around Piazza Santa Maria in Trastevere. The area to the east of Viale di Trastevere is less gentrified, with warehouses dating back to the days when this was the home of the Tiber's dockers.

**Best for**
*Daytime strolling and shopping and night-time bars*

**Home to**
*Santa Maria in Trastevere*

**Experience**
*The centre of Rome's social life*

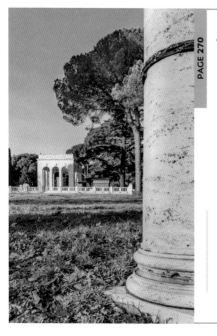

# JANICULUM

PAGE 270

The highest of Rome's hills – though not one of the original seven – the Janiculum is a great place to go for a walk and views of the city, and can be approached from either the Vatican or Trastevere. The main focus is Piazzale Giuseppe Garibaldi, a wide, cobbled space with snack vans and a puppet show booth, at its busiest in the early evening as people gather to watch the sunset over the city. Head to Villa Farnesina for beautiful paintings and frescoes by Raphael and his pupils.

**Best for**
*A bracing walk after a day in the Vatican Museums*

**Home to**
*The Renaissance Villa Farnesina*

**Experience**
*A view of Rome at sunset*

→

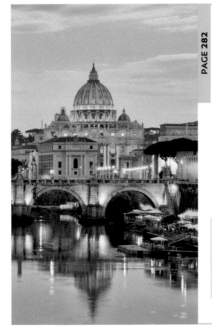

PAGE 282

# VATICAN

With St Peter's basilica, the centre of the Roman Catholic faith, and the Vatican Museums, housing some of the world's greatest art collections, the Vatican is a must for pilgrims and art lovers. The area around the world's smallest sovereign state is full of busy streets lined with souvenir shops selling ecclesiastical memorabilia and hawkers flogging Sistine Chapel T-shirts and plaster Pietàs. Cobbled, pedestrianized Borgo Pio is the most attractive street, retaining some old-world charm and authentic places to eat.

**Best for**
*World-famous art and sculpture*

**Home to**
*St Peter's; the Vatican Museums and Sistine Chapel; Castel Sant'Angelo*

**Experience**
*A Papal Audience on Piazza San Pietro*

PAGE 306

# VIA VENETO

The focus of the decadent and glamorous night scene of the late 1950s and 60s that inspired Fellini's film *La Dolce Vita*, Via Veneto is but a shadow of its former self, though the street retains its elegance and is home to some of the city's most luxurious hotels. The fascinating, though macabre, Capuchin Crypt, with thousands of human bones as well as mummified corpses decorating its walls and ceilings, comes as a surprise underneath the 17th-century Santa Maria della Concezione church.

**Best for**
*Scary skeletal sculptures and mummies*

**Home to**
*The Capuchin Crypt; Palazzo Barberini; Santa Maria della Vittoria*

**Experience**
*A cocktail in Il Giardino rooftop bar at the Hotel Eden*

# BEYOND THE CENTRE

Rome has a small, compact centre – you can walk from one side to the other in a couple of hours – and keen walkers can easily cover some of the city's peripheral sights on foot too. Ranging from Roman catacombs to the 21st-century MAXXI art gallery, and from ancient churches to the futuristic suburb of EUR and fantasy quarter of Coppedè, delving outside the centre not only brings you to sights off the beaten track, but into residential neighbourhoods where you can get a real sense of everyday life in Rome.

**Best for**
Discovering the Art Nouveau architecture of the Coppedè Quarter

**Home to**
Ostia Antica; MAXXI; Villa Ada park; Via Appia Antica

**Experience**
A classical or jazz concert at the Auditorium Parco della Musica; Roma Incontra il Mondo world music festival at Villa Ada in July

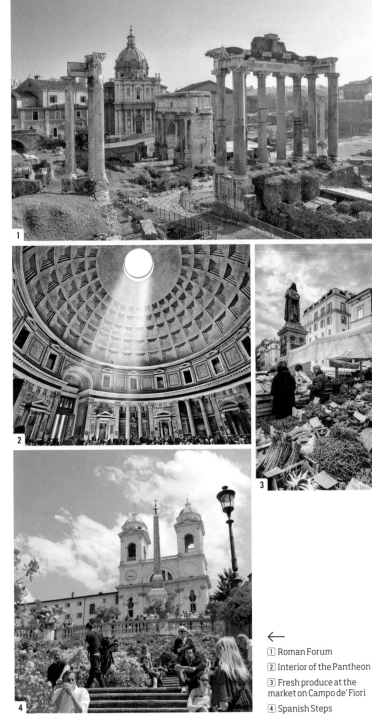

←

[1] Roman Forum

[2] Interior of the Pantheon

[3] Fresh produce at the market on Campo de' Fiori

[4] Spanish Steps

Whether you are in Rome for several days or just want a brief flavour of this great city, these itineraries will help you make the most of your time.

# 24 HOURS

## Morning

Do as the Romans do, and breakfast on a coffee and pastry in a café-bar, while you plot a route by foot or by bus to the Colosseum *(p88)*. Try to get there early – it opens at 8.30am. If the queues are long when you arrive, content yourself with a walk around the building to view its world-famous tiers of arches. Wander past the Roman Forum *(p80)*, and up the Capitoline Hill *(p62)*; pop in to see the breathtaking equestrian statue of Marcus Aurelius in the Capitoline Museums *(p66)*, or just admire the replica in the centre of Michelangelo's Piazza del Campidoglio, before treating yourself to a coffee with sweeping views from the museums' rooftop bar, Caffetteria dei Musei Capitolini. Next, head over to Palazzo Valentini *(p98)* to view the ruins of two Roman houses and see them restored to their former glory as part of an interesting audio-visual presentation, then stroll through the Jewish Ghetto to Campo de' Fiori with its open-air market *(p164)*, stopping for lunch at Ar Galletto restaurant (Piazza Farnese 104).

## Afternoon

Wind across to Piazza Navona *(p124)* to make a circuit of its spectacular fountains before crossing over to visit the Pantheon *(p106)*. Buy an ice cream from Giolitti *(p116)*, then wander the narrow cobbled streets, window-shopping your way to the Trevi Fountain *(p184)*. Head north to Piazza di Spagna *(p140)* to join the crowds on the Spanish Steps, then walk along Via Trinità dei Monti, from where there are sweeping views over the multi-domed skyline of Rome to St Peter's.

## Evening

Reward yourself with an *aperitivo* on the panoramic terrace of Ciampini al Café du Jardin (Piazza Trinità dei Monti), which is open between April and October – it's a bit touristy, but the views at sunset are worth it. In winter, when the café is closed, head back to Piazza di Spagna and join the smart set for a cocktail at the Hotel de Russie's Stravinskij Bar. Then move on to Babette (Via Margutta 3) for a dinner of delicious traditional Italian cuisine.

$\rightarrow$

1 St Peter's Square

2 The Colosseum

3 Pavement tables at a typical café

4 *Rape of Proserpine* by Bernini in Galleria Borghese

# 3 DAYS

## Day 1

**Morning** Get up at dawn for the unforgettable experience of an almost empty Piazza San Pietro, and enter the Basilica, along with nuns, priests and pilgrims, at 7am (p286). The spiral steps winding up inside the shell of the dome to the cupola open at 8am – having the views to yourself is magical. Book a slot to the Vatican Museums online in advance (p291), and take in the glories of the Cortile della Pigna over breakfast in the café. See the Sistine Chapel ceiling, then select your other highlights in the museums, breaking for lunch in the pizzeria outside the Carriage Pavilion.

**Afternoon** Clear your mind with a long, bracing walk up the Janiculum Hill (p270) for fabulous views over the city, winding down past Bramante's Tempietto (p277) into Trastevere (p257) to browse its boutiques. Marvel at the splendid mosaics in the church of Santa Maria in Trastevere (p260).

**Evening** Enjoy a well-earned *aperitivo* on Piazza Santa Maria in Trastevere, followed by dinner at Enoteca Ferrara (p267).

## Day 2

**Morning** Explore the Colosseum (p88), then head to the Palatine (p94). With pine trees shading its slopes and wild flowers surrounding its ruins, this is one of the most evocative of Rome's ancient sites. Don't miss the lovely Farnese Gardens or the surviving section of Emperor Nero's Cryptoporticus tunnel (p96). Walk downhill into the Roman Forum (p80), and see if you can spot the melted coins fused to the pavement of the Basilica Aemilia and the gameboards carved into the steps of Basilica Julia. Treat yourself to lunch at the bistro, La Bottega del Caffè, on Monti's traffic-free Piazza Madonna dei Monti.

**Afternoon** Stroll up past the quirky fashion boutiques of Via dei Serpenti to Trajan's Markets (p92), an ancient Roman shopping mall, and the digitally reconstructed Roman villas below Palazzo Valentini (p98). See superb frescoes at Palazzo Massimo alle Terme (p186).

**Evening** Collapse over a fine glass of wine at the Trimani Il Wine Bar (p192), followed by a dinner of inventive Italian dishes at L'Asino d'Oro (p194).

## Day 3

**Morning** Start with a leisurely caffè latte at the Antico Caffè Vitti on pretty Piazza San Lorenzo in Lucina, then browse the chic shops of Via Campo Marzio, Via del Leone and Piazzetta della Toretta; strike across Piazza del Parlamento to Piazza del Montecitorio – watch politicians and lobbyists coming and going from the parliament building, then zig-zag down to the Pantheon (p106), taking in little Piazza delle Coppelle. See Caravaggio canvasses in San Luigi dei Francesi (p127) and the ingenious courtyard of Sant'Ivo alla Sapienza (p129), then cross Piazza Navona for lunch at Chiostro del Bramante Bistro (Arco della Pace 5).

**Afternoon** Head up to Villa Borghese to see world-famous sculptures by Bernini in the Galleria Borghese (p146), and, if you are not too tired, the incredible Etruscan collection at Villa Giulia (p148).

**Evening** Wind down with an *aperitivo* on the garden terrace of the Galleria d'Arte Nazionale Moderna's Caffè delle Belle Arti (p146), then walk to Dal Pollarolo restaurant for a dinner of local Italian pasta dishes (Via di Ripetta 4–5).

←

1 Ancient ruins of the Baths of Caracalla

2 Hall of Mirrors, Palazzo Doria Pamphilj

3 Bramante's Tempietto

4 Pavement eatery in Trastevere

# 5 DAYS

## Day 1

**Morning** Explore the Forum *(p80)* and walk up through the Imperial ruins of the Palatine Hill *(p94)*. If you are here at the weekend, pick up supplies for sandwiches at the Circo Massimo farmers' market *(p51)*.

**Afternoon** See iconic ancient sculptures at the Capitoline Museums *(p66)*, then head to the Crypta Balbi museum *(p172)*.

**Evening** Stroll through the Jewish Ghetto, stopping for an *aperitivo* at Roscioli, then dine on *cucina romana* at Piperno *(p175)*.

## Day 2

**Morning** Search out traces of the Teatro di Pompeo *(p166)*, then dive underground to see the remains of the Roman stadium beneath Piazza Navona *(p121)*. Take an audio tour through Palazzo Doria Pamphilj *(p116)*, narrated by the current Prince, Jonathan. Treat yourself to lunch in the palazzo's café.

**Afternoon** After marvelling at the dizzying frescoes in Sant'Ignazio di Loyola *(p111)* indulge in some retail therapy on Via Condotti *(p150)*, then visit the room where John Keats spent his final months at the Keats-Shelley Memorial House *(p140)* before seeing the wonderful frescoes in Villa Medici *(p151)*.

**Evening** Enjoy a cocktail and dinner at Doney Café *(p310)* on nearby Via Veneto.

## Day 3

**Morning** Take in the splendour of Santa Maria Maggiore *(p204)*, then pick up picnic supplies at nearby Panella (Via Merulana 59) and stroll through the Colle Oppio park, past the ruins of the Baths of Trajan *(p210)*. Stop off for some time travel through the strata of San Clemente *(p218)* before heading up to the Villa Celimontana park *(p235)* for a picnic.

**Afternoon** Walk over the Celian Hill to visit the Baths of Caracalla *(p232)*. Then catch bus 118 along the Via Appia Antica to the Catacombs of San Callisto and continue on foot to the Tomb of Cecilia Metella *(p323)*.

**Evening** Dine on fine Mediterranean cuisine at Ristorante L'Archeologia (Via Appia Antica 139).

## Day 4

**Morning** Amble past the pretty gardens and villas of the Aventine to Testaccio. After wandering around Monte Testaccio *(p250)* explore the numerous stalls in the Mercato di Testaccio *(p51)*. Lunch on delicious street food at the market.

**Afternoon** Cross the Tiber and stroll along the pine-shaded paths through the Villa Sciarra park *(p266)* to Bramante's Tempietto *(p277)*.

**Evening** Dine on Roman dishes at Antica Pesa (Via Garibaldi 18), followed by a nightcap and live jazz at Big Mama *(p267)*.

## Day 5

**Morning** Explore Villa Borghese park on foot, by bike or by rickshaw, making time for a row on the lake and a visit to Museo Carlo Bilotti *(p145)*. Treat yourself to a lunch of handmade ravioli on the elegant travertine terrace of Galleria Nazionale d'Arte Moderna's Caffè delle Belle Arti *(p146)*.

**Afternoon** Visit the Galleria Borghese *(p146)* before walking through the Salaria neighbourhood to Coppedè for some fanciful architecture *(p319)*. Take tram 3 from nearby Piazza Buenos Aires back into town to Trastevere – the ideal neighbourhood in which to spend your last evening in Rome.

**Evening** Sip a Prosecco accompanied by live music at Ombre Rosse *(p267)*, then head to Antico Arco *(p277)* for a gourmet dinner.

### ▽ Ancient Frescoes

Head to Palazzo Massimo alle Terme *(p188)* to see the exquisite frescoes of garden scenes from the house of Emperor Augustus's wife Livia. A sense of the role that art played in the lives of more ordinary Romans can be seen at Ostia Antica in the frescoes depicting carrots and chickpeas on the wall of a bar *(p317)*.

### △ Early Christian Mosaics

Mosaic reached its zenith in the 6th–9th centuries as Rome fell under the influence of Byzantine art. See one of the finest mosaics in Rome in the apse of Santa Cecilia in Trastevere *(p266)*, a superb example of 9th-century Byzantine style.

# ROME FOR
# ART LOVERS

As a power-centre first of the Roman Empire and then of the Catholic Church Rome has always been a magnet for those with immense wealth and ambition. Over the centuries emperors, popes and aristocrats have displayed their riches by commissioning works from the greatest artists of their time.

### △ Renaissance Masterpieces

Many major artists of the Renaissance were attracted to Rome. For some of the most splendid art, see the frescoes on the Sistine Chapel ceiling created by Michelangelo for Pope Julius II and Pope Paul III Farnese *(p294)*. Head to Villa Farnesina for glorious mythological frescoes painted by Raphael for super-wealthy banker Agostino Chigi.

## ▽ Early Baroque Painting

Caravaggio worked for both church and aristocracy in Rome, often introducing an iconoclastic secularism to religious works. Look out for the sexualized angel and the very realistic depiction of trees, leaves and stones in *The Flight to Egypt* in the art gallery in Palazzo Doria Pamphilj *(p116)*.

## ▷ Baroque Flamboyance

Rome's wealth and power were at their height in the late 17th century, propelling a massive restyling of the city. Hundreds of churches, palaces and piazzas were redesigned in a flamboyant Baroque style. Look out in particular for magnificent fountains, many designed by Bernini, such as the Fontana del Tritone, which pepper the centre of the city. To see some of Bernini's most ground-breaking, emotive sculptures, created for Cardinal Scipione Borghese, visit the Galleria Borghese *(p146)*.

## △ Modern and Contemporary Art

For 20th-century art, head to Galleria Nazionale d'Arte Moderna *(p146)*, which has works by De Chirico, such as *Spettacolo Misterioso* (1971), and by the Italian Futurists. Museo Carlo Bilotti *(p145)* also has paintings by De Chirico. For contemporary art, visit the futuristic MAXXI *(p318)*.

---

**TOP 5 ARTISTS IN ROME**

**Michelangelo**
Remarkable sculptor, painter and architect

**Raphael**
Supreme painter of the High Renaissance

**Caravaggio**
Pioneer of dramatic Baroque painting

**Bernini**
Architect and the leading sculptor of his age

**Artemisia**
She painted women from myths and the Bible.

### Coffee

The average Italian visits simple café-bars at least twice a day - for breakfast and after lunch. Around Piazzas Navona, Spagna and Rotonda, ordinary café-bars are scarce, but there is one on almost every street corner elsewhere. Most Italians drink while standing up at the bar. For an authentic coffee experience, try Bar del Cappuccino on Via Arenula 50.

←

Traditional way of drinking coffee, standing at the bar

# ROME FOR
# FOODIES

There are few more enduring pleasures than lingering over a leisurely al fresco meal in a piazza in the Eternal City. Roman food is tasty, nutritious, simple and extremely varied. Menus tend to be seasonal and food is redolent of aromatic herbs, olive oil, garlic and onion.

### INSIDER TIP
### Gelato

Legend has it that the art of ice-cream making was brought to Sicily in the 16th century by its medieval Arab rulers who introduced the technique of blending fruit syrups and flower essences with snow taken from the slopes of Mount Etna. Gourmet ice creams made with organic ingredients have taken Rome by storm - try the delicious offerings at San Crispino *gelateria* on Via della Panetteria 42.

### Traditional Roman Dishes

Originating in working-class areas such as Testaccio, traditional Roman food is based on cheap cuts of meat and offal and simple pasta dishes such as *cacio e pepe* (pecorino cheese and black pepper). *Carciofi alla giudia* (deep-fried artichokes) is a key delicacy introduced by the Jewish community of the Ghetto.

→

A traditional Roman restaurant on Via Arco di San Calisto in Trastevere

↑ *Aperitivo* drinks at a pavement bar in Trastevere

## EAT

Dine on creative dishes at one of Rome's chic new-wave eateries.

**Casa Coppelle**
This Franco-Roman restaurant offers a tempting range of dishes. The rack of lamb is a highlight.

🗺 U2 📍 Piazza delle Coppelle 49
🌐 casacoppelle.com

€€€

**Bistrot64**
One of the most affordable Michelin-starred restaurants in Italy, Bistrot64 specializes in flavours inspired by Italy and Japan.

📍 Via G Calderini 62/64
🌐 bistrot.it

€€€

## Aperitivo and Wine Bars

The *aperitivo*, a pre-dinner glass of wine, Aperol or Campari Spritz, served with snacks, is a tradition rooted in northern cities such as Turin and Milan, but is very popular in Rome too. At the very least there will be crisps, olives and peanuts to accompany the drinks, but often there are abundant buffets such as the one in Vin Allegro in Trastevere on Piazza Giuditta Tavani Arquati.

## Food to Take Away

Hot takeaway food has been a feature of Italian life since Roman times. Taste hot focaccia dripping with Ligurian olive oil or a slice of pizza fresh from the oven *(pizza a taglio)*, topped with anchovies and *puntarelle* (chicory shoots) or courgette flowers and ricotta, available at bakeries. Enjoy aubergine parmigiana (fried aubergines with cheese and tomato sauce) or herby roast chicken and golden-crusted savoury pies at *rosticceria*.

Entrance to Antico Forno Roscioli, *(inset)* chefs preparing *pizza a taglio* ↑

### ▽ Interactive Tour of Roman Houses Under Palazzo Valentini
Computer technology, light and sound effects, films and projections reconstruct the remains of two grand Roman villas discovered beneath Palazzo Valentini *(p98)*.

### △ Family Audio Guide at the Vatican Museums
Explore the collections of the Vatican's museums *(p290)* by renting the Family Audioguide, which is engagingly narrated by a series of characters ranging from an angel to a grumpy Michelangelo. For a break, head to the museum's pizzeria.

# ROME FOR
# FAMILIES

With its spectacular ancient ruins, Egyptian obelisks, and theatrical piazzas and fountains, Rome is a city that brings history to life like no other. Peppered with parks, ice cream parlours and takeaway pizzerias, it is also a fun city for families, with children made welcome everywhere.

### △ Gladiator School
W gruppostoricoromano.it
Learn how to fight like a gladiator in a re-created arena at Via Appia Antica 18. Lessons are held by members of a historical re-enactment society.

## ▽ Cycling the Appia Antica
🌐 parcoappiaantica.it

Encompassing open countryside, the Parco Regionale dell'Appia Antica makes for a great day trip. The park rents out bikes and toddler seats. Go on a Sunday, when there are often kids' events, including nature trails, insect-spotting and bird-watching.

### Did You Know?

All kids under the age of 18 get free entry to national museums.

## ▷ Places to Let Off Steam

Rome's piazzas are great fun to run around in. Head to the huge Piazza Navona, where there is always something going on - from street mime to fire-jugglers to the annual Christmas fair and carnival. It is also home to one of Rome's best toy shops, Al Sogno (no. 53). For playgrounds, head to Villa Borghese (p144), where bikes can be hired, Parco Adriano (p286), Villa Celimontana (p235) and the huge Villa Doria Pamphilj (p327).

## ▽ Technotown
📍 J5 🏠 Via Lazaro Spallanzani 1A
🕐 9am-7pm Tue-Sun
🌐 technotown.it

Experiment with 3D printers, a camera obscura, photography and film effects at this small science museum. Don't miss the Lego laboratory, where kids (and adults) can create robots.

## △ Baths of Caracalla

Experience one of the biggest and most spectacular baths complexes in ancient Rome through virtual reality headsets (p232). The complex is surrounded by grass and umbrella pines - ideal for a run-around.

## Modern Rome

The 20th century opened in Rome with the Art Nouveau fantasies of the Coppodè Quarter (p319), followed by Futuristic - even dystopian - EUR, founded by Mussolini (p323). Watch out too for buildings designed by contemporary international architects, such as Renzo Piano's Auditorium Parco della Musica and Zaha Hadid's MAXXI (p318). See ancient sculptures juxtaposed with the turbines of a former power plant at Centrale Montemartini (p325).

MAXXI contemporary art museum, designed by Zaha Hadid ↓

# ROME'S
# ARCHITECTURE

Explore Rome on an incredible journey through the history of Western architecture. Ancient Roman relics are strewn throughout the city cheek-by-jowl with medieval basilicas, Renaissance palaces and extravagant Baroque piazzas, churches and fountains.

## Ancient Rome

The architects of Imperial Rome combined the Classical styles of ancient Greece with innovative new forms such as the arch, the vault and the dome. Visit the Pantheon to see the world's largest unreinforced concrete dome. Note the three storeys of Doric, Ionic and Corinthian columns on the Colosseum, imitated in façades of palaces and churches throughout the world.

The Colosseum, a
↓ prime example of
ancient architecture

## Christian Rome

The first places of worship were simply houses belonging to Christians or sites of martyrdoms. Visit San Crisogono *(p263)* to see the excavations of a private home that was used as an early Christian church. The first purpose-built churches were based on the Roman basilica, with three naves and an apse. To see Rome's main basilicas, visit St Peter's *(p286)*, San Giovanni in Laterano *(p216)* and Santa Maria Maggiore *(p204)*. More flamboyant Baroque innovations are Sant'Ivo alla Sapienza *(p129)* and San Carlo alle Quattro Fontane *(p192)*, designed by Borromini, and Bernini's Sant'Andrea al Quirinale *(p191)*.

### THE LAYERS OF SAN CLEMENTE

Around 200 AD an aristrocrat built a temple to the god Mithras in the central room of his house. In the 4th century the temple and house were filled in, and a church dedicated to Christian martyr San Clemente was built on top. In the 12th century this was filled with rubble to form the foundation for yet another church.

↑ St Peter's, one of the world's most iconic churches

### Renaissance and Baroque Rome

Rome is an extravaganza of Baroque piazzas, fountains and stairways, and enticing glimpses of frescoed ceilings through the windows of vast noble palaces. For spectacular views of Rome's buildings and piazzas, take a walk at night to see them lit up in the dark. The interiors of Palazzo Doria Pamphilj *(p116)*, Galleria Borghese *(p146)* and Villa Farnesina *(p274)* give a wonderful taste of glamour.

↑ The Baroque Palazzo Doria Pamphilj and *(inset)* its entrance

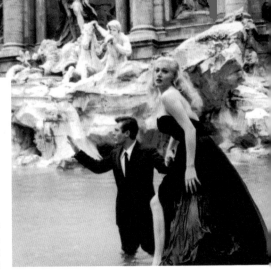

**La Dolce Vita
(Federico Fellini, 1960)**
A paparazzo, played by Marcello Mastroianni, looks for love among the decadent nightlife of Rome in this iconic Fellini film. In a famous scene, Anita Ekberg, playing a Swedish film star, takes a dip in the Trevi fountain.

→

Anita Ekberg and Marcello Mastroianni in the Trevi Fountain in *La Dolce Vita*

# ROME FOR
# INSPIRATION

Home of the Roman Empire and a major centre of the Renaissance, Rome has captured the imagination of many great writers and film makers. Trace the steps of some of the most famous films and books set in Rome.

## ON THE PAGE

### Lord Byron (1788-1824)
Byron's experiences in Rome in 1817 were the inspiration for several episodes in his epic poem *Childe Harold's Pilgrimage*. The Tomb of Cecilia Metella inspired the line: "But who was she, the lady of the dead, Tomb'd in a palace?"

### Edith Wharton (1862-1937)
Edith Wharton's short story *Roman Fever,* published in 1934, is set in Rome. The Forum is described as the "accumulated wreckage of passion and splendour", acting as a metaphor for the main characters.

### Dan Brown (1964- )
In Dan Brown's best-selling thriller *Angels and Demons*, published in 2000, a cardinal is murdered in the church of Santa Maria della Vittoria and another is drowned in the Fontana dei Quattro Fiumi.

## Charles Dickens
Charles Dickens visited Rome in 1844-45, witnessing an execution, Carnival, an Easter ceremony in which the Pope washed the feet of 13 men and a fireworks display at Castel Sant' Angelo. He published an account of his travels in *Pictures from Italy* in 1846.

Fireworks at Castel Sant'Angelo during Sts Peter and Paul celebrations ↑

## Roman Holiday
### (William Wyler, 1953)

Starring Audrey Hepburn as a princess and Gregory Peck as an American journalist, *Roman Holiday* gives a sightseeing tour of Rome, featuring Vespa-riding and romantic scenes at the Colosseum, Trevi Fountain and Spanish Steps.

↓ Audrey Hepburn riding a scooter in *Roman Holiday*

ON FILM

### Roma
### (Federico Fellini, 1972)

Fellini's surreal and ironic *homage* to his adopted city features a bizarre fashion show in the Vatican with outrageously dressed priests and nuns on the catwalk.

### L'Eclisse
### (Michelangelo Antonioni, 1962)

Starring Monica Vitti and Alain Delon, this disturbing film about a doomed love affair opens with Vitti splitting up with her lover in the deserted streets of EUR.

### The Bicycle Thieves
### (Vittorio De Sica, 1948)

This film centres on a desperate father searching the markets of Rome for his stolen bicycle (without which he will be unable to work). Rubbish collectors give him a lift across the Tiber to Porta Portese.

### Eat Pray Love
### (Ryan Murphy, 2010)

Julia Roberts plays author Elizabeth Gilbert, who comes to Rome to rediscover the joy of eating after the breakup of her marriage. She wanders through the city, indulging in gastronomic delicacies.

## John Keats

In 1820 Keats rented a house with his friend Joseph Severn at the foot of the Spanish Steps, where he died of consumption the following year, aged only 25. His death inspired Shelley's poem, *Adonaïs*. Visit the house where Keats lived, now a museum containing original letters and other mementoes, including those of fellow romantic poets, notably Percy Bysshe Shelley.

↑ The Keats-Shelley Museum, on Piazza di Spagna

## Classical Concerts, Ballet and Theatre

The Auditorium Parco della Musica (p318) is a much-loved focus of Rome's music scene. Many churches also host classical concerts, while Teatro Olimpico on Piazza Gentile da Fabriano 17 is Rome's principal venue for modern dance. Main theatres include Teatro Palladium on Piazza Bartolomeo Romano 8 and Teatro Argentina (p170).

←

Classical music concert at Auditorium Parco della Musica

# ROME
# AFTER DARK

An after-dark *passeggiata* taking in the lively street life of the historic centre is hard to beat, with bars and cafés galore to choose from. In summer ancient sites, parks and piazzas become outdoor theatres for live music, while throughout the year there is a packed programme of theatre and festivals.

## Opera

A highlight of Rome's opera scene is the sheer spectacle of the summer open-air operas at the Baths of Caracalla (p232). The main season runs from November to January at the Teatro dell'Opera, moving outdoors in July and August. Book tickets online at www.operaroma.it.

↓ Verdi's opera *Nabucco* at the Baths of Caracalla

## ESTATE ROMANA

Rome's summer-long cultural festival (p52) includes pop-up bars and restaurants along the banks of the Tiber – an atmospheric place to spend an evening.

Outdoor dining after dark on Piazza Navona ↓

## Street and Piazza Life

One of the most enjoyable things to do in Rome at night is simply to stroll through the historic centre, around Piazza Navona, Piazza di Spagna, Campo de' Fiori and Trastevere, while people-watching, window-shopping and pausing for a drink in a pavement café. Many shops around Piazza Navona stay open late, while Piazza Navona itself becomes a magnet for mime artists and other street performers.

## Rock and Jazz

Jazz, indie rock and world-music artists perform frequently at the Auditorium Parco della Musica, while mainstream mega concerts are staged in sports arenas such as the Palalottamatica on Piazzale Pier Luigi Nervi 1 and Stadio Olimpico on Viale dei Gladiatori.

←

Jazz musicians performing in the street in summer

## Street Festivals

Rome has a venerable tradition of street celebrations, many with their origins in religious festivals, others born of left-wing politics, notably in the working class San Giovanni area, where the free pop concerts on 1 May and 24 June are a Rome institution. New Year is ushered in with fireworks and free concerts, while Chinese New Year sees stunning fireworks on Piazza del Popolo.

→

New Year fireworks at the Colosseum

# ROME FOR
# SHOPPERS

In Rome, haute couture and chic boutiques rub shoulders with artisans' studios and small neighbourhood shops. Have fun exploring designer stores, large emporia and crafts workshops. The most interesting shops are in the old centre, so you can combine shopping with sightseeing.

**Laura Biagiotti**
Rome's queen of classic couture specializes in knitwear and silk.

**Silvia Venturini Fendi**
The only family member still working at the Fendi fashion house is famous for designing the iconic baguette bag.

**Stella Jean**
A fusion of Italian style with Caribbean themes reflects Stella Jean's Creole heritage.

**Valentino**
A high priest of fashion, Valentino is famous for stunning evening wear.

## Leather

Gucci (Via dei Condotti 8), Fendi (Largo Goldoni 420) and Ferragamo (Via dei Condotti 65) have beautiful boutiques in Rome, as do trendy mid-range brands such as Mandarina Duck (Via dei Due Macelli 59). For more artisanal leather goods, try Ibiz (Via dei Chiavari 39) near Campo de' Fiori, La Sella (Via della Cuccagna 16), or have a pair of glamorous, bejewelled Capri-style sandals made to measure at Di San Giacomo (Via Tor di Millina 10/11 off Piazza Navona).

Shelves stacked with leather gloves in a vast array of colours ↑

## Designer Fashion

The meccas are Valentino and Fendi, occupying entire palazzi on Piazza di Spagna 35/38 and Largo Goldoni 420, respectively. Queen of cashmere Laura Biagiotti's flagship store is at Via Belsiana 57 near Piazza di Spagna. Via Condotti, Via Frattina and Via Borgognona are lined with other international fashion designer boutiques, all with jaw-dropping window displays.

← Famous fashion street Via dei Condotti, with Gucci's flagship store and other major designer boutiques

### INSIDER TIP
### Shopping Areas

Head to Via del Corso and Via Cola di Rienzo for high-street chains; Via dei Condotti and the pedestrianized streets off Piazza di Spagna for big-name designers; and Monti and Trastevere for vintage, alternative and new designers. COIN (Via Cola di Rienzo) and Rinascente (Via del Tritone) are Rome's main department stores.

## Jewellery

Traditional artisan goldsmiths and silversmiths work to order in tiny studios concentrated in the old Jewish Ghetto and around Campo de' Fiori, on Via Giulia and Piazza Monte di Pietà. For classic designer jewellery, visit Rome's oldest jewellery house, Massoni (Via Margutta 54A). For costume jewellery head to Granuzzo at Via dei Coronari 193 or Nicotra di San Giacomo at Via del Governo Vecchio 128.

← Window display of fine jewellery at a shop in the centre of Rome

## Antiques and Memorabilia

The cream of antiques shops are concentrated in Via dei Coronari, the historic centre of the antiques trade, and Via Margutta and Via del Babuino, known for their fine art galleries. Via Giulia also has high-end antiques shops, while the parallel Via Monserrato and nearby Via dei Banchi Vecchi are worth scouring for more affordable pieces.

↑ Comics Bazar, crammed full of antiques, at Via dei Banchi Vecchi 127

### Foro Italico

Visit the Stadio dei Marmi, the stadium of the Fascist-era Foro Italico, built by Mussolini in the vain hope of securing the 1944 Olympic Games. Equally chilling and kitsch, the stadium is surrounded by 60 colosssal, idealized statues of athletes *(see p324)*.

Stadio dei Marmi, part of the Fascist-era Foro Italico ↑

## ROME
# OFF THE
# BEATEN TRACK

There are a host of lesser known sights and neighbourhoods all over Rome that will allow you to experience the city like a local. Get away from the crowds and discover a different, more unusual side of Rome.

### EUR

Built by Mussolini in the 1930s to show the world an ideal Fascist metropolis, EUR is not merely one of the most Futuristic places of 20th-century Europe, but is also home to the Museo della Civiltà, with a reconstructed room from Ostia Antica *(p323)*, and an Olympic-sized swimming pool *(p324)*. The stark Palazzo della Civiltà del Lavoro now houses the headquarters of Fendi.

←

Palazzo della Civiltà del Lavoro, EUR, an icon of Fascist architecture

## Gardens on the Aventine Hill

Escape the crowds in the small picturesque gardens on the Aventine Hill, such as the Rose Garden (Roseto Comunale di Roma) and Parco Savello (also known as Giardino degli Aranci), with its orange trees and beautiful views of St Peter's.

→
St Peter's seen from Parco Savello on the Aventine Hill

# EAT

Italy's links with its former colonies, Eritrea and Ethiopia, have led to restaurants in Rome from the Horn of Africa.

### Enqutatash
Seasoned dishes served with spiced wine.

⌂ Viale della Stazione Prenestina 55
☎ 06-273767

€ €€

---

### Mesob
Feast on spicy vegetable and pulse dishes with flatbread.

⌂ Via Prenestina 118
ⓦ mesob.it

€ €€

Unusual, elaborate architecture in the
↓ Quartiere Coppedè

💬 INSIDER TIP
**Craft Beer**

World-famous for wine, Italy also produces superb craft beer. Beer aficionados should seek out Open Baladin (Via degli Specchi 6) in the Campo de' Fiori area, which has over 40 craft and 200 bottled beers, or L'Oasi della Birra (Piazza Testaccio 38/41), a bar and restaurant serving craft and vintage beers.

## Quartiere Coppedè

To see part of Rome that few people imagine, head to the little cluster of upscale streets between Piazza Buenos Aires and Via Tagliamento, and discover a perfectly preserved quarter of fantastic villas and fairytale palaces created by architect Gino Coppedè in the early 20th century, influenced by Art Nouveau, medieval and Baroque styles *(p319)*.

St Peter's dome and Rome's rooftops seen from above ↓

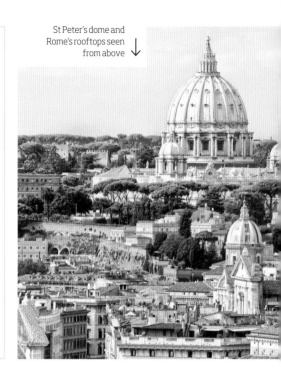

# ROME
# ON A SHOESTRING

Although expensive, Rome's historic centre is compact, so it can mostly be seen on foot. Ancient sites, piazzas, palace façades and beautiful parks can be enjoyed without spending any money, while the city's churches are free to enter.

### Food and Drink

Rome is full of marvellous delicatessens, bakeries and takeaway pizzerias where you can get fabulous food for a fraction of the prices charged in cafés and restaurants. Parks make good locations for picnics. Look out for bars advertising *aperitivo* or "happy hours", where you pay a set price for a drink and can help yourself from an ample buffet. To save money at other times, order and drink at the bar to avoid paying for table service.

Selection of salamis at a ↓ delicatessen

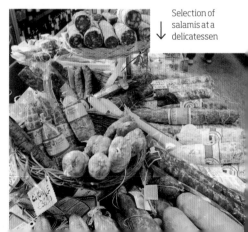

## Sights and Views

The Pantheon is the only one of Rome's ancient monuments to which entry is free, thanks to having been converted into a church in the Byzantine era. Many visitors find the Colosseum more impressive from without than within. Entry to the Victor Emmanuel Monument – with some of the best views in Rome – is free, though to see the view from the very top you have to pay a small fee for the lift. There are other great city views from the Pincio Gardens and Janiculum Hill. There is no charge to get close to Trajan's Column – use the zoom on your phone or camera to see details of the marble carving up close. Access to St Peter's is free, allowing you to see famous works such Michelangelo's *Pietà* and Bernini's Baldacchino.

💬 INSIDER TIP
**Free Entry to Museums**

State and city museums are free for all visitors who are under the age of 18. The Vatican Museums are free for everybody on the last Sunday of every month.

↑ Mosaics of a blue-and-gold-walled heaven in the apse of Santa Prassede

## Art

See Michelangelo's muscular *Moses* masterpiece for free at San Pietro in Vincoli. Marvel at magnificent Byzantine mosaics in Santa Prassede. Entering the church's tiny Chapel of St Zeno is akin to walking into a jewel box. Although entry is charged for exhibitions at MAXXI and MACRO, there are usually free video presentations, and large parts of the buildings, such as MACRO Peroni's roof terrace, can be entered for no charge.

↑ MACRO contemporary art gallery, converted from a former Peroni beer factory

### ▽ Campo de' Fiori
**⊙ T4 ⊙ 7am-1:30pm Mon-Sat**

This market has been held in Campo de' Fiori for centuries. The piazza is transformed by stalls selling fruit and vegetables, all beautifully displayed. The piazza's excellent delicatessens and bakery complement the market, making it a great place to pick up supplies for a picnic.

# ROME FOR
# MARKETS

Soak up the vibrant atmosphere of Rome's numerous markets, ranging from those on small neighbourhood piazzas designed to serve local residents to the large, famous Testaccio and Porta Portese markets.

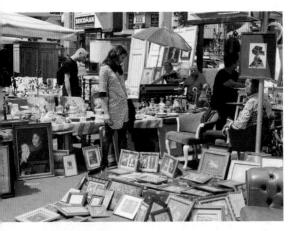

### △ Porta Portese
**⊙ F8 ⊡ Piazza di Porta Portese ⊙ 7am-2pm Sun**

Said to have grown out of the thriving black market of World War II, Porta Portese is where anything and everything seems to be for sale, from vintage and new clothes, shoes, prints and books to chandeliers, household linens and other housewares.

## NEIGHBOURHOOD MARKETS

### Piazza delle Coppelle
**⊙ U2 ⊙ 7am-2pm Mon-Sat**

With its fruit and flower stalls, Piazza delle Coppelle, near the Pantheon, is probably the most delightful of the small food markets scattered around Rome.

### Piazza San Cosimato
**⊙ F7 ⊙ 6am-1:30pm Mon-Sat**

In the heart of Trastevere, this market has abundant fruit and vegetables and excellent cheeses, hams and salamis.

### ▽ Circo Massimo Farmers' Market
**� H7 ⌂ Via di San Teodoro ⌚ 8am–3pm Sat & Sun**

A mecca for foodies, this market attracts niche producers from all over central Italy. It has artisan cheeses, hams, craft breads and beers and unusual pulses, vegetables and fruits.

### △ Mercato delle Stampe
**⊙ U1 ⌂ Largo della Fontanella di Borghese ⌚ 7am–1pm Mon–Sat**

A treasure-trove for lovers of old prints, books, magazines, comics and other printed ephemera, this market is a fabulous place to seek out a special souvenir of Rome, such as a Piranesi reproduction of your favourite vista, ruin or church.

### ▷ Nuovo Mercato Esquilino
**⊙ M6 ⌂ Via Principe Amedeo ⌚ 7am–2pm Mon–Sat**

Housed in purpose-built covered premises, this remains the most authentic of Rome's markets – where locals come for kilos of fruit and vegetables at knock-down prices. It is also the best place in Rome to seek out international ingredients and spices, with African and Asian stalls catering to the area's diverse community.

### ◁ Mercato di Testaccio
**⊙ G9 ⌂ Via Lorenzo Ghiberti ⌚ 7am–3:30pm Mon–Sat**

Locals flock here to purchase the freshest ingredients. Visit at lunchtime to sample everything from traditional tripe sandwiches to gourmet morsels by top chefs as you go.

# A YEAR IN
# ROME

**As you would expect from the home of the Roman Catholic church, Rome celebrates Christian festivals with a bang. But, as well as Easter and Christmas, the city's calendar is punctuated by springtime sporting events, summer foodie festivals and winter music gigs.**

## Spring

After the excitement of Christmas and the New Year has passed, Romans hunker down. Sporting events and indoor concerts pass the time as temperatures steadily climb and the days draw longer. Easter marks the beginning of the tourist season, with Catholics flocking to St Peter's for the Pope's Easter Sunday address, while the less devout take advantage of the mild weather.

*1. Italy's national rugby team competing in a Six Nations match*

## Summer

This is the season to get outdoors. Throughout the summer, pop-up stalls, cafés and restaurants line the banks of the River Tiber, and open-air concerts, cinema screenings and dance festivals take over the city's piazzas and ancient ruins.

### SPORTING EVENTS

Romans have a long history of enjoying sport, beginning with the gladiator games in the 1st century AD. Highlights of the sporting calendar include Six Nations rugby matches in spring, the Piazza di Siena summer horse show and the Rally di Roma car race in July.

As daytime temperatures soar, festivities are relegated to nighttime. On La Notta di San Lorenzo, on 10 August, Romans flock to the Pincio Gardens to catch sight of meteor showers.

*2. Summertime stalls lining the River Tiber*

## Autumn

For much of September, it's still warm enough to sit outside for lunch and – this being harvest time – menus are filled with local produce, including cheeses, chestnuts and, of course, wines. As the nights get steadily chillier, art, film and music festivals move indoors. With the arrival of All Saints' Day on 1 November, winter seems right around the corner.

*3. A street seller roasting chestnuts in the city centre*

## Winter

The run-up to Christmas is magical. *Presepi* (manger scenes) are set up in many churches and piazzas, and from mid-December to Twelfth Night, Piazza Navona hosts a buzzing market, with colourful stalls and a dizzying carousel. Christmas itself is a family event, but New Year's Eve is one big party – free concerts take place throughout the city and everyone takes to the streets to drink sparkling wine and watch the fireworks.

*4. The Christmas market in Piazza Navona, and (inset) New Year's Eve fireworks above the Castel Sant'Angelo*

TOP **5** **CHRISTIAN EVENTS**

**La Befana (Epiphany)**
The Christmas witch brings presents to children on 6 January.

**Carnival**
Dressing up, parties and pranks in February.

**Easter Week**
Good Friday procession at the Colosseum and Easter Sunday blessing from St Peter's balcony.

**Madonna della Neve**
Commemorating a papal vision, a sound-and-light show at Santa Maria Maggiore ends in a "snow-storm" of white petals on 5 August.

**Christmas**
At noon on 25 December, the Pope gives a blessing on Piazza San Pietro.

3

4

# A BRIEF
# HISTORY

Retaining layers of buildings spanning over two millennia, Rome has been continuously inhabited since it was founded. As the headquarters of the Roman Empire and then of the Catholic Church, the city has played a leading role in history, not just of Europe, but the entire world.

### The Beginning

Rome began as an Iron-Age village in the mid-8th century BC, founded according to legend by twin brothers, Romulus and Remus. In 616 BC the Etruscans seized power and dominated the Italian peninsula. In 509 BC the Roman people rebelled and founded a Republic. Over the centuries Rome fought its way south into North Africa; by 146 BC it was the biggest power in the world.

Julius Caesar emerged as a formidable military leader, and, in 44 BC, was declared "dictator of Rome for life". Appalled to see power in the hands of a single individual, a group of Republicans led by Brutus and Cassius assassinated Caesar that same year.

1 Painting of the Colosseum (c 1842)

2 The She-Wolf, Capitoline Museums

3 Illustration of Emperor Augustus riding in procession through the streets of Rome

4 Mosaic of Emperor Constantine I (c 274–337)

## Timeline of events

**753 BC**
Legendary foundation of Rome by brothers Romulus and Remus.

**616 BC**
Etruscans seize power in Rome.

**44 BC**
Julius Caesar is assassinated on 15 March in the Curia of Pompey.

**509 BC**
Etruscans expelled and Roman Republic founded.

**27 BC**
Augustus becomes Emperor.

## The Age of Augustus

The murder of Caesar threw Rome into turmoil. Caesar's deputy, Mark Antony, joined forces with Caesar's adopted son, Octavian, and defeated an army led by Brutus and Cassius. Civil war raged on until 27 BC, when Octavian, now known as Augustus, became Rome's first emperor. Augustus ruled for 40 years, transforming Rome from "a city of brick to a city of marble", creating the first Imperial Forum, and filling the Campus Martius (now the *centro storico*) with temples, theatres and monuments.

## The Fall of Rome

After years of prosperity the sheer logistics of keeping such a large empire running was taking its toll. By the 3rd century AD, Rome was falling apart and Christianity was on the rise. Emperor Diocletian had hundreds of Christians killed as he attempted to extinguish the religion. But Christianity flourished, and in AD 313 Emperor Constantine became a Christian himself and shifted the capital of the Empire to Byzantium. In AD 455 and 475 Rome was attacked by Goths and Vandals, the city decayed, the population shrank and disease was rife. The glory days seemed over for ever.

### ROMAN WOMEN

In ancient Rome, women were granted little power, although Rome itself was created by vestal virgin Rea Silvia. A woman's role was to look after the home. Widow Cornelia (c 200 BC) exemplifies the perfect Roman matron. She refused to marry the future King of Egypt, Tolomaeus, to educate her 12 children instead. Later, she established a literary salon in her home near Amalfi.

**AD 313**
Emperor Constantine declares Christianity to be the official religion of the Roman Empire.

**AD 537**
Rome's aqueducts destroyed by Goths. Population drops by 90 percent.

**AD 608**
The Pantheon is converted into a Christian church.

**AD 64**
Fire destroys much of Rome - Emperor Nero is blamed.

**AD 410**
Rome attacked by Goths for the first time.

## The Rise of the Papacy

In the 7th century Pope Gregory the Great turned Rome's fortunes around, sending out missionaries to spread the word of the Church, and drawing hordes of pilgrims to the city. New churches were built, and the pope and his city became the power centre of the Christian world. When Frankish ruler Charlemagne invaded Italy in AD 800 he was crowned the first Holy Roman Emperor in St Peter's. Over the centuries, however, conflicts between the pope and the Holy Roman Emperor weakened the papacy. The 10th–12th centuries were among the bleakest in Roman history: violent invaders left Rome poverty-stricken and the constantly warring local barons tore apart what remained of the city. Despite this, the first Holy Year was declared in 1300 and thousands of pilgrims arrived in Rome; only nine years later though, the papacy was forced to move to Avignon, leaving Rome to slide into further squalor and strife.

## The Renaissance

Pope Nicholas V came to the throne in 1447 determined to make Rome a city fit for the papacy. Among his successors, men like Julius II and Leo X eagerly followed his lead, and the

↑ Portrait of Pope Nicholas V (c 1450), who was pope from 1447 to 1455

## Timeline of events

**AD 800**
Charlemagne is crowned Holy Roman Emperor in St Peter's.

**1452**
Demolition of old St Peter's basilica begins.

**1506**
Work begins on new St Peter's basilica.

**1300**
Pope Boniface VIII declares the first ever Holy Year and pilgrims flock to Rome.

**1508**
Michelangelo begins work on Sistine Chapel ceiling.

city's appearance was transformed. The Classical ideals of the Renaissance inspired artists and architects, such as Michelangelo, Bramante and Raphael, to build and decorate churches and palaces, influenced by the styles of recently rediscovered ancient Roman buildings, statues and frescoes. In 1527, however, the continuing power struggle between the Holy Roman Empire and the papacy resulted in the Sack of Rome, when the unruly troops of the Holy Roman Emperor Charles V rampaged throughout the city, burning and looting palaces and churches, leaving behind just a fraction of its former splendour.

## The Counter-Reformation and the Baroque

In northern Europe, opposition to the fabulously rich (and famously corrupt) papacy was growing, and people began to embrace the Protestant movement. In response, the Catholic Church burned controversial books, tortured radical thinkers and told artists exactly what they were and were not allowed to paint. As the Church regained confidence – although not political power – popes such as Sixtus V, Urban VIII and Innocent X commissioned the extravagant Baroque piazzas, fountains, palaces and churches that define the city of Rome today.

1 Constantine on horseback sculpture by Bernini (1670), St Peter's ↑

2 Map of Rome in the Middle Ages

3 Miniature of Pope Gregory the Great (7th century)

4 The sack of Rome by Holy Roman Emperor Charles V, May 1527, attributed to Pieter Brueghel the Elder (16th century)

---

*1527*

Troops of Holy Roman Emperor Charles V sack Rome, marking the end of the Roman Renaissance.

*1568*

Jesuits build the Gesù church.

*1585*

Rome's streets are replanned by Pope Sixtus V.

*1626*

New St Peter's basilica completed on the site of the old basilica commissioned by Emperor Constantine.

*1651*

Bernini designs the Fontana dei Quattro Fiumi on Piazza Navona.

## A Capital Again

In the mid-18th century the Italian peninsula was still a collection of city-states and principalities and Rome was but a minor player on the world stage. In 1797 Napoleon conquered the city and briefly united Italy, but in 1815 the pre-Napoleonic patchwork of independent governments was restored. The brief taste of unification was never forgotten. On 20 September 1870 Italian troops, spearheaded by Giuseppe Mazzini, Count Camillo Cavour and Giuseppe Garibaldi, entered the city and Rome was declared capital of the new Italy, under King Vittorio Emanuele II.

## Mussolini and Post-War Rome

After World War I, disillusionment, national debt and social unrest culminated in massive support for the ex-Socialist politician Benito Mussolini. In October 1922, Mussolini marched on Rome with his Blackshirts and, within just three years, was running a Fascist dictatorship. Mussolini began constructing an imposing new suburb, EUR, south of Rome.

In 1940, Italy joined World War II on the side of Nazi Germany. In September 1943, two months after the Allies had landed in Sicily, the king took power away from Mussolini and Italy

↑ Portrait of Vittorio Emanuele II, the first king of a united Italy

## Timeline of events

**1797**
Napoleon captures Rome.

**1861**
Kingdom of Italy founded with capital in Turin.

**1870**
Royalist troops take Rome, which becomes capital of unified Italy.

**1922**
Fascists march on Rome; Mussolini becomes Prime Minister.

**1929**
Lateran Treaty creates the Vatican State.

**1940**
Italy enters World War II on the side of Germany.

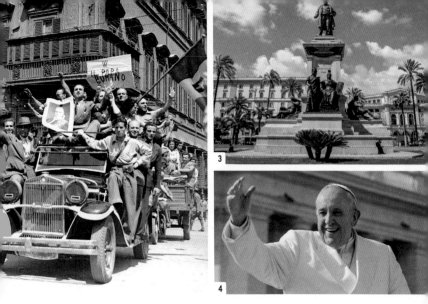

switched allegiance to the Allies. Rome was bombed by both sides before being liberated by the Allies on 4 June 1944.

In the chaos after the war, Rome was riven by divisions between left- and right-wing parties, and by the 1970s terrorism held the country to ransom. After more than 50 changes of government, the 1990s saw the rise of Silvio Berlusconi, who, despite many scandals, became Italy's longest-serving post-war prime minister until he was made to resign on corruption charges in 2012.

## Rome Today

Famous for its past, Rome is embracing the future: much of the historic centre is closed to local traffic, and radical new buildings, such as MAXXI (p318), have been erected, while digital technology is transforming museums and ancient sights. In 2016, Virginia Raggi of the anti-establishment Five Star Movement (M5S) was the first woman to be elected Mayor of Rome. The national elections in March 2018 followed, with M5S winning one-third of the votes. In 2020, Italy became the first western country to be hit by the Corona virus pandemic, with a very high rate of victims. The long and very strict lockdown that resulted from that took a heavy toll on the economy.

1 Church of Santi Pietro e Paolo in the EUR, a suburb designed by Mussolini ↑

2 Liberation of Rome by the Allies in June 1944

3 Statue of Count Camillo Cavour, a leading figure in the movement towards Italian Unification

4 Pope Francis greeting the faithful

**1944**
Allied Forces liberate Rome.

**1946**
National Referendum establishes Italy as a Republic; King Umberto II exiled.

**1978**
Premier Aldo Moro kidnapped, then killed, by Red Brigades.

**2004**
A new constitution of the European Union is signed in Rome.

**2013**
Pope Francis elected.

**2016**
Virginia Raggi of the populist 5 Star Movement elected first female mayor of Rome.

# EXPERIENCE

Interior of St Peter's basilica

# CAPITOL

The Temple of Jupiter on the Capitol, the southern summit of the Capitoline Hill, was the centre of the Roman world. Reached by a zig-zag path up from the Forum, the temple was the scene of all the most sacred religious and political ceremonies. The hill and its temple came to symbolize Rome's authority as *caput mundi*, head of the world, and the Capitol gave its name to the seat of the US Congress. Throughout the city's history, the Capitol (Campidoglio) has remained the seat of municipal government. Today's city council, the Comune di Roma, meets in the Renaissance splendour of Palazzo Senatorio. The Capitol also serves as Rome's Registry Office. Rome's position as a modern capital is forcefully expressed in the enormous Victor Emmanuel Monument, which unfortunately blots out the view of the Capitol from Piazza Venezia. The present arrangement on the hill dates from the 16th century, when Michelangelo created a beautiful piazza reached by a flight of steps, the Cordonata. Two of the buildings around the piazza now house the Capitoline Museums.

# CAPITOL

**Must See**

❶ Capitoline Museums

**Experience More**

❷ Piazza del Campidoglio
❸ Santa Maria in Aracoeli
❹ Roman Insula
❺ Cordonata
❻ Tarpeian Rock
❼ Temple of Jupiter
❽ Victor Emmanuel Monument (Il Vittoriano)
❾ Palazzo Venezia and Museum
❿ San Marco

**Eat**

① Caffetteria dei Musei Capitolini

PIAZZA DEL
COLLEGIO ROMANO

Palazzo
Odescalchi

PIAZZA SANTI APOSTOLI

W

VIA DEL CORSO

Museo
delle Cere

Palazzo
Colonna

3

VIA QUATTRO NOVEMBRE

V. C. BATTISTI

**PIAZZA DELLA
ROTONDA**
*p102*

VIA DEL PLEBISCITO

**FORUM AND
PALATINE**
*p76*

VIA D. FORNARI

Gesù

VIA DEGLI ASTALLI

Palazzo Venezia
and Museum

**9**

**10**

San
Marco

PIAZZA
SAN MARCO

PIAZZA
VENEZIA

VIA DEI FORI IMPERIALI

Foro di
Traiano

4

VIA DI SAN MARCO

VIA
D'ARACOELI

VIA SAN VENANZIO

VIA DEL TEATRO DI MARCELLO

Victor Emmanuel
Monument (Il Vittoriano)

**8**

VIA DI SAN PIETRO IN CARCERE

PIAZZA
MARGANA

PIAZZA
D'ARACOELI

Roman
Insula

**4**

Santa Maria
in Aracoeli

**3**

Foro di
Cesare

Aracoeli
Staircase

Museo Centrale
del Risorgimento

**CAMPO DE' FIORI**
*p160*

Cordonata

**5**

VIA DELLE TRE PILE

Capitoline Museums -
Palazzo Nuovo

**1**

PIAZZALE
CAFFARELLI

VIA DI VILLA CAFFARELLI

Piazza del
Campidoglio

**2**

Palazzo
Senatorio

Arco di Settimio
Severo

VIA DEL TEATRO DI MARCELLO

Capitoline Museums -
Palazzo dei Conservatori

**1**

Rostra

Tempio
di Giove

①

Temple of Jupiter

**7**

VIA DEL TEMPIO DI GIOVE

Tempio di
Saturno

VIA DI MONTE TARPEO

5

Basilica
Giulia

Tarpeian
Rock

**6**

PIAZZA DELLA CONSOLAZIONE

VIA DEL FORO ROMANO

VICO JUGARIO

VIA DEI FIENILI

VIA DEI FIENILI

VIA DEI FORAGGI

**AVENTINE**
*p242*

0 metres          100

0 yards           100

N

V

W

# CAPITOLINE MUSEUMS

**◉W5 △Piazza del Campidoglio 1 ▢63, 70, 75, 81, 87, 160, 170, 204, 628, 716 and other routes to Piazza Venezia ▦8 ◷9:30am-7:30pm daily ▣museicapitolini.org**

**This museum of Classical sculpture is housed in two palaces – Palazzo dei Conservatori and Palazzo Nuovo – either side of Piazza del Campidoglio.**

The Capitoline collection began in 1471 when Pope Sixtus IV donated several Classical bronze statues from his personal collection, including the She-Wolf, to the city. The She-Wolf was displayed on the façade of the Palazzo dei Conservatori, and rapidly became the symbol of Rome. Located in two majestic palaces, both with façades designed by Michelangelo, the collection has grown over the centuries to become Rome's finest and most famous assemblage of Classical sculpture. Palazzo dei Conservatori also houses a lovely gallery of Renaissance art. In 1734 Pope Clement XII Corsini decreed that the collection be turned into what is considered to be the world's first public museum.

## MUSEUM GUIDE

The main entrance to the two buildings is via Palazzo dei Conservatori. The ground and first floors of this palazzo hold Classical statues, while the second floor is home to a gallery of Renaissance paintings. A tunnel links the Palazzo dei Conservatori with the Palazzo Nuovo, where more Classical sculptures are exhibited on the two main floors.

### c.117–138

△ Found at Hadrian's Villa in Tivoli, this faun, sculpted in marble the colour of bresaola, is a version of a Greek original. It is an example of Hadrian's fondness for all things Greek.

### c.312–315

△ The foot of a 12 m- (40 ft-) high statue of emperor Constantine I has survived, along with a hand and other body fragments.

### c.11th–12th centuries

△ This bronze portrays the She-Wolf suckling Rome's legendary founders Romulus and Remus. The twins were probably added in the 15th century.

### 1640s

△ Bernini's dramatic bust of the mythological Medusa shows her caught in the moment of metamorphosis from human to stone.

# EAT & DRINK

**Caffetteria dei Musei Capitolini**
The big draw of this café-restaurant on the top floor of the Capitoline Museums is its vast terrace with a panoramic view taking in rooftops and assorted ruins. The vista is especially spectacular at sundown. Opt for superior coffee and cake or an *aperitivo* and a snack. The café is also open to non-ticket-holders via a separate entrance on Piazzale Caffarelli.

📍W5 ⬛Piazzale Caffarelli 4
🌐museicapitolini.org/ it/oltre_il_museo/ caffetteria

↑ Piazza del Campidoglio with the Palazzo Nuovo and a replica of the equestrian statue of Marcus Aurelius

The frescoed interior of the Palazzo dei Conservatori ↑

# PALAZZO DEI CONSERVATORI

Dramatically displayed in the centre of a grand glass-roofed gallery at the heart of the palazzo is the gilded bronze equestrian statue of Marcus Aurelius that once stood in Piazza del Campidoglio (where it has been replaced by a replica). Standing at

## Did You Know?

The Marcus Aurelius bronze is much more life-like than other statues of emperors, which were idealized.

← Spinario, a 1st-century AD bronze of a boy removing a thorn from his foot

4 m (11 ft) high, it is extraordinarily true to life. Among the most significant works in the Palazzo dei Conservatori are the She-Wolf, the ancient Spinario and a wonderfully Baroque snake-haired Medusa by Bernini. The courtyard is home to several marble body parts belonging to a statue of Constantine (p67).

### Pinacoteca

The Pinacoteca on the second floor holds a small collection of Renaissance art, which includes works by Caravaggio, Tintoretto and Titian. Perhaps the most remarkable is Caravaggio's *Saint John the Baptist*, painted in 1602 for a noble Roman family, the Mattei. The freedom of a private (rather than Church) commission is evident, with John the Baptist represented as a nude adolescent in a posture inspired by the Ignudi of Michelangelo's Sistine Chapel ceiling. The other

↑ Caravaggio's highly unorthodox painting of St John the Baptist

Caravaggio shows a gypsy girl reading the palm (and possibly stealing the ring) of a foppish young man. Apparently, spotting the girl on the street, Caravaggio decided to paint her in order to prove the then revolutionary idea that art could be made from life, not simply from copying Classical models.

> The Pinacoteca on the second floor holds a small collection of Renaissance art, which includes works by Caravaggio, Tintoretto and Titian.

# PALAZZO NUOVO

A tunnel connects the two palazzi. Signs will take you past the gloomy relics of a 2nd-century BC temple dedicated to Veiovis, god of the underworld, to the Tabularium, the ancient city's Public Records Office. Up on the ground floor, don't miss the room just off the courtyard which has a collection of Egyptian statues, including a granite crocodile and two monkeys, found in the streets around Piazza Minerva, where there was once a temple to Egyptian goddess Isis *(p113)*. The main collection is on the first floor. Most of the finest works are Roman copies of Greek masterpieces.

**GREAT VIEW**
**Tabularium**
You can enjoy one of the best views in Rome of the Forum from a window in the ruins of the Tabularium, or ancient Roman Public Records Office, in the basement of the Palazzo Nuovo.

↑ The marble Capitoline Venus dating from around AD 100–150

## Key Works

Entering the main sculpture galleries of the Palazzo Nuovo is to step into a chandelier-lit world of marble figures. Some are instantly recognizable – the Capitoline Venus emerging from her bath, or the wounded, tousle-haired Dying Gaul – both Roman copies of celebrated Greek works. Others, less famous, are equally compelling. Wander among the statues and see who grabs your attention – a haggard, drunk old Hellenistic woman; a sour-faced Roman matron dressed (or rather undressed) as Venus; Caracalla as a toddler, happily strangling a snake; or the sentimental statue of a little Roman girl playing with a pet dove. Other highlights include the Red Faun, sculpted for Hadrian's Villa in Tivoli *(p326)*; and the Wounded Warrior by 18th-century French sculptor Monnot, in which the twisted torso of a Greek discus-thrower was transformed into a fallen warrior by being tilted on his side and given a shield.

## Halls of Philosophers and Emperors

In these two rather intimate, exquisitely decorated halls, the busts of Greek politicians, philosophers, writers and scientists, and Roman emperors, empresses and members of the Imperial family are displayed on elegant marble shelves.

↑ Hall of Emperors and *(inset)* a close-up of a bust

↑ Piazza del Campidoglio, designed in the 16th century by Michelangelo

# EXPERIENCE MORE

## ❷
### Piazza del Campidoglio

⬛W5 🚌40, 62, 63, 64, 110, 170 🚋8

When the Holy Roman Emperor Charles V visited Rome in 1536, Pope Paul III Farnese was so embarrassed by the muddy state of the Capitol that he asked Michelangelo to draw up plans for repaving the piazza, and for renovating the façades of the Palazzo dei Conservatori and Palazzo Senatorio.

Michelangelo proposed adding the Palazzo Nuovo to form a piazza in the shape of a trapezium, embellished with Classical sculptures chosen for their relevance to Rome. Building started in 1546 but progressed so slowly that Michelangelo only lived to oversee the double flight of steps at the entrance of Palazzo Senatorio. The piazza was completed in the 17th century, the design remaining largely faithful to the original. Pilasters two storeys high and balustrades interspersed with statues link the buildings thematically. The piazza faces west towards St Peter's, the Christian equivalent of the Capitol. At its centre stands a replica of a statue of Marcus Aurelius. The original is in the Palazzo dei Conservatori (p68).

## ❸
### Santa Maria in Aracoeli

⬛W4 📍Piazza d'Aracoeli (entrances via Aracoeli Staircase and door behind Palazzo Nuovo) ☎06-6976 3837 🚌40, 62, 63, 64, 110, 170 🚋8 🕐Summer: 9am–6:30pm daily; winter: 9am–5:30pm daily

Dating from at least the 6th century, the church of Santa Maria in Aracoeli, or St Mary of the Altar in the Sky, stands on the northern summit of the Capitoline, on the site of the ancient temple to Juno. Its

> **Popular belief has it that all those who climb the steps of Santa Maria in Aracoeli on their knees will win the Italian national lottery.**

22 columns were taken from various ancient buildings; the inscription on the third column to the left tells us that it comes "*a cubiculo Augustorum*" – from the bedroom of the emperors.

The church of the Roman senators and people, Santa Maria in Aracoeli has been used to celebrate many triumphs over adversity. Its ceiling, with naval motifs, commemorates the Battle of Lepanto (1571), and was built under Pope Gregory XIII Boncompagni, whose family crest, the dragon, can be seen towards the altar end. Many other Roman families and individuals are honoured by memorials in the church. To the right of the entrance door, the tombstone of archdeacon Giovanni Crivelli, rather than being set into the floor of the church, stands eternally to attention, partly so that the signature "Donatelli" (by Donatello) can be read at eye-level.

The frescoes in the first chapel on the right, painted by Pinturicchio in the 1480s in the beautifully clear style of the early Renaissance, depict St Bernardino of Siena. On the left wall, the perspective of *The Burial of the Saint* slants to the right, taking into account the position of the viewer just outside the chapel. The church is most famous, however, for an icon with apparently miraculous powers, the Santo Bambino. Its powers are said to include resurrecting the dead, and it is sometimes summoned to the bedsides of the gravely ill. Other than at Christmas when the Christ icon sits in the centre of a crib in the second chapel on the left, it is usually to be found in the sacristy, as is the panel of the *Holy Family* from the workshop of Giulio Romano.

The famed Aracoeli Staircase leading to the church numbers 124 marble steps (122 if you start from the right) and was completed

in 1348, some say in thanks for the passing of the Black Death, but probably in view of the Holy Year of 1350.

The 14th-century tribune-turned-tyrant Cola di Rienzo used to harangue the masses from the Aracoeli Staircase; in the 17th century foreigners used to sleep on the steps, until Prince Caffarelli, who lived on the hill, scared them off by rolling barrels filled with stones down them.

Popular belief has it that all those who climb the steps of Santa Maria in Aracoeli on their knees will win the Italian national lottery. From the top there is a good view of Rome, with the domes of Sant'Andrea della Valle and St Peter's slightly to the right.

## ➍ Roman Insula

🔲 W4  🏛 Piazza d'Aracoeli  🚌 40, 62, 63, 64, 110, 170  🚋 8  🔒 To the public

Two thousand years ago the urban poor of Rome used to make their homes in *insulae* – apartment blocks. These were often badly maintained by landlords, and expensive to rent in a city where land costs were high. This 2nd-century AD tenement block, of barrel-vault construction, is the only survivor in Rome from that era. The fourth, fifth and part of the sixth storey remain

above current ground level. It is closed to the public but you can view its exterior from the street. In the Middle Ages, a section of the upper storeys was converted into a church; look out for the bell tower and 14th-century Madonna.

During the Fascist years, the area was cleared, and three lower floors emerged. Some 380 people may have lived in the tenement, in the squalid conditions described by the 1st-century AD satirical writers Martial and Juvenal. The latter mentions that he had to climb 200 steps to reach his garret.

This *insula* may once have had more storeys. The higher you lived, the more dismal the conditions, as the poky spaces of the building's upper levels testify.

## ➎ Cordonata

🔲 W5  🚌 40, 62, 63, 64, 110, 170  🚋 8

From Piazza Venezia, the Capitol is approached by a gently rising, subtly widening ramp – the Cordonata. At the foot is a pair of granite Egyptian lions, and on the left a 19th-century monument to Cola di Rienzo, close to where the dashing 14th-century tyrant was executed. The top of the ramp is guarded by Classical statues of the Dioscuri – Castor and Pollux.

→

The top of the marble Aracoeli Staircase, with a view across the city

## ❻

### Tarpeian Rock

📍 W5 🏛 Via di Monte Caprino and Via del Tempio di Giove 🚌 40, 62, 63, 64, 110, 170 🚋 8

The steep cliff on the southern tip of the Capitoline is called the Tarpeian Rock (Rupe Tarpea), after Tarpeia, the young daughter of Spurius Tarpeius, defender of the Capitol in the 8th-century BC Sabine War.

The Sabines, bent on vengeance for the rape of their women by Romulus and his men, bribed Tarpeia to let them up on to the Capitol. As the Augustan historian Livy records, the Sabines used to wear heavy gold bracelets and jewelled rings on their left hands, and Tarpeia's reward for her treachery was to be given "what they wore on their shield-arms".

The Sabines kept to the letter of the bargain if not to its spirit – they repaid Tarpeia not with their jewellery but by crushing her to death between their shields. Tarpeia was possibly the only casualty of her act of treachery – as the invading warriors met the Roman defenders, the Sabine women leapt between the two opposing armies, forcing a reconciliation. The site was subsequently used as a place of execution: traitors and other condemned criminals were thrown over the sheer face of the rock.

## ❼

### Temple of Jupiter

📍 W5 🏛 Via del Tempio di Giove 🚌 40, 62, 63, 64, 110, 170 🕐 9am-5pm, Sat, Sun & Mon

The Temple of Jupiter, the most important in ancient Rome, was founded in honour of the arch-god around 509 BC on the southern summit of the Capitoline Hill. From the few traces that remain, archaeologists have been able to reconstruct the rectangular, Greek appearance of the temple as it once stood. In places it is possible to see remnants of its particularly Roman feature, the podium. Most of this lies beneath the Museo Nuovo wing of the Palazzo dei Conservatori (p68).

By walking around the site, from the podium's southwestern corner in Via del Tempio di Giove to its southeastern corner in Piazzale Caffarelli, you can see that the temple was about the same size as the Pantheon.

---

## ❽

### Victor Emmanuel Monument

📍 W4 🏛 Piazza Venezia 📞 06-678 3587 🚌 40, 62, 63, 64, 110, 170 🚋 8 🕐 Summer: 9:30am-7:30pm daily; (last adm: 45 mins before closing)

Known as Il Vittoriano, this monument was begun in 1885 and inaugurated in 1911 in honour of Victor Emmanuel II of Savoy, the first king of a unified Italy. The king is depicted here in a gilt bronze equestrian statue, oversized like the monument itself – the statue is 12 m (39 ft) long.

The edifice also contains a museum of the Risorgimento, the events that led to unification (p58). Built in white Brescian marble, the "wedding cake" (just one of its many nicknames) can be seen from almost every part of Rome and will never mellow into the ochre tones of surrounding buildings. It is widely held to be the epitome of self-important, insensitive architecture, though the views it offers are spectacular. A glass lift at the back of the building takes visitors to the very top.

---

**9**

## Palazzo Venezia and Museum

🔲 V4 🏛 Via del Plebiscito 118 📞 06-6780131 🚌 40, 62, 63, 64, 110, 170 🚋 8 🕐 9:30am-7:30pm Tue-Sun (last adm: 1 hr before closing) 🚫 1 Jan, 1 May, 25 Dec

The arched windows and doors of this Renaissance civic building are so harmonious that the façade was once attributed to the great Humanist architect Leon Battista Alberti (1404–72). It was more probably built by Giuliano da Maiano, who is known to have carved the fine doorway on to the piazza.

Palazzo Venezia was built in 1455–64 for the Venetian cardinal Pietro Barbo, who later became Pope Paul II. It was at times a papal residence, but it also served as the Venetian Embassy to Rome before passing into French hands in 1797. Since 1916 it has belonged to the state; in the Fascist era,

← 

The huge, white marble Victor Emmanuel Monument in Rome's Piazza Venezia

↑ *The Immaculate Conception* by Pier Francesco Mola (1612-66) in the San Marco basilica

Mussolini used Palazzo Venezia as his headquarters and addressed crowds from the central balcony.

The interior is best seen by visiting the Museo del Palazzo Venezia, Rome's most underrated museum. It holds first-class collections of early Renaissance painting; painted wood sculptures and Renaissance chests from Italy; tapestries from all over Europe; majolica; silver; Neapolitan ceramic figurines; Renaissance bronzes; arms and armour; Baroque terracotta sculptures by Bernini, Algardi and others; and 17th- and 18th-century Italian painting. There is a marble screen from the Aracoeli convent, destroyed to make way for the huge Victor Emmanuel Monument, as well as a bust of Paul II, showing him to rank with Martin V and Leo X among the fattest-ever popes. The building also hosts major temporary exhibitions.

**10**

## San Marco

🔲 W4 🏛 Piazza San Marco 48 📞 06-679 5205 🚌 40, 62, 63, 64, 110, 170 🚋 8 🕐 10am-1pm & 4-6pm Tue-Sun (Sat & Sun: to 8pm)

The basilica of San Marco was founded in 336 by Pope Mark, in honour of St Mark the Evangelist. The Pope's relics lie under the altar. The church was restored by Pope Gregory IV in the 9th century.

Further major rebuilding took place in 1455–71, when Pope Paul II Barbo made San Marco the church of the Venetian community in Rome. The blue and gold coffered ceiling is decorated with Pope Paul's heraldic crest, the lion rampant, recalling the lion of St Mark. The appearance of the rest of the interior, with its colonnades of Sicilian jasper, was largely the creation of Filippo Barigioni in the 1740s.

# A SHORT WALK
# THE CAPITOL AND PIAZZA VENEZIA

**Distance** 1 km (0.6 mile) **Nearest bus** 40, 62, 63, 64, 110, 170 **Time** 20 minutes

The absence of cars on the Capitol makes the hill a welcome retreat for a short stroll. Climb up the broad flight of steps (the Cordonata) to Michelangelo's spectacular Piazza del Campidoglio. This is flanked by the Palazzo Nuovo and Palazzo dei Conservatori, housing the Capitoline Museums with their fine collections of sculptures and paintings. It's worth braving the traffic on the piazza to visit Palazzo Venezia and its museum.

The huge white marble Victor Emmanuel monument to Italy's first king was completed in 1911.

PIAZZA VENEZIA

PIAZZA VENEZIA

START

VIA DEL TEAT

San Marco, the church for Venetian expatriates in Rome, has a fine 9th-century apse mosaic (p73).

The Palazzo Venezia museum's finest exhibits date from the late Middle Ages (p73).

The Roman Insula is a ruined apartment block dating from Imperial Rome (p71).

0 metres 100
0 yards 100

N

← The Aracoeli Staircase leading to Santa Maria in Aracoeli

The treasures hidden behind the church of Santa Maria Aracoeli's brick façade include a 15th-century fresco of the Funeral of St Bernardino by Pinturicchio (p70).

The Palazzo Nuovo, part of the Capitoline Museums, houses many fine Classical sculptures (p69).

Palazzo Senatorio was used by the Roman Senate from about the 12th century. It now houses the offices of the mayor.

Michelangelo designed both the geometric paving and the façades of the buildings on Piazza del Campidoglio (p70).

When it was built in 1348, the Aracoeli Staircase became a centre for political debate (p71).

VIA DI SAN PIETRO IN CARCERE

FINISH

Palazzo dei Conservatori, part of the Capitoline Museums, displays a fine series of reliefs from the Temple of Hadrian in the courtyard (p68).

Michelangelo's great Cordonata staircase changed the orientation of the Capitol towards the west (p71).

VIA DEL TEMPIO DI GIOVE

RCELLO

Ruins of the Temple of Jupiter, the most important temple in ancient Rome (p72).

In ancient Rome traitors were thrown to their death from the Tarpeian Rock on the Capitol (p72).

# FORUM AND PALATINE

Although the relics of ancient Rome are strewn throughout the city, the most concentrated and fully excavated cluster lie on the flat, once marshy area between the Capitoline, Esquiline and Palatine hills, home to the original Roman Forum, the Colosseum and the Imperial Fora. The Roman Forum was the official heart of the ancient city, the centre of political, commercial and judicial life, and according to the playwright Plautus, teemed with "lawyers and litigants, bankers and brokers, shopkeepers and strumpets, good-for-nothings waiting for a tip from the rich". Nearby, the Colosseum was the centre of entertainment. As Rome's population boomed, the original Forum became too small, and in 46 BC Julius Caesar built an extension, setting a precedent followed by emperors from Augustus to Trajan. Looking down on all this, the Palatine Hill was the most desirable residential area in Rome, home to some of the city's most famous inhabitants. The great orator Cicero had a house here, as did the lyric poet Catullus. Augustus was born on the hill and continued to live here even when he became emperor.

# FORUM AND PALATINE

## Must Sees
1 The Roman Forum
2 Colosseum
3 Trajan's Markets
4 Palatine

## Experience More
5 Trajan's Column
6 Palazzo Valentini
7 Forum of Nerva
8 Forum of Caesar
9 Forum of Augustus
10 Mamertine Prison
11 Arch of Constantine

## Eat
1 Terre e Domus della Provincia di Roma

SS. Apostoli

Palazzo Colonna

VIA IV NOVEMBRE

Palazzo Valentini 1

6

FORO TRAIANO

Trajan's Column 5

VIA DEI

Forum of Caesar 8

CAPITOL p62

Mamertine Prison 10

Curia

Arch of Septimius Severus

Rostra

Temple of Saturn

Column of Phocas

Basilica Julia

Temple of Castor and Pollux

FORO ROMANO

San Teodoro

Arco di Giano

Orti Farnesiani

House of Livia

Huts of Romulus

House of Augustus

AVENTINE p242

REGOLA

LUNGOTEVERE DEI CENCI

Isola Tiberina

Ponte Fabricio

Ponte Cestio

Ponte Palatino

Santa Maria in Cosmedin

TRASTEVERE

San Michele a Ripa Grande

Parco di Savello

VIA DEL CIRCO MASSIMO

RIPA

Santa Sabina

**J**

VIA XXIV MAGGIO

VIA NAZIONALE

**K**

**5**

MONTI

Banca d'Italia

VIA

VIA DEI

VIA PANISPERNA

FORUM AND PALATINE

**QUIRINAL AND MONTI** *p180*

Torre delle Milizie

VIA MAZZARINO

VIA SERPENTI

VIA GIOVANNI

VIA IN SELCI

**3** Trajan's Markets

Casa dei Cavalieri di Rodi

ALESSANDRINA

V. TOR DE CONTI

VIA BACCINA

CAVOUR

VIA D. SETTE SALE

**6**

**9** Forum of Augustus

VIA EUDOSIANA

MONTEOPPIO

**7** Forum of Nerva

LARGO CORRADO RICCI

VIA DEL COLOSSEO

VIA

DEL

FORI IMPERIALI

**ESQUILINE** *p200*

Domus Aurea

Basilica Aemilia

VIA DEI FORI IMPERIALI

VIA SACRA

Temple of Antoninus and Faustina

Temple of Romulus and Santi Cosma e Damiano

Basilica of Constantine and Maxentius

VIA DEL COLOSSEO

Colosseo **M**

VIA TERME DI TITO VIALE

VIA NICOLA SALVI

**1** **ROMAN FORUM**

Temple of Vesta

Santa Francesca Romana

House of the Vestal Virgins

Antiquarium Forense

Temple of Venus and Rome

Arch of Titus

VIA SACRA

PIAZZA DEL COLOSSEO

VIALE DOMUS

Farnese Gardens

**CAMPITELLI**

**2** Colosseum

**LATERAN** *p212*

**7**

Cryptoporticus

**11** Arch of Constantine

Temple of Cybele

VIA CELIO VIBENNA

VIA CAPO D'AFRICA

VIA CLAUDIA

Domus Flavia

Domus Augustana

**CARACALLA** *p228*

Tempio di Claudio

Santi Giovanni e Paolo

**4** **PALATINE**

Stadium

VIA DI SAN GREGORIO

CLIVO DI SCAURO

V. S. PAOLO DELLA CROCE

CERCHI

San Gregorio Magno

**8**

*Parco del Circo Massimo*

Circo Massimo

PIAZZA DI PORTA CAPENA

0 metres 200

0 yards 200

N ↑

**J**

**K**

❶ ⊗ ⊗ ⊗

# THE ROMAN FORUM

📍 J6 🏛 Via della Salara Vecchia 5/6 🚌 85, 87, 117, 175, 186, 810 🚊 3 Ⓜ Colosseo
🕐 10:30am–1 hour before sunset 🌐 coopculture.it

**The Roman Forum was the scene of public meetings, law courts and gladiatorial combats and was lined with shops and open-air markets. It was also the site of many of the city's key temples and monuments.**

In the early days of the Republic, the Roman Forum was like a large piazza – a hive of social activity – containing shops, food stalls, temples and the Senate House. By the 2nd century BC it was decided that Rome required a more salubrious centre, and the food stalls were replaced by business centres and law courts. The Forum remained the ceremonial centre of the city under the Empire. Emperors repeatedly renovated old buildings and erected new temples and monuments.

To appreciate the vast layout of the Forum before visiting its confusing patchwork of ruined temples and basilicas, it is best to view the whole area from above, from the Piazza del Campidoglio (*p70*). Excavation of the Forum continues today, and the ruins uncovered date from many different periods of Roman history.

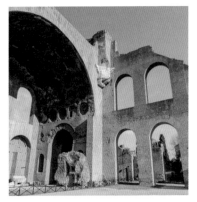

↑ Basilica of Constantine and Maxentius, once the largest building in the Forum

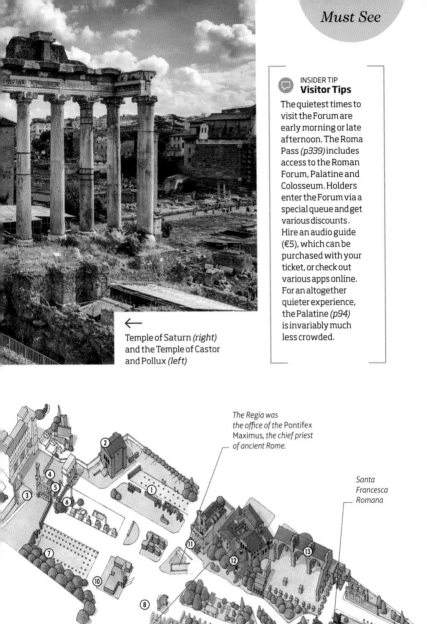

← Temple of Saturn *(right)* and the Temple of Castor and Pollux *(left)*

💬 INSIDER TIP
**Visitor Tips**

The quietest times to visit the Forum are early morning or late afternoon. The Roma Pass *(p339)* includes access to the Roman Forum, Palatine and Colosseum. Holders enter the Forum via a special queue and get various discounts. Hire an audio guide (€5), which can be purchased with your ticket, or check out various apps online. For an altogether quieter experience, the Palatine *(p94)* is invariably much less crowded.

*The Regia was the office of the* Pontifex Maximus, *the chief priest of ancient Rome.*

Santa Francesca Romana

*An early Iron Age necropolis was found here in 1902. Finds from it are on view in the Antiquarium.*

↑ Plan showing the key buildings of the Roman Forum

# ① Basilica Aemilia

This building was once a rectangular colonnaded hall, with a multicoloured marble floor and a bronze-tiled roof. It was built by the consuls Marcus Aemilius Lepidus and Marcus Fulvius Nobilor in 179 BC. The two consuls, who were elected annually, exercised supreme power over the Republic.

Basilicas in ancient Rome served no religious purpose; they were meeting halls for politicians, moneylenders and *publicani* (businessmen contracted by the state to collect taxes). A consortium agreed to hand over a specified sum to the state, but its members were allowed to collect as much as they could and keep the difference. This is why tax-collectors in the Bible were so loathed.

The basilica was rebuilt many times; it was finally burned down when the Visigoths sacked Rome in AD 410.

---

# ② Curia

A modern restoration now stands over the ruins of the hall where Rome's Senate (chief council of state) used to meet. The first Curia stood on the site now occupied by the church of Santi Luca e Martina, but after the building was destroyed by fire in 52 BC, Julius Caesar built a new Curia at the edge of the Forum. This was restored by Domitian in AD 94 and, after another fire, rebuilt by Diocletian in the 3rd century. The current building is a 1937 restoration of Diocletian's Curia. Inside are two relief panels commissioned by Trajan to decorate the Rostra.

→

The Curia, or the Court of Rome, rebuilt by Diocletian in the 3rd century

### MELTED COINS

Business seems to have carried on until the last minute at the Basilica Aemilia. You can still spot Roman coins melted into its pavement from the 5th century AD when the Visigoths invaded and set it on fire.

# ③ Rostra

Speeches were delivered from this dais, the most famous (thanks to Shakespeare) being Mark Antony's "Friends, Romans, Countrymen" oration after the assassination of Julius Caesar in 44 BC. Caesar himself had just reorganized the Forum and this speech was made from the newly sited Rostra, where the ruins now stand. In the following year the head and hands of Cicero were put on show here after he was put to death by the second Triumvirate (Augustus, Mark Antony and Marcus Lepidus). Fulvia, Mark Antony's wife, stabbed the great orator's tongue with a hairpin.

The dais took its name from the ships' prows *(rostra)* with which it was decorated. Sheathed in iron (for ramming enemy vessels), these came from ships captured at the Battle of Antium in 338 BC.

### ④
## Arch of Septimius Severus

This triumphal arch was built in AD 203 to celebrate the tenth anniversary of the accession of Septimius Severus. The relief panels – largely eroded – celebrate the emperor's victories in Parthia (modern-day Iraq and Iran) and Arabia. Originally, the inscription along the top of the arch was to Septimius and his two sons, Caracalla and Geta, but after Septimius died Caracalla murdered Geta, and had his brother's name removed. Even so, the holes into which the letters of his name were pegged are still visible.

### ⑤
## Temple of Saturn

The most prominent of the ruins in the fenced-off area between the Forum and the Capitoline Hill is the Temple of Saturn. It consists of a high platform, eight columns and a section of entablature. There was a temple dedicated to Saturn here as early as 497 BC, but it had to be rebuilt many times and the current remains date only from 42 BC.

Saturn was the mythical god-king of Italy, said to have presided over a prosperous and peaceful Golden Age from which slavery, private property, crime and war were absent. As such, he appealed particularly to the lower and enslaved classes. Every year, between 17 December and 23 December, Saturn's reign was remembered in a week of sacrifices and feasting, known as the Saturnalia. As long as the revels lasted, the normal social order was turned upside down. Enslaved people were permitted to drink and dine with (and sometimes even be served by) their masters. Senators and other high-ranking Romans would abandon the aristocratic togas that they usually wore to distinguish themselves from the lower classes and wear more democratic, loose-fitting gowns. During the holidays, all the courts of law and schools in the city were closed. No prisoner could be punished, and no war could be declared. People also celebrated the

Saturnalia in their own homes: they exchanged gifts and played light-hearted gambling games, the stakes usually being nuts, a symbol of fruitfulness. Much of the spirit and many of the rituals of the Saturnalia have been preserved in the Christian celebration of Christmas.

↑ The Arch of Septimius Severus, one of the best-preserved ruins

### ⑥
## Column of Phocas

This column is one of the few to have remained upright since the day it was put up. It is the youngest of the Forum's monuments, erected in AD 608 in honour of the Byzantine emperor, Phocas, who had just paid a visit to Rome. The column may have been placed here as a mark of gratitude to Phocas for giving the Pantheon to the pope (*p106*).

> **Much of the spirit and many of the rituals of the Saturnalia have been preserved in the Christian celebration of Christmas.**

### ⑦
## Basilica Julia

This immense basilica was begun by Julius Caesar in 54 BC and completed after his death by his great-nephew Augustus. It was damaged by fire almost immediately afterwards in 9 BC, but was subsequently repaired. After numerous sackings only the steps, pavement and column stumps remain. The basilica had a central hall, surrounded by a double portico. The hall was on three floors, while the outer portico had only two.

The Basilica Julia was the seat of the *centumviri*, a body of 180 magistrates who tried civil law cases. They were split into four chambers of 45 men, and unless a case was very complicated they would all sit separately. The four courts were divided only by screens or curtains. Lawyers hired crowds of spectators, who applauded every time the lawyer who was paying them made a point and jeered at his opponents. Scratched into the steps are gameboards where the clappers and booers played dice and other gambling games to while away the time between cases.

### ⑧
## Temple of Vesta

The Forum's most elegant temple, a circular building originally surrounded by a ring of 20 fine fluted columns, dates from the 4th century AD, though there had been a temple on the site for far longer. It was partially reconstructed in 1930.

### ⑨
## House of the Vestal Virgins

As soon as a girl became a Vestal she came to live in the House of the Vestal Virgins. This was once an enormous complex with about 50 rooms on three storeys. The only remains today are some of the rooms around the central courtyard. This space is perhaps the most evocative part of the Forum. Overlooking ponds of water lilies and goldfish is a row of eroded, and mostly headless, statues of senior Vestals, dating from the 3rd and 4th centuries AD. The better-preserved examples are in the Palazzo Massimo alle Terme (*p188*).

Ring of Corinthian columns

Cella (sacred inner chamber)

Sacred flame

↑ The Temple of Vesta was circular in shape and had 20 Corinthian columns

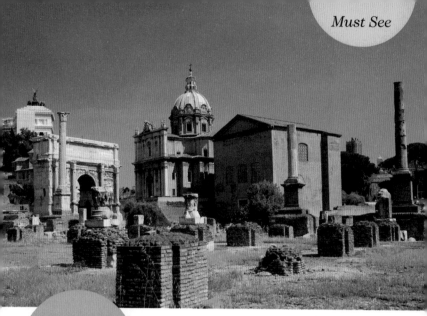

### Did You Know?

Vestal Virgins had their hair cut off and hung on a lotus tree as an offering to the gods.

⑩

## Temple of Castor and Pollux

The three slender fluted columns of this temple form one of the Forum's most beautiful ruins. The first temple here was probably dedicated in 484 BC in honour of the mythical twins and patrons of horsemanship, Castor and Pollux. During the battle of Lake Regillus (499 BC) against the ousted Tarquin kings, the Roman dictator Postumius promised to build a temple to the twins if the Romans were victorious. Some said the twins appeared on the battlefield, helped the Romans to victory and then materialized in the Forum – the temple marks the spot – to announce the news. The three surviving columns date from the last occasion on which the temple was rebuilt – by the Emperor Tiberius after a fire in AD 6.

⑪

## Temple of Antoninus and Faustina

One of the Forum's oddest sights is the Baroque façade of the church of San Lorenzo in Miranda rising above the porch of a Roman temple. First dedicated in AD 141 by Emperor Antoninus Pius to his late wife Faustina, the temple was rededicated to them both on the death of the emperor. In the 11th century it was converted into a church because it was believed that San Lorenzo had been condemned to death there. The current church dates from 1601.

↑ Remains of the Basilica Julia, a Roman court of civil law

### THE VESTAL VIRGINS

The cult of Vesta, the goddess of fire, dates back to at least the 8th century BC. Six virgins kept the sacred flame of Vesta burning in her circular temple. The girls, who came from noble families, were selected when they were between 6 and 10 years old, and served for 30 years. They had high status and financial security, but were buried alive if they lost their virginity and whipped by the high priest if the sacred flame died out. Although they were permitted to marry after finishing their service, few did so.

## ⑫
### Temple of Romulus and Santi Cosma e Damiano

No one is exactly sure to whom the Temple of Romulus was dedicated, but it was probably to the son of Emperor Maxentius, and not to Rome's founder.

The temple is a circular brick building, topped by a cupola, with two rectangular side rooms and a concave porch. The heavy, dull bronze doors are original.

Since the 6th century the temple has acted as a vestibule to the church of Santi Cosma e Damiano, which itself occupies an ancient building – a hall in Vespasian's Forum of Peace. The entrance to the church is on Via dei Fori Imperiali. The beautiful carved figures of its 18th-century Neapolitan *presepio*

(crib or Nativity scene) are on view, and the church has a vivid Byzantine apse mosaic with Christ pictured against orange clouds.

## ⑬
### Basilica of Constantine and Maxentius

The basilica's three vast, coffered barrel vaults are powerful relics of what was the largest building in the Forum. Work began in AD 308 under Emperor Maxentius. When he was deposed by Constantine after the Battle of the Milvian Bridge in AD 312, work on the massive project continued under the new regime. The building, which, like other Roman basilicas, was used for the administration of justice and for carrying on business, is often

referred to simply as the Basilica of Constantine. The area covered by the basilica was roughly 100 m by 65 m (330 ft by 215 ft). It was originally designed to have a long nave and aisles running from east to west, but Constantine switched the axis around to create three short broad aisles with the main entrance in the centre of the long south wall. The height of the building was 35 m (115 ft). In the apse at the western end, where it could be seen

> ### Did You Know?
>
> It was not until the 18th century that excavations of the Roman Forum began, revealing what can be seen today.

The octagonal coffers in the vaulted ceiling were originally faced with stucco.

The three barrel-vaulted aisles of the basilica were used as law courts.

The roof was supported by eight massive Corinthian columns. One now stands in Piazza Santa Maria Maggiore.

The main entrance was added by Constantine in AD 313.

↑ Basilica of Contantine and Maxentius

from all over the building, stood a 12 m- (39 ft-) statue of the emperor, made partly of wood and partly of marble. The giant head, hand and foot are on display in the courtyard of the Palazzo dei Conservatori (p68). The roof of the basilica glittered with gilded tiles until the 7th century when they were stripped off to cover the roof of the old St Peter's.

---

⑭

## Arch of Titus

This triumphal arch was erected in AD 81 by the Emperor Domitian in honour of the victories of his brother Titus and his father Vespasian in the Jewish War in Judaea. In AD 66 the Jews, who were weary of being exploited by unscrupulous Roman officials, rebelled. A bitter war broke out which ended four years later in the sacking of Solomon's temple in Jerusalem, the fall of Jerusalem after the city was completely destroyed, and the Jewish Diaspora.

Although the reliefs inside the arch are somewhat eroded, you can make out a triumphant procession of Roman soldiers carrying off spoils from the Temple of Jerusalem. The booty includes the altar, silver trumpets and the menorah, a golden seven-branched candelabrum.

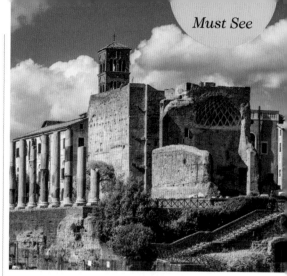

↑ Temple of Venus and Rome, designed by Emperor Hadrian and inaugurated in 121 AD

⑮

## Temple of Venus and Rome

The Emperor Hadrian designed this temple himself. The temple, thought to have been the largest and most splendid in ancient Rome, was dedicated to Roma, the personification of the city, and to Venus Felix, ancestor of the Roman people and bringer of good fortune. Each goddess had her own *cella* (shrine). When the architect Apollodorus allegedly pointed out that the seated statues in the niches were too big (had

they tried to "stand" their heads would have hit the vaults), Hadrian had him put to death. The temple has had extensive restoration, and a number of the columns have been re-erected. There are excellent views of the Colosseum from here.

---

### SANTA FRANCESCA ROMANA

Santa Francesca Romana was a 14th-century housewife, who became convinced of the constant presence of a guardian angel lighting the road before her whenever she travelled. For this reason, in 1925, she was made the patron saint of motorists. On her feast day, 9 March, the city's trams and buses are blessed, and the road outside her church next to the Temple of Venus and Rome is packed with cars whose drivers are seeking her blessing.

↑ Detail of a marble relief on the Arch of Titus showing a triumphal procession

# COLOSSEUM

📍 K7  🏛 Piazza del Colosseo 1  🚌 75, 81, 85, 87, 117, 673, 810  🚊 3 to Piazza del Colosseo  Ⓜ Colosseo  🕐 10:30am–approx 1 hour before sunset daily (last admission 1 hour before closing)  🌐 coopculture.it

**Rome's greatest amphitheatre was commissioned by Emperor Vespasian in AD 72. This magnificent structure was where the Imperial passion for bloody spectacle reached its peak of excess.**

Built by enslaved Jews on the marshy site of a lake in the grounds of Nero's palace, the Domus Aurea (p208), the Colosseum was the arena where deadly gladiatorial combats and wild animal fights were staged by the emperor and wealthy citizens for public viewing, free of charge. The Colosseum was built to a practical design, with its 80 arched entrances allowing easy access to 55,000 spectators, but it is also a building of great beauty. It was one of several similar amphitheatres built in the Roman Empire – other surviving examples are at El Djem in North Africa, Nîmes and Arles in France, and Verona in northern Italy. Despite being damaged over the years by neglect and theft, the Roman Colosseum remains a majestic sight.

---

💬 INSIDER TIP
**Ticket Holders**

General tickets include access to the Colosseum, Palatine and Forum. Roma Pass (p339) holders and those with tickets bought in advance online gain preferential access. However, you still need to collect tickets at the ticket office. The quietest times to visit are 30 minutes before opening, early in the morning, or just before closing.

---

## Timeline

**72**
△ Emperor Vespasian begins work on the Colosseum.

**80**
Vespasian's son, Titus, stages inaugural festival in the amphitheatre lasting 100 days.

**81–96**
Amphitheatre completed in reign of Domitian.

**404**
▽ Gladiatorial combats banned.

**442**
Building damaged in an earthquake.

**523**
△ Wild animal fights banned.

**1200s**
Frangipane family turns Colosseum into a fortress.

↑ The Colosseum at sunset and *(inset)* its internal corridors

**1312**
▲ Emperor Henry VII gives Colosseum to the Senate and people of Rome.

**15th–16th centuries**
Ruins used as quarry; travertine blocks recycled by popes.

**1870**
All vegetation removed.

**1893–6**
▼ Structure below arena revealed.

↑ The Colosseum amphitheatre seen from above

## How Fights were Staged in the Arena

The emperors held shows here, which often began with animals performing circus tricks. Then on came the gladiators, who fought each other to the death. When one was killed, attendants dressed as Charon, the mythical ferryman of the dead, carried his body off on a stretcher, and sand was raked over the blood ready for the next bout. A badly wounded gladiator would surrender his fate to the crowd. Legend has it that the "thumbs up" sign from the emperor meant he could live, "thumbs down" that he die. The victor became a hero. Roman gladiators were usually enslaved people, prisoners of war or condemned criminals. Most were men, but there were a few female gladiators.

Animals were brought here from as far away as North Africa and the Middle East. The games held in AD 248 to mark the 1,000th anniversary of Rome's founding saw the death of a host of lions, elephants, hippos, zebras and elks in wild-animal hunting spectacles.

A complex of rooms, passages and lifts over several floors lies underneath the arena. Metal fencing kept animals penned in, while archers stood by just in case any escaped. A winch brought the animal cages up to arena level when they were due to fight. A ramp and trap door enabled the animal to reach the arena.

### SEA BATTLES IN THE ARENA

Historian Cassius Dio, writing in the 3rd century AD, relates how, 150 years earlier, the Colosseum's arena was flooded on one occasion to stage a mock sea battle. This type of spectacle took place regularly in the Naumachia of Augustus, a water-filled arena across the Tiber in Trastevere.

*The velarium was a huge awning which shaded spectators from the sun.*

→ Drawing of the Colosseum showing how it looked at the time of its opening in AD 80

*The outer walls are made of travertine. Stone plundered from the façade during the Renaissance was used to build several palaces, bridges and parts of St Peter's.*

*The vomitorium was the exit used from each numbered section.*

↑ Lithograph from 1881 of gladiators in the Colosseum

*Arched entrances (80 in total) were numbered to speed up the entry of the vast crowds.*

↑ Inside view of the Colosseum showing remains of the underground rooms where animals were kept

*The podium was a large terrace where the emperor and the wealthy upper classes had their seats.*

*Entry routes to take the spectators to their seats were reached by staircases to the various levels.*

*The internal corridors were designed to allow the large and often unruly crowd to move freely and to be seated promptly.*

Corinthian pilasters

Ionic pilasters

Doric pilasters

## Did You Know?

The founder of the Colosseum, Vespasian, was a professional soldier.

**3** ⚡ 🏛

# TRAJAN'S MARKETS

📍 J6 🏠 Via IV Novembre 94 📞 06-0608 🚌 64, 70, 170 and routes to Piazza Venezia ⏰ 9:30am–7:30pm daily (last admission 1 hour before closing) 🌐 mercatiditraiano.it

Originally considered among the wonders of the Classical world, this visionary complex of 150 shops and offices was built by Emperor Trajan and architect Apollodorus of Damascus in the 2nd century AD.

The ancient Roman equivalent of the modern shopping mall, Trajan's Markets was a complex of shops on five levels, selling everything from silks and spices imported from the Middle East to fresh fish, fruit, flowers, wine, oil and fabrics. The top tier was occupied by welfare offices that administered the free corn ration to Roman men and boys. Via Biberatica, the main street, is named after the drinking inns that once lined it. The Torre delle Milizie, the large tower above the Markets, was built in the Middle Ages. The Museo dei Fori Imperiali charts the growth of the extensions to the Roman Forum from Julius Caesar onwards.

## MARKET SHOPPING

Shops opened early and closed at about noon. The most upmarket stores were decorated with mosaics of goods they sold. Almost all the shopping was done by men, although women visited dressmakers and cobblers. The traders were also almost all male, according to employment records for the period AD 117–193.

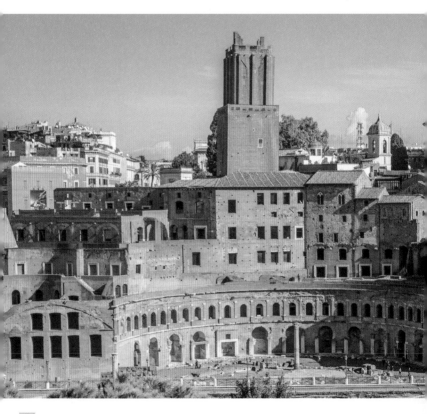

Cross vaulting

Main Hall
Twelve shops
were built on two
floors, and the
corn dole was
shared out on the
upper storey – a
free corn ration
given to men to
prevent hunger.

Small semicircle
of shops

Via Biberatica
The main street running
through the market is
named after the drinking
inns which once lined it.

Upper Corridor
Shops on this upper
level were thought
to have sold wine
and oil.

A terrace over the
archway spanning
Via Biberatica
has a good view of the
Forum of Trajan.

Staircase

Wall dividing market area
from Forum of Trajan

Market Shops were built
with arched entrances,
with rectangular portals
and windows.

Forum of Trajan, built in
front of the markets in
AD 107–113, was flanked
by the Basilica Ulpia.

Large hall
with
semidomed
ceiling

Illustration of Trajan's
Market, detailing where
the shops were housed ↑

# EAT

**Terre e Domus della
Provincia di Roma**
Right by Trajan's
Markets, this small
modern restaurant
serves Roman cuisine
made with the freshest
local ingredients. The
*cacio e pepe* (cheese
and pepper) pasta is
especially good, and
there's a very strong
wine list.

**▣ H5 ▢ Foro Traiano 82
Ⓦ palazzovalentini.it/
terre-domus**

€€€

←
The red-brick Trajan's
Markets complex, the
world's first shopping mall

4 ⟨⟩ ⟨M3⟩

# PALATINE

⦿ J7  🏠 Via di San Gregorio 30  🚌 75, 80, 81, 175, 673, 850  🚃 3  Ⓜ Colosseo  🕐 10:30am–1 hour before sunset  🌐 coopculture.it

The Palatine, the centremost of the seven hills of Rome, was once the residence of emperors and aristocrats and is the most pleasant of Rome's ancient sites. Towering over the Roman Forum and the Circus Maximus, the hill's ruins include the simple house in which Augustus is thought to have lived and the Domus Flavia and Domus Augustana, the public and private wings of a luxurious palace built by Domitian.

The remains of elaborate fountains, colourful marble floors, fine stone carvings, columns, stuccoes and frescoes can be seen within the magnificent walls of the Imperial palaces. The Palatine Hill is a green haven, shaded by pines, with wild flowers growing among the ancient ruins. The hill offers fantastic views of the Roman Forum, the Colosseum, the Capitoline Hill and the Circus Maximus. In the 16th century the first private botanical gardens in Europe were built by the Farnese family on the Palatine – the area was dug up during excavations and re-landscaped.

↑ The Palatine Hill viewed through an arch of the neighbouring Colosseum

## A History of the Palatine Hill

### The Founding

According to legend, the twins Romulus and Remus were brought up on the Palatine by a wolf. Romulus, having killed his brother, is said to have founded the village that was destined to become Rome. Traces of mud huts dating back to the 8th century BC have been found on the hill, lending archaeological support to the legend.

### The Republic

By the 1st century BC the Palatine was the most desirable address in Rome and home to the leading citizens of the Republic. Its aristocractic residents were notoriously indulgent and their villas were magnificent dwellings with doors of ivory, floors of bronze and frescoed walls.

### The Empire

The first emperor, Augustus, was born on the Palatine in 63 BC and lived here in a modest house. Domitian's house, the Domus Flavia and its private quarters, Domus Augustana, remained the official residence of future emperors (who were referred to as "Augustus") for over 300 years.

The remains of elaborate fountains, colourful marble floors, fine stone carvings, columns, stuccoes and frescoes can be seen within the magnificent walls of the Imperial palaces.

↑ ⑨
*To Farnese Gardens*

↓ Plan of the
Palatine Hill

The 16th-century
Farnese Gardens on the
northern side of the hill

## ① Domus Flavia

In AD 81 Domitian, the third of the Flavian dynasty of emperors, decided to build a splendid new palace on the Palatine Hill. The palace had an official wing (Domus Flavia) and a private house (Domus Augustana). It was the main Imperial palace for 300 years.

At the front of the Domus Flavia, the surviving fragments of columns and walls trace the shapes of three adjoining rooms. The Basilica was where the emperor presided over legal cases. The central Aula Regia was a throne room decorated with 12 black basalt statues. The Lararium (now covered with corrugated plastic) contained a shrine for the household gods known as Lares (usually the owner's ancestors). It may have been used for official ceremonies or by the palace guards.

Fearing assassination, Domitian had the walls of the courtyard covered with shiny marble slabs designed to act as mirrors so that he could see anyone lurking behind him. In the event, he was assassinated in his bedroom, possibly on the orders of his wife, Domitia. The courtyard is now a pleasant place; the flower beds follow the maze pattern of a sunken fountain pool.

## ② Domus Augustana

This part of Domitian's palace was called the Domus Augustana because it was the private residence of the "august" emperors. On the upper level a high brick wall remains, and you can make out the shape of its two court-yards. The far lower level is closed to the public, though you can look down on its sunken courtyard with the geometric foundations of a fountain in its centre. Sadly, you cannot see the stairs linking the two levels (once lit by sunlight falling on a mirror-paved pool), nor the surrounding rooms, paved with coloured marble.

---

## ③ Cryptoporticus

The Cryptoporticus, a series of underground corridors, was built by Nero to connect his Domus Aurea *(p208)* with the palaces of earlier emperors on the Palatine. Its vaults are decorated with delicate stucco reliefs – copies of originals now kept in the Palatine's museum.

The Domus Flavia, the official wing of what was once a vast emperor's palace

## ④ Garden

For a long time from the 19th century it was believed that this structure was a stadium, but it is now thought that it was almost certainly a large sunken garden adjoining the Palace of Domitian.

↑ Ruins of a bath building in the sunken garden of the Palace of Domitian

## ⑤ House of Livia

Dating from the 1st century BC, this was probably the house in which the Emperor Augustus and his wife Livia lived and is one of the best preserved houses on the Palatine. In comparison with later Imperial palaces, it is a relatively modest home. According to Suetonius, the biographer of Rome's early emperors, Augustus slept in the same small bedroom for 40 years on a low bed.

A flight of steps leads down to a courtyard off which are three small reception rooms. The frescoes in the central one include a faded scene of Hermes rescuing Zeus's beloved Io. In the left-hand room are frescoed griffins and

other beasts, while the decor in the right-hand room includes landscapes and cityscapes.

## ⑥ House of Augustus

Painted in about 30 BC, the frescoes in the House of Augustus are among the most impressive existing examples of Roman wall paintings, similar in quality to those found in Pompeii and Herculaneum. In vivid shades of red, blue and ochre, they include *trompe l'oeil* effects, such as a room whose walls are painted to resemble a stage with side doors, and a garden vista. This is where Augustus (or Octavian, as he was then known) lived before assuming supreme power as Rome's first emperor.

## ⑦ Temple of Cybele

Other than a platform with a few column stumps and capitals, there is little to see of the temple, a popular fertility goddess imported to Rome from Asia. The priests of the cult castrated themselves in the belief that if they

sacrificed their own fertility it would guarantee that of the natural world. The annual festival of Cybele, in spring, culminated with eunuch-priests slashing their bodies to offer up their blood to the goddess, and the ceremonial castration of novice priests.

## ⑧ Huts of Romulus

According to legend, after killing his brother Remus, Romulus founded a village on the Palatine. In the 1940s a series of holes was found, and archaeologists deduced that these must originally have held the supporting poles of three Iron-Age huts – the first foundations of Rome.

## ⑨ Farnese Gardens

Tree-lined avenues, rose gardens and elegant pavilions grace part of what was once an extensive pleasure-garden, designed by architect Vignola and built in the 16th century for Cardinal Alessandro Farnese over the ruins of Tiberius's palace.

**29**

European languages whose word for "palace" derives from the Palatine.

# EXPERIENCE MORE

## ⑤ Trajan's Column

**⊙ H6  ⚲ Via dei Fori Imperiali 🚌 64, 70, 170 and routes to Piazza Venezia**

This elegant marble column was inaugurated by Trajan in AD 113, and celebrates his two campaigns in Dacia (Romania) in AD 101–3 and AD 107–8. The column, base and pedestal are 40 m (131 ft) tall – precisely the same height as the spur of Quirinal Hill excavated to make room for Trajan's Forum.

Spiralling up the column are minutely detailed scenes from the campaigns. The column is pierced with small windows to illuminate its internal spiral staircase (closed to the public).

When Trajan died in AD 117 his ashes were placed in a golden urn in the hollow base of the column. The column's survival was largely due to the intervention of Pope Gregory the Great (reigned 590–604). He was so moved by a relief of Trajan helping a woman whose son had been killed that he begged God to release the emperor's soul from hell. God duly appeared to the pope to say that Trajan had been rescued, but asked him not to pray for the souls of any more pagans. Legend has it that when Trajan's ashes were exhumed his skull and tongue were not only intact, but his tongue told of his release from hell. The land around the column was then declared sacred and the column was

↑ The remains of the Forum of Caesar, the first of Rome's Imperial fora

←

Trajan's Column topped with a statue of St Peter

> **INSIDER TIP**
> **Trajan's Column**
>
> At Palazzo Valentini there are screenings of a brilliant animation of the bas-reliefs of Trajan's Column. Be sure to book in advance.

spared. In 1587, the statue of Trajan atop the column was replaced with one of St Peter.

## ⑥  Palazzo Valentini

**⊙ H5  ⚲ Via IV Novembre 119/a  🚫 Closed due to COVID-19 with no date for reopening 🌐 palazzo valentini.it**

During maintenance work in the basement of Palazzo Valentini in 2005, the remains of two houses belonging to a leading patrician family of Imperial ancient Rome were discovered. Elegant living rooms, courtyards, a kitchen and a private baths complex were revealed, complete with traces of their elaborate original decorations – mosaics, frescoes and coloured marbles.

Using digital technology, light and sound effects, film and projections, the houses have been "reconstructed", creating a virtual-reality museum. There are tours in English and Italian.

## ⑦ Forum of Nerva

**⊙ J6  ⚲ Piazza del Grillo 1 (via the Forum of Augustus) 📞 06-0608  🚌 85, 87, 186, 810  🚫 To the public but viewable from above**

The Forum of Nerva was begun by his predecessor, Domitian, and completed in AD 97. Little more than a long corridor with a colonnade along the sides and a Temple of Minerva at one end, it was also known as the Forum Transitorium because it lay between the Forum of Peace, built by Vespasian in AD 70, and the Forum of Augustus. Vespasian's forum is almost completely covered by Via dei Fori Imperiali, as is much of the Forum of Nerva. Excavations have unearthed shops and taverns, but only part of the forum can be seen.

## ⑧ Forum of Caesar

**⊙ H6  ⚲ Via del Carcere Tulliano 📞 06-0608  🚌 85, 87, 186, 810, 850  🚫 By appt only**

The first of Rome's Imperial fora was built by Julius Caesar. He spent a fortune buying up and demolishing houses on the site. Pride of place went to a temple dedicated in 46 BC to the goddess Venus Genetrix, from whom Caesar claimed descent. The temple contained statues of Caesar and Cleopatra as well as of Venus. All that remains is a platform and three Corinthian columns. The forum was enclosed by a double colonnade sheltering a row of shops, but this burned down in AD 80 and was rebuilt by Domitian and Trajan.

Some parts are visible from above in Via dei Fori Imperiali.

---

### 9
### Forum of Augustus

J6  Piazza del Grillo 1  06-0608  64, 70, 170 and routes to Piazza Venezia  To the public but viewable from above

The Forum of Augustus was built to celebrate Augustus's victory over Julius Caesar's assassins, Brutus and Cassius, at the Battle of Philippi in 41 BC. The temple in its centre was dedicated to Mars the Avenger. The forum stretched from a high wall at the foot of the sleazy Suburra quarter to the edge of the Forum of Caesar. At least half of it is now concealed below Mussolini's Via dei Fori Imperiali. The temple is easily identified, with its cracked steps and four Corinthian columns. Originally it had a statue of Mars which looked very like Augustus.

---

### 10
### Mamertine Prison

H6  Clivo Argentario 1  06-698 96375  85, 87, 186, 810  Closed due to COVID-19 with no date for reopening

Below the 16th-century church of San Giuseppe dei Falegnami (St Joseph of the Carpenters) is a dank dungeon in which, according to Christian legend, St Peter was imprisoned. He is said to have caused a spring to bubble up into the cell, using the water to baptize his guards. The prison was in an old cistern with access to the city's main sewer (the Cloaca Maxima). The lower cell was used for executions and bodies were thrown into the sewer. The Gaulish leader Vercingetorix, defeated by Julius Caesar in 52 BC, was executed here.

---

### 11
### Arch of Constantine

J7  Between Via di San Gregorio and Piazza del Colosseo  75, 85, 87, 673, 810  3  Colosseo

This arch was dedicated in AD 315 to mark Constantine's victory three years before over his co-emperor, Maxentius. Constantine claimed he owed his victory to a vision of Christ, but there is nothing Christian about the arch – most of the medallions, reliefs and statues were scavenged from earlier monuments. Inside the arch are reliefs of Trajan's victory over the Dacians, probably by the same artist who worked on Trajan's Column.

# A LONG WALK
# ROME'S TRIUMPHAL ARCHES

**Distance** 2.5 km (1.5 miles)  **Walking time** 1 hour
**Nearest metro** Colosseo

Rome's greatest gift to architecture was the arch, and the Roman people's highest tribute to their victorious generals was the triumphal arch. This walk is a celebration of that tribute. In Imperial times, arches were erected to honour an emperor's campaign victories almost as a matter of course, promoting his personal cult and ensuring his subsequent deification. Spectacular processions passed through these arches. Conquering generals, cheered by rapturous crowds, processed in their chariots to the Capitol, accompanied by their legions bearing spoils from their campaigns.

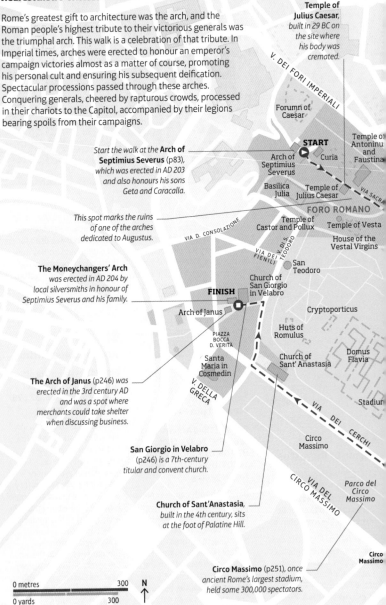

**Temple of Julius Caesar**, built in 29 BC on the site where his body was cremated.

Start the walk at the **Arch of Septimius Severus** (p83), which was erected in AD 203 and also honours his sons Geta and Caracalla.

This spot marks the ruins of one of the arches dedicated to Augustus.

**The Moneychangers' Arch** was erected in AD 204 by local silversmiths in honour of Septimius Severus and his family.

**The Arch of Janus** (p246) was erected in the 3rd century AD and was a spot where merchants could take shelter when discussing business.

**San Giorgio in Velabro** (p246) is a 7th-century titular and convent church.

**Church of Sant'Anastasia**, built in the 4th century, sits at the foot of Palatine Hill.

**Circo Massimo** (p251), once ancient Rome's largest stadium, held some 300,000 spectators.

START

Forum of Caesar

Arch of Septimius Severus

Curia

Temple of Antoninus and Faustina

Basilica Julia

Temple of Julius Caesar

VIA SACRA

FORO ROMANO

Temple of Castor and Pollux

Temple of Vesta

House of the Vestal Virgins

VIA D. CONSOLAZIONE

VIA DEI FIENILI

VIA D. S. TEODORO

San Teodoro

FINISH

Arch of Janus

Church of San Giorgio in Velabro

Cryptoporticus

Huts of Romulus

PIAZZA BOCCA D. VERITÀ

Santa Maria in Cosmedin

Church of Sant'Anastasia

Domus Flavia

V. DELLA GRECA

VIA DEI CERCHI

Stadium

Circo Massimo

VIA DEL CIRCO MASSIMO

Parco del Circo Massimo

Circo Massimo

V. DEI FORI IMPERIALI

0 metres          300
0 yards           300

N ↑

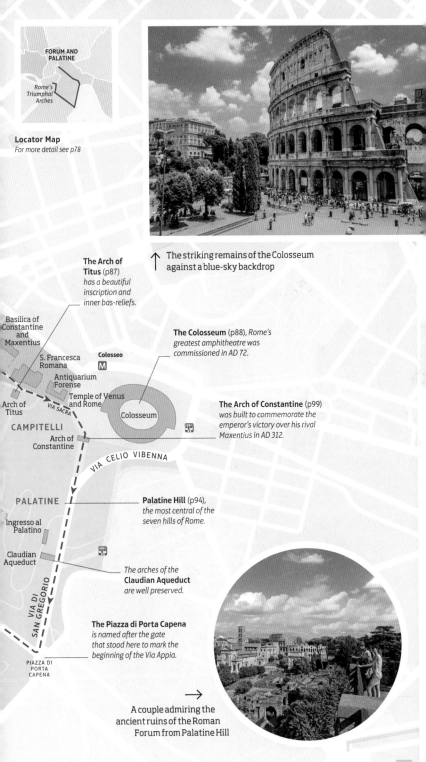

**Locator Map**
For more detail see p78

FORUM AND PALATINE

Rome's Triumphal Arches

↑ The striking remains of the Colosseum against a blue-sky backdrop

**The Arch of Titus** (p87) has a beautiful inscription and inner bas-reliefs.

Basilica of Constantine and Maxentius

S. Francesca Romana

Antiquarium Forense

Temple of Venus and Rome

Arch of Titus

VIA SACRA

CAMPITELLI

Arch of Constantine

Colosseo Ⓜ

Colosseum

**The Colosseum** (p88), Rome's greatest amphitheatre was commissioned in AD 72.

**The Arch of Constantine** (p99) was built to commemorate the emperor's victory over his rival Maxentius in AD 312.

VIA CELIO VIBENNA

PALATINE

Ingresso al Palatino

Claudian Aqueduct

VIA DI SAN GREGORIO

PIAZZA DI PORTA CAPENA

**Palatine Hill** (p94), the most central of the seven hills of Rome.

The arches of the **Claudian Aqueduct** are well preserved.

**The Piazza di Porta Capena** is named after the gate that stood here to mark the beginning of the Via Appia.

→ A couple admiring the ancient ruins of the Roman Forum from Palatine Hill

# PIAZZA DELLA ROTONDA

The Pantheon, one of the great buildings in the history of European architecture, has stood at the heart of Rome for nearly 2,000 years. The historic area around it has seen uninterrupted economic and political activity throughout that time. Palazzo di Montecitorio, built for Pope Innocent XII as a papal tribunal in 1694, is now the Italian parliament and many nearby buildings are government offices. This is also the main financial district of Rome, housing banking headquarters and the stock exchange. Not many people live in the area, but in the evenings, Romans stroll in the narrow streets and fill the bustling restaurants and cafés that make this a focus for the city's social life.

# PIAZZA DELLA ROTONDA

## Must Sees
**1** Pantheon
**2** Gesù

## Experience More
**3** Temple of Hadrian
**4** Piazza di Sant'Ignazio
**5** Sant' Ignazio di Loyola
**6** Palazzo del Collegio Romano
**7** Palazzo Baldassini
**8** La Maddalena
**9** Sant'Eustachio
**10** Santa Maria sopra Minerva
**11** Pie' di Marmo
**12** Palazzo di Montecitorio
**13** Obelisk of Montecitorio
**14** Palazzo Borghese
**15** Santa Maria in Campo Marzio
**16** Column of Marcus Aurelius
**17** Palazzo Doria Pamphilj
**18** Via della Gatta
**19** Palazzo Capranica
**20** San Lorenzo in Lucina
**21** Fontanella del Facchino
**22** Palazzo Altieri

## Eat
**1** Armando al Pantheon
**2** Osteria dell'Ingegno

## Drink
**3** Caffè Sant'Eustachio
**4** Tazza d'Oro

## Gelaterie
**5** Cremeria Monteforte
**6** Giolitti
**7** San Crispino
**8** Gunther Gelato Italiano

# PANTHEON

🗺 U3  📍 Piazza della Rotonda  🚌 116 and routes along Via del Corso, Corso Vittorio Emanuele II and Corso del Rinascimento  🕐 9am-7pm daily, 9am-1pm public hols  🌐 pantheonroma.com

With its awe-inspiring domed interior, the Pantheon – the Roman temple of "all the gods" – is the best-preserved ancient building in Rome. Unlike many other Roman structures that fell into disrepair, it became a church in the 7th century, ensuring its continued use and conservation.

↑ The immense portico, built on the foundations of Agrippa's temple

## Inside the Pantheon

The interior of the church is dominated by the vast hemispherical dome, which has both a height and diameter of 43.3 m (142 ft). The hole at the top of the dome, the oculus, provides the only light; we owe this marvel of engineering to the Emperor Hadrian, who designed the structure (AD 118–125) to replace an earlier temple built by Marcus Agrippa, son-in-law of Augustus. The shrines that line the wall of the Pantheon range from the Tomb of Raphael to those of the kings of Italy.

## Did You Know?

The Pantheon's dome remains the largest unreinforced concrete dome in the world.

*The walls of the drum supporting the dome are 6 m (19 ft) thick.*

*118–25*

Hadrian builds
new Pantheon.

*609*

▽ Pope Boniface IV
consecrates Pantheon
as church of Santa
Maria ad Martyres.

*1309–77*

While the papal seat
is in Avignon, the
Pantheon is used as
a poultry market.

*27–25 BC*

△ Marcus Agrippa
builds first
Pantheon.

*663*

Byzantine Emperor
Constans II strips
gilded tiles from
the roof.

*1632*

△ Urban VIII melts
bronze from the
portico for the
baldacchino.

Oculus

Oculus and coffered
interior of the
Pantheon's dome →

*The dome was cast
by pouring concrete
mixed with tufa
and pumice over a
temporary wooden
framework.*

*The Tomb of
Raphael rests
below a Madonna
sculpture by
Lorenzetto (1520).*

← Illustration of
the Pantheon

# ❷ GESÙ

📍V4 🏛Piazza del Gesù 📞06-697 001 🚌H, 46, 62, 64, 70, 81, 87, 186, 492, 628, 810 and other routes 🚊8
🕐7am–12:30pm & 5–7:30pm daily (to 8pm Sun)

Dating from between 1568 and 1584, the Gesù was the first Jesuit church to be built in Rome. Its design has been much imitated throughout the Catholic world.

Epitomizing Counter-Reformation and Baroque architecture, the layout proclaims the church's two major functions: a large nave with side pulpits for preaching to crowds, and a main altar as the centrepiece for the celebration of the Mass. By providing people with prayer books and filling the nave with enough light for people to read, the Jesuits hoped to increase the popularity of Catholicism during the Thirty Years' War when Catholics were losing followers to the Protestants. The illusionistic decoration by Il Baciccia in the nave and dome was added after the war in the late 17th century. Its message is clear and triumphant: faithful Catholic worshippers will be joyfully uplifted into the heavens while Protestants and other heretics are flung into hell's fires.

←

The façade of the Gesù church, designed by Giacomo della Porta

→

Stuccoes by Antonio Raggi, designed by Il Baciccia to complement the figures on his own nave frescoes

## Timeline

**1540** ▲ Founding of the Society of Jesus (the Jesuits).

**1568–71** ▲ Vignola builds the church, under the patronage of Cardinal Alessandro Farnese.

**1571** Giacomo della Porta's design chosen for the façade.

**1584** Church's consecration.

**1622** ▽ Ignatius of Loyola is canonized.

**1773** Pope Clement XIV orders the suppression of the Jesuit order.

## ST IGNATIUS AND THE JESUIT ORDER

Spanish soldier Ignatius of Loyola (1491–1556) joined the Church after being wounded in battle in 1521. He came to Rome in 1537 and founded the Jesuits, sending missionaries and teachers all over the world to win souls for Catholicism.

↑ The splendid, highly ornate main nave and altar inside the Gesù

# EXPERIENCE MORE

### 3

#### Temple of Hadrian

V2 La Borsa, Piazza di Pietra 117, 119, 492 and routes along Via del Corso or stopping at Piazza San Silvestro For exhibitions

This temple honours the Emperor Hadrian as a god and was dedicated by his son and successor, Antoninus Pius in AD 145. The remains of the temple are visible on the southern side of Piazza di Pietra, incorporated in a 17th-century building. This was originally a papal customs house, completed by Carlo

Fontana and his son in the 1690s. Today the building houses the Roman stock exchange (La Borsa).

Eleven marble Corinthian columns 15 m (49 ft) high stand on a base of *peperino*, a volcanic rock quarried from the Alban hills, to the south of Rome. The columns decorated the northern flank of the temple enclosing its inner shrine, the *cella*. The *peperino* wall of the *cella* is still visible behind the columns, as is part of the coffered portico ceiling.

A number of reliefs from the temple, representing conquered Roman provinces, are now in the courtyard of

the Palazzo dei Conservatori (*p68*). They reflect the mostly peaceful foreign policy of Emperor Hadrian's reign.

---

### 4

#### Piazza di Sant'Ignazio

V2 & 3 117, 119, 492 and routes along Via del Corso or stopping at Piazza San Silvestro

One of the major works of the Roman Rococo, Piazza di Sant'Ignazio (1727–8) is Filippo Raguzzini's master-piece. It offsets the imposing façade of the church of Sant'Ignazio with the intimacy of the houses belonging to the bourgeoisie. The theatrical setting, the cur-vilinear design and the playful forms of its windows, balco-nies and balusters mark the piazza as one of a highly

> The Piazza di Sant'Ignazio offsets the imposing façade of the church of Sant'Ignazio with the intimacy of the houses belonging to the bourgeoisie.

↑ The exuberant frescoed ceiling of Sant'Ignazio di Loyola

**EAT**

**Armando al Pantheon**

Just steps away from the Pantheon, this wood-panelled trattoria has been going strong since 1961, never straying from its menu of Roman dishes cooked to perfection – from *spaghetti all'amatriciana* to *coda alla vaccinara* (oxtail stew). It's deservedly popular, so book ahead.

📍U3 🏠Salita de' Crescenzi 31 🌐armandoal pantheon.it

€€€

───────────

**Osteria dell'Ingegno**

In a picture-perfect little piazza, this buzzing restaurant has a menu of traditional dishes with a modern twist, such as duck with mandarin and endive, and pasta with lamb and juniper sauce. The arty interior and jazz soundtrack add to the appeal.

📍V2 🏠Piazza di Pietra 45 🌐osteriadel lingegno.com

€€€

one of a highly distinct group of structures. Along with Palazzo Doria Pamphilj (1731), the façade of La Maddalena (1735) and the aristocratic Spanish Steps (1723), it belongs to the moment when Rome's opulent Rococo triumphed over conservative Classicism.

───────────

**5**

### Sant'Ignazio di Loyola

📍V3 🏠Piazza di Sant'Ignazio 📞06-679 4406 🚌117, 119, 492 and routes along Via del Corso 🕐7:30am-7pm Mon-Sat, 9am-7pm Sun

The church was built by Pope Gregory XV in 1626 in honour of St Ignatius of Loyola, founder of the Society of Jesus and the man who most embodied the zeal of the Counter-Reformation.

Together with the Gesù (p108), Sant'Ignazio forms the centre of the Jesuit area in Rome. Built in Baroque style, Sant'Ignazio di Loyola's vast interior, lined with precious stones, marble, stucco and gilt, creates a sense of theatre. The church has a Latin-cross plan, with an apse and many side chapels. A cupola was planned but never built, so the space it would have filled was covered by a vast fake perspective painting by Andrea Pozzo. The stunning *trompe l'oeil* frescoes give the illusion of a cupola open to a bright sky on the nave ceiling.

───────────

**6**

### Palazzo del Collegio Romano

📍V3 🏠Piazza del Collegio Romano 🚌117, 119, 492 and routes along Via del Corso or stopping at Piazza Venezia 🚫To the public

On the same block as the church of Sant'Ignazio is the majestic palazzo used by Jesuits as a college where many future bishops, cardinals and popes studied. The college was confiscated in 1870 and turned into an ordinary school. The façade is adorned with a bell, a clock and two sundials. On the right is a tower built in 1787 as a meteorological observatory. Until 1925 its time signal regulated all the clocks within the city.

### ⑦

## Palazzo Baldassini

📍U2 🏛Via delle Coppelle 35 📞06-684 0421 🚍116 and many routes along Via del Corso and Corso Rinascimento 🚫To the public

Melchiorre Baldassini commissioned architect Antonio da Sangallo the Younger to build his home in Florentine Renaissance style in 1514–20. With its cornices marking the different floors and wrought-iron window grilles, this is one of the best examples of an early 16th-century Roman palazzo. It stands in the part of Rome still known as the Renaissance Quarter, which flourished around the long, straight streets such as Via di Ripetta and Via della Scrofa, built at the time of Pope Leo X (reigned 1513–21).

### ⑧

## La Maddalena

📍U2 🏛Piazza della Madda-lena 📞06-899 281 🚍116 and many routes along Via del Corso and Corso Vittorio Emanuele II 🕐7am–noon & 5-8pm Mon-Fri; 9:30am-noon & 5-8pm Sat & Sun

Situated in a small piazza near the Pantheon, the Maddalena, built in 1735, has a Rococo façade that epitomizes the love of light and movement of the late Baroque. Its curves are reminiscent of Borromini's San Carlo alle Quattro Fontane (p192). The façade has been lovingly restored, although die-hard Neo-Classicists dismiss its painted stucco as icing sugar.

The small size of the Maddalena did not deter the 17th- and 18th-century decorators who filled the interior with ornaments from the floor to the top of the elegant cupola. The organ loft

↑ The church of Sant'Eustachio seen from Via della Palombella, which links Piazza della Minerva with Piazza Sant'Eustachio

and choir are particularly powerful examples of the Baroque's desire to fire the imagination of the faithful.

Many of the paintings and sculptures found within the Maddalena adopt the Christian imagery of the Counter-Reformation. In the niches of the nave, the statues are personifications of virtues such as Humility and Simplicity. There are also scenes from the life of St Camillus de Lellis, who died in the adjacent convent in 1614. The church belonged to his followers, the Camillians, a preaching order active in Rome's hospitals. Like the Jesuits, they commissioned powerful works of art to convey the force of their religious message.

### ⑨

## Sant'Eustachio

📍U3 🏛Piazza Sant'Eustachio 📞06-686 5334 🚍116 and routes along Corso Vittorio Emanuele II 🕐7:45am-noon & 4–8pm daily

The origins of this church date back to early Christian times, when it offered relief to the poor. In the medieval period, many charitable brother-hoods elected St Eustace as their patron. The church's Romanesque bell tower is one of the few surviving remains of the medieval church, which was completely redecorated in the 17th and 18th centuries.

Nearby is the excellent Caffè Sant'Eustachio (p115).

**10**

## Santa Maria sopra Minerva

**V3** **Piazza della Minerva 42** **06-679 3926** **116 and routes along Via del Corso, Via del Plebiscito and Corso Vittorio Emanuele II** **10:30am–12:30pm & 3–7pm daily**

Few other churches display such a complete and impressive record of Italian art. Dating from the 13th century, the Minerva is one of the few examples of Gothic architecture in Rome. It was the traditional stronghold of the Dominicans, whose anti-heretical zeal earned them the nickname of *Domini Canes* (the hounds of the Lord).

Built on ancient ruins, supposed to have been the Temple of Minerva, the simple T-shaped vaulted building acquired rich chapels and works of art by which its many patrons wished to be remembered. Note the Cosmatesque 13th-century tombs and the exquisite works of 15th-century Tuscan and Venetian artists. Local talent of the period can be admired in Antoniazzo Romano's *Annunciation*, featuring Cardinal Juan de Torquemada, uncle of the infamous Spanish Inquisitor.

The more monumental style of the Roman Renaissance can be seen in the tombs of the 16th-century

Medici popes, Leo X and his cousin Clement VII, and in the richly decorated Aldobrandini Chapel. Near the steps of the choir is the celebrated sculpture of the *Risen Christ*, started by Michelangelo but completed by Raffaello da Montelupo in 1521. There are also splendid works of art from the Baroque period, including a tomb and a bust by Bernini.

The church also contains the tombs of many famous Italians: St Catherine of Siena, who died here in 1380; the Venetian sculptor Andrea Bregno (died 1506); the Humanist Cardinal Pietro Bembo (died 1547); and Fra Angelico, the Dominican friar and painter, who died in Rome in 1455.

Originally meant to decorate Palazzo Barberini as a joke, the elephant and obelisk sculpture in front of the church is typical of Bernini's inexhaustible imagination. (The elephant was actually sculpted by Ercole Ferrata to Bernini's design.) When the ancient obelisk was found in the garden of the monastery of Santa Maria sopra Minerva, the friars wanted the monument erected in their piazza. Despite opposition from Bernini, the elephant was

provided with a cube underneath it (partly covered by an enormous saddle-cloth) at the insistance of a friar, who was Bernini's rival. The friar claimed that the gap under the animal's abdomen would undermine its stability. Bernini knew better, however: you need only look at the Fontana dei Quattro Fiumi in Piazza Navona *(p124)* to appreciate his use of empty space.

———

**11**

## Pie' di Marmo

**V3** **Via Santo Stefano del Cacco** **62, 63, 64, 70, 81, 87, 116, 186, 492 and other routes along Via del Corso, Via del Plebiscito and Corso Vittorio Emanuele II**

Bronze and marble statues filled the streets of ancient Rome. Fragments of these giants, usually gods or emperors, are still scattered over the city. This piece, a colossal sandalled marble foot *(pie' di marmo)* in a small side-street, comes from an area dedicated to the Egyptian gods Isis and Serapis and was probably part of a temple statue. In ancient times statues were painted and covered with jewels and clothes given by the faithful, which posed a great fire risk with unattended burning tapers.

### SYMBOLISM OF THE ELEPHANT

In the 1600s elephants were thought by the Catholic church to be a model of strength, intelligence and sexual morality because they took only one partner and mated for just five days every two years. The elephant bearing the Obelisk of Santa Maria sopra Minerva was designed by Bernini for Pope Alexander VII in 1667. Obelisks were thought to represent wisdom; hence Alexander had an inscription added to the base: "A robust intelligence is required to support solid wisdom."

## 12 🚶‍♂️ ♿

# Palazzo di Montecitorio

📍V2 🏛Piazza di Monte Citorio 🚌116 and all routes along Via del Corso or stopping at Piazza San Silvestro 🕐Usually 1st Sun each month (except Jul & Aug); ticket office opens 9:30am, with first guided visit 10:30am & last entry 3:30pm 🌐camera.it

The palazzo's first architect, Bernini, was appointed after he presented a silver model of his design to the wife of his patron, Prince Ludovisi. The building was completed in 1694 by Carlo Fontana and became the Papal Tribunal of Justice. In 1871 it was chosen to be Italy's new Chamber of Deputies, and by 1927 it had doubled in size, with a second grand façade. The 630 members of the Italian parliament are elected by a majority system with proportional representation. Guided tours take in the plenary hall and reception rooms.

## 13

# Obelisk of Montecitorio

📍V2 🏛Piazza di Monte Citorio 33 🚌116 and routes along Via del Corso or to Piazza San Silvestro

The measurement of time in ancient Rome was always a hit-and-miss affair: for many years the Romans relied on an imported, inaccurate sundial, a trophy from the conquest of Sicily. In 10 BC the Emperor Augustus laid out an enormous sundial in the Campus Martius. The shadow was cast by a huge granite obelisk that he had brought back from Heliopolis in Egypt. Unfortunately, this sundial, too, became inaccurate after only 50 years, possibly owing to subsidence.

The obelisk was still in the piazza in the 9th century, but then disappeared until it was rediscovered lying under medieval houses in the reign of Pope Julius II (1503–13). However, it was only under Pope Benedict XIV (reigned 1740–58) that the obelisk

was finally unearthed. It was erected in its present location in 1792 by Pope Pius VI.

## 14

# Palazzo Borghese

📍U1 🏛Largo della Fontanella di Borghese 🚌81, 117, 492, 628 🚫To the public

The palazzo was acquired in about 1605 by Cardinal Camillo Borghese, just before he became Pope Paul V. Flaminio Ponzio was hired to enlarge the building and give it the grandeur appropriate to the pope's family. He added a wing overlooking Piazza Borghese and the delightful porticoed courtyard inside. Subsequent enlargements included the building and decoration of a great *nymphaeum* known as the Bath of Venus. For more than two centuries this palazzo housed the Borghese family's famed collection of paintings, which was bought by the Italian state in 1902 and transferred to the Galleria Borghese (*p146*).

→ The façade of Palazzo Montecitorio, the Italian Chamber of Deputies

# DRINK

## Caffè Sant'Eustachio

Many Romans believe that Sant'Eustachio serves the city's best coffee – hence the hordes of locals that throng this tiny bar from morning till late. There's also a tempting selection of coffee-flavoured cakes.

📍U3 🏠Piazza di Sant'Eustachio 82 🌐santeustachioil caffe.com

---

## Tazza d'Oro

Right next to the Pantheon, this historic bar has a fabulously retro interior and serves excellent coffee and pastries, as well as *granita di caffè* – a cooling treat on a hot day.

📍U2 🏠Via degli Orfani 84 🌐tazzadoro coffeeshop.com

---

## Santa Maria in Campo Marzio

📍U2 🏠Piazza di Campo Marzio 45 📞06-6979 7542 🚌116 and routes on Via del Corso and Corso Rinascimento ⏱Group tours by appt only

Access to the church interior is restricted to groups, but it is still worth visiting to see the courtyard by Baroque architect Giovanni Antonio de Rossi, who used an architectural illusion to make it look wider than it is. Around the courtyard there are fascinating remnants of medieval houses. The church itself was rebuilt in 1685 by De Rossi, using a square Greek-cross plan with a cupola.

The Column of Marcus Aurelius celebrating his victories and *(right)* a detail of the carving ↑

## 16 Column of Marcus Aurelius

📍V2 🏠Piazza Colonna 🚌116 and routes along Via del Corso or to Piazza San Silvestro

Clearly an imitation of the column of Trajan *(p98)*, this monument was erected after the death of Marcus Aurelius in AD 180 to commemorate his victories over the barbarian tribes of the Danube. The 80-year lapse between the two works produced a great artistic change: the military campaigns of Marcus Aurelius are rendered with simplified pictures in stronger relief for clarity and immediacy. The spirit of the work is more akin to the 4th-century Arch of Constantine *(p99)* than to Trajan's monument. A new emphasis on the supernatural points to the end of the Hellenistic tradition and the beginning of Christianity.

Composed of 28 drums of marble, the column was restored in 1588 by Domenico Fontana on the orders of Pope Sixtus V. The emperor's statue on the summit was replaced by a bronze of St Paul. The 20 spirals of the low relief detail the German Marcommanic War (AD 172–3), and those of the upper half the Sarmatic War (AD 174–5). The column is nearly 30 m (100 ft) high and 3.7 m (12 ft) in diameter, with an internal spiral staircase, which is closed to the public.

## ⑰ ⚡ Ⓜ ▢ 🛍

### Palazzo Doria Pamphilj

📍 V3 🏛 Via del Corso 305
🚌 64, 81, 85, 117, 119, 492
and many other routes
🕐 9am–7pm daily, by appt
only 🚫 1 Jan, Easter Sun,
25 Dec 🌐 doriapamphilj.it

Palazzo Doria Pamphilj is a great island of stone in the heart of Rome, the oldest parts dating from 1435. Through the Corso entrance you can see the pretty 18th-century courtyard planted with citrus trees. The Aldobrandini were the next owners after the Della Rovere. Between 1601 and 1647 the mansion acquired a second courtyard and flanking wings at the expense of a public bath that stood nearby.

When the Pamphilj family took over, they completed the Piazza del Collegio Romano façade and the Via della Gatta wing, a splendid chapel and a theatre inaugurated by Queen Christina of Sweden in 1684.

In the first half of the 1700s, Gabriele Valvassori created the gallery above the courtyard and a new façade along the Corso, using the highly decorative style of the Rococo period, which now dominates the building. The stairways and salons, the Mirror Gallery and the picture gallery all give a sense of light and space.

The family collection in the Doria Pamphilj gallery has over 400 paintings dating

↑ A courtyard with orange trees in the Palazzo Doria Pamphilj

from the 15th to the 18th century, including the famous portrait of Pope Innocent X Pamphilj by Velázquez. There are also works by Titian, Caravaggio, Lorenzo Lotto and Guercino. The rooms in the private apartment have many of their original furnishings, including splendid Brussels and Gobelin tapestries.

---

### ⑱
### Via della Gatta

📍 V3 🚌 62, 63, 64, 70, 81,
87, 186, 492 and routes
along Via del Plebiscito and
Corso Vittorio Emanuele II

This narrow street runs between the Palazzo Doria Pamphilj and the smaller Palazzo Grazioli. The ancient marble sculpture of a cat (gatta) that gives the street its name is on the first cornice on the corner of Palazzo Grazioli.

---

### ⑲
### Palazzo Capranica

📍 U2 🏛 Piazza Capranica
101 🚌 116 and routes
along Via del Corso or to
Piazza San Silvestro
🚫 To the public

One of Rome's small number of surviving 15th-century buildings, the palazzo was commissioned by Cardinal Domenico Capranica both as his family residence and as a college for higher education. Its fortress-like appearance is a patchwork of subsequent additions, not unusual in the late 15th century, when Rome was still hovering between medieval and Renaissance

# EAT

A scoop of artisanal ice cream is a must. Do as the Romans do, and top it with whipped cream.

**Cremeria Monteforte**
📍 U3 🏛 Via della
Rotonda 22
📞 06-686 7720

---

**Giolitti**
📍 U2 🏛 Via degli Uffici
del Vicario 40
🌐 giolitti.it

---

**San Crispino**
📍 U2 🏛 Piazza della
Maddalena 3
🌐 ilgelatodisan
crispino.com

---

**Gunther Gelato Italiano**
📍 U3 🏛 Piazza di
Sant'Eustachio 47
🌐 gunthergelato
italiano.com

← The ancient marble cat sculpture from which Via della Gatta takes its name

↑ The main altar in the ancient Roman basilica of San Lorenzo in Lucina

taste. The Gothic-looking windows on the right of the building show the cardinal's coat of arms, and the date 1451 is inscribed on the doorway underneath. The palazzo now houses a conference centre.

## ⑳ San Lorenzo in Lucina

📍 V1 🏠 Via in Lucina 16A 📞 06-687 1494 🚌 81, 117, 492, 628 🕒 8am–8pm daily

The church is one of Rome's oldest Christian places of worship, and was probably built on a well sacred to Juno, protectress of women. It was rebuilt during the 12th century, and today's external appearance is quite typical of the period, featuring a portico with reused Roman columns crowned by medieval capitals, a plain triangular pediment and a Romanesque bell tower with coloured marble inlay.

The interior was totally rebuilt in 1856–8. The old basilica plan was destroyed and the two side naves were replaced by Baroque chapels. Do not miss the fine bust in the Fonseca Chapel, designed by Bernini, or the *Crucifixion* by Guido Reni above the main altar. There is also a 19th-century monument honouring French painter Nicolas Poussin, who died in Rome in 1655 and was buried in the church.

## ㉑ Fontanella del Facchino

📍 V3 🏠 Via Lata 🚌 64, 81, 85, 117, 119, 492 and many other routes

Il Facchino (the Porter), once in the Corso, now set in the wall of the Banco di Roma, was one of Rome's "talking statues" like Pasquino (*p128*). Created around 1590, the fountain may have been based on a drawing by painter Jacopino del Conte. The statue of a man holding a barrel most likely represents a member of the Università degli Acquaroli (Fraternity of Water-carriers), though it is also said to be of Martin Luther, or of the porter Abbondio Rizzio, who died carrying a barrel.

## ㉒ Palazzo Altieri

📍 V4 🏠 Via del Gesù 49 🚌 46, 62, 63, 64, 70, 81, 87, 186, 492 and routes along Via del Plebiscito and Corso Vittorio Emanuele II 🚊 8 🚪 To the public

The Altieri family first appears in Rome's history in the 9th century. This palazzo was built by the last male heirs, the brothers Cardinal Giambattista di Lorenzo Altieri and Cardinal Emilio Altieri, who later became Pope Clement X (reigned 1670–76). Many surrounding houses were demolished, but an old woman called Berta refused to leave, so her hovel was incorporated into the palazzo. Its windows are still visible on the west end of the building.

# A SHORT WALK
# PIAZZA DELLA ROTONDA

**Distance** 0.7 km (0.4 mile)  **Nearest bus** 116 and other routes along Corso del Rinascimento  **Time** 15 minutes

If you wander through this area, sooner or later you will emerge into Piazza della Rotonda with its jumble of open-air café tables in front of the Pantheon. The refreshing splash of the fountain makes it a welcome resting place. In this warren of narrow streets, it can be hard to realize just how close you are to some of Rome's finest sights. The magnificent art collection of Palazzo Doria Pamphilj and the Baroque splendour of the Gesù are just a few minutes' walk from the Pantheon. At night there is always a lively buzz of activity, as people dine in style or enjoy the coffee and ice cream for which the area is famous.

Andrea Pozzo painted the glorious Baroque ceiling in Sant Ignazio di Loyola in 1685 to celebrate St Ignatius and the Jesuit order (p111).

Piazza di Sant'Ignazio is a rare example of stylish domestic architecture from the early 18th century (p110).

The columns of the ancient Roman Temple of Hadrian now form the façade of the Chamber of Commerce.

La Tazza d'Oro enjoys a reputation for the potent coffee consumed on its premises as well as for its freshly ground coffee to take away.

The awe-inspiring interior of Rome's best-preserved ancient temple, the Pantheon, is only hinted at from the outside (p106).

Obelisk of Santa Maria sopra Minerva – in 1667 Bernini dreamed up the idea of mounting a recently discovered obelisk on the back of a marble elephant (p113).

The rich decoration of Rome's only Gothic church, Santa Maria Sopra Minerva, was added in the 19th century.

PIAZZA DI SANT'IGNAZIO

VIA DI SANT IGNAZIO

VIA DEL SEMINARIO

PIAZZA DELLA ROTONDA

START

PIAZZA DELLA MINERVA

↑ The Pantheon and the Obeslisk of Santa Maria sopra Minerva on Piazza della Rotonda

**Locator Map**
*For more detail see p102*

**Did You Know?**

If you visit the Pantheon when it's raining you can see rain falling through the dome's oculus.

The water in the small 16th-century Fontanella del Facchino fountain spurts from a barrel held by a porter.

Up until 1870, the college in the Palazzo del Collegio Romano educated many leading figures in the Catholic Church (p111).

Among the masterpieces in the art gallery of the magnificent Palazzo Doria Pamphilj (p116) is a portrait of Pope Innocent X by Velázquez (1650).

The Via della Gatta is named after the statue of a cat (p116).

The enormous 17th-century Palazzo Altieri is decorated with the arms of Pope Clement X (p117).

The design of the first-ever Jesuit church, the Gesù, had a great impact on religious architecture (p108).

The Pie' di Marmo, a marble foot, is a stray fragment from a gigantic Roman statue (p113).

**FINISH**

PIAZZA DEL COLLEGIO ROMANO

VIA DELLA GATTA

VIA DEL MARMO

DEL GESÙ

VIA DEL PLEBISCITO

0 metres 75

0 yards 75

N

# PIAZZA NAVONA

The foundations of the buildings surrounding the elongated oval of Piazza Navona were the ruined grandstands of the vast ancient Stadium of Domitian. The piazza still provides a dramatic spectacle today, with the obelisk of the Fontana dei Quattro Fiumi in front of the church of Sant'Agnese in Agone as its focal point. The predominant style of the area is Baroque, many of its finest buildings dating from the reign of Innocent X Pamphilj (1644–55), patron of Bernini and Borromini. Of special interest is the complex of the Chiesa Nuova, headquarters of the Filippini, the order founded by San Filippo Neri, the 16th-century "Apostle of Rome".

# PIAZZA NAVONA

## Must See
**1** Piazza Navona

## Experience More
**2** Santa Maria della Pace
**3** Palazzo Madama
**4** San Luigi dei Francesi
**5** Sant'Agostino
**6** Palazzo Pamphilj
**7** Palazzo Massimo alle Colonne
**8** Pasquino
**9** Sant'Ivo alla Sapienza
**10** Palazzo Braschi
**11** Sant'Andrea della Valle
**12** Via del Governo Vecchio
**13** Torre dell'Orologio
**14** Chiesa Nuova
**15** Oratorio dei Filippini
**16** Palazzo del Banco di Santo Spirito
**17** San Salvatore in Lauro
**18** Museo Napoleonico
**19** Via dei Coronari
**20** Palazzo Altemps

## Eat
**1** Tre Scalini
**2** Lo Zozzone
**3** Osteria del Pegno
**4** Casa Bleve
**5** Ristorante La Campana

## Stay
**6** Hotel Raphael

## Shop
**7** Antica Libreria Cascianelli
**8** Delfina Delettrez

**❶**

# PIAZZA NAVONA

🚇 T2 🚌 46, 62, 64, 70, 81, 87, 116, 492, 628

No other piazza in Rome can rival the theatricality of Piazza Navona. The social centre of the city, the piazza buzzes with life day and night.

Rome's most famous and theatrical piazza is surrounded by cafés and dominated by the Egyptian obelisk, cascading waters and gleaming marble statues of Bernini's Fontana dei Quattro Fiumi. Located on the site of an ancient Roman stadium, the oval piazza has long been a lively part of Rome. In the Renaissance years there was a market here. Today the square is equally bustling, and is especially spectacular at night when the fountains are flood-lit and the café-terraces illuminated with flame-throwing lamps.

> **DOMITIAN'S STADIUM**
> ⊘ 🚇 T2 🏛 Via di Tor Sanguigna 3
> 🕙 10am-7pm Sun-Fri, 10am-8pm Sat
> 🌐 stadiodomiziano.com
>
> A section of the massive underground brickwork ruins of Domitian's Stadium can be seen at this museum. Video reconstructions in 3D and an audio guide bring the story of the stadium to life.

## Timeline

**1500–1600**
Rome's city market is transferred from the Campidoglio to Piazza Navona.

**1655–1866**
Every August, the fountain outlets are plugged and the piazza flooded. The lower classes swim in the square while aristocrats look on.

**1–100 AD**
△ A stadium is built for athletic contests (agones), chariot races and other sports. Piazza Navona will follow the shape of this stadium.

**1644–1655**
△ Pope Innocent X commissions a new church, palace and fountain for the square.

**1869**
Rome's city market moves to the nearby Campo de' Fiori.

↑ Piazza Navona, with the Fontana del Moro in the foreground

## Fountains

Work on Bernini's Fontana dei Quattro Fiumi in the centre of the square started in 1648, and was financed by a tax levied on bread, even though there was a famine at the time. The fountain is thought to symbolize the power of the papacy over the entire world, represented by the four rivers (Plate, Ganges, Nile and Danube). The obelisk originally stood on the Appian Way, and sits on a sculpted rock, decorated with the dove and olive branch emblems from Pope Innocent X's coat of arms.

Featuring a Moor wrestling with a dolphin, the Fontana del Moro at the southern end was originally designed by Giacomo della Porta and consisted simply of the dolphin and four Tritons. In 1653, Bernini embellished it by designing the statue of a Moor to straddle the dolphin. In 1874, the original was moved to the Galleria Borghese and replaced with a copy.

At the northern end of the square, the Fontana del Nettuno began as a public drinking and washing fountain, with a basin designed by Giacomo della Porta. In the late 19th century Romans no longer depended on public fountains for their water supplies, and the fountain became a purely decorative one.

↑ The square's centrepiece, Fontana dei Quattro Fiumi, designed by Bernini

## Sant'Agnese in Agone

This Baroque church, on the left-hand side of the square, has a concave façade designed by Borromini in 1657. It stands on the site where, according to legend, in 304 AD Agnese, a 13-year-old girl from an early Christian family, was exposed naked to the spectators in Domitian's Stadium for refusing to marry and renounce her faith. Story has it that her hair grew miraculously, cascading over her body and concealing it from the crowds. Agnese was then condemned to death and martyred.

←

Statues of Neptune and the Nereids in the Fontana del Nettuno

# EXPERIENCE MORE

## ❷
### Santa Maria della Pace

**⚲ T2 ⌂ Vicolo dell' Arco della Pace 5** 🚌 46, 62, 64, 70, 81, 87, 116, 492, 628 **🕐 9:30am–6:30pm daily**

A drunken soldier allegedly pierced the breast of a painted Madonna on this site, causing it to bleed. Pope Sixtus IV della Rovere (reigned 1471–84) placated the Virgin by ordering Baccio Pontelli to build her a church if she would bring the war with Turkey to an end. Peace was restored and the church was named Santa Maria della Pace (St Mary of Peace).

The cloister was added by Bramante in 1504. As in his famous round chapel, the Tempietto (p277), he scrupulously followed Classical rules of proportion and achieved a monumental effect in a relatively small space. Pietro da Cortona may have had Bramante's Tempietto in mind when he added the church's charming semicircular portico in 1656. The interior, a short nave ending under an octagonal cupola, houses Raphael's famous frescoes of four *Sybils*, and four *Prophets* by his pupil Timoteo Viti, painted for the banker Agostino Chigi in 1514. Baldassarre Peruzzi

also did some work in the church (he painted the fresco in the first chapel on the left), as did the architect Antonio da Sangallo the Younger, who designed the second chapel on the right.

---

## ❸
### Palazzo Madama

**⚲ U3 ⌂ Corso del Rinascimento** 🚌 70, 81, 87, 116, 186, 492, 628 **🔒 Closed due to COVID-19 with no date for reopening** 🌐 senato.it

This 16th-century palazzo was built for the Medici family. It was the residence of Medici cousins Giovanni and Giuliano, both of whom became popes: Giovanni as Leo X and Giuliano as Clement VII. Caterina de' Medici, Clement VII's niece, also lived here before she was married to Henri, son of King François I of France, in 1533.

The palazzo takes its name from Madama Margherita of Austria, illegitimate daughter of Emperor Charles V, who married Alessandro de' Medici and, after his death, Ottavio Farnese. Thus, part of the art collection of the Florentine Medici family was inherited by the Roman Farnese family.

The spectacular façade was built in the mid-17th century by Cigoli and Paolo Maruccelli. The latter gave it an ornate cornice and whimsical decorative details on the roof. Since 1871 the palazzo has been the seat of the upper house of the Italian parliament.

←

Detail of Raphael's fresco depicting four *Sibyls* (c 1514), in the Chigi Chapel of Santa Maria della Pace

> **All three Caravaggios in San Luigi dei Francesi display very disquieting realism and a highly dramatic use of light.**

The Baroque decoration on the ceiling and columns inside the church of San Luigi dei Francesi

## ④ San Luigi dei Francesi

🗺 U2 🏛 Piazza di San Luigi dei Francesi 5 📞 06-688 271 🚌 70, 81, 87, 116, 186, 492, 628 🕐 9:30am-12:45pm & 2:30-6:30pm daily (Sat: to 12:15pm; Sun: from 11:30am)

The French national church was founded in 1518, but it took until 1589 to complete. It holds the tombs of many illustrious French people, including Chateaubriand's lover Pauline de Beaumont, who died in Rome in 1805.

Three Caravaggio masterpieces hang in the fifth chapel on the left, all dedicated to St Matthew. Painted between 1597 and 1602, these were Caravaggio's first great religious works: the *Calling of St Matthew*, the *Martyrdom of St Matthew* and *St Matthew and the Angel*. The first version of this last painting was rejected because of its vivid realism; never before had a saint been shown as a tired old man with dirty feet. All three Caravaggios in San Luigi dei Francesi display very disquieting realism and a highly dramatic use of light.

## ⑤ Sant'Agostino

🗺 U2 🏛 Piazza di Sant' Agostino 80 🚌 70, 81, 87, 116, 186, 492, 628 🕐 7:30am-noon & 4:30-7:30pm daily

One of the earliest of Rome's Renaissance churches – and with a façade made of travertine taken from the Colosseum – Sant'Agostino is associated with mothers, thanks to a statue of the Madonna del Parto (Pregnant Madonna) by Jacopo Sansovino that is believed to have the power to help pregnant women. The Virgin's Classical features and heavy drapery suggest she may have been inspired by a statue of Juno Lucina, the Roman goddess of childbirth. Don't miss the extraordinary *Madonna di Loreto* by Caravaggio. Depicting a peasant-like Madonna standing in a doorway welcoming two pilgrims, it is remarkably – and, at the time, controversially – realistic. The soles of the pilgrims' feet are filthy, and even the Madonna has dirty toenails.

---

## ⑥  Palazzo Pamphilj

🗺 T3 🏛 Piazza Navona 14 🚌 46, 62, 64, 70, 81, 87, 116, 492, 628 🕐 For guided tours only (in Italian and Portuguese) 🌐 roma.itamaraty. gov.br

In 1644 Giovanni Battista Pamphilj became Pope Innocent X. During his ten-year reign, he heaped riches on his own family, especially his domineering sister-in-law, Olimpia Maidalchini. The "talking statue" Pasquino (p128) gave her the nickname "Olim-Pia", Latin for "formerly virtuous". She lived in the grand Palazzo Pamphilj, which has wonderful 17th-century frescoes by Pietro da Cortona depicting scenes from the life of Aeneas and a gallery by Borromini. The building now houses the Brazilian embassy and cultural centre.

---

### COURTESANS AT SANT'AGOSTINO

Sant'Agostino was a notoriously popular church with 16th-century courtesans, for whom going to a "society" church, dressed in all their finery, was a crucial publicity exercise. The women looked magnificent, dripping with jewellery and dressed in the latest, most ostentatious styles, with their hair bleached blonde and elaborately curled. Crowds of young men would gather outside the church, waiting for them to arrive. A priest from Sant'Agostino would hear their confessions. "Just think, Your Excellency, what a lot of fine things he must have heard...," wrote one courtesan, Beatrice Ferrarese, to her lover Lorenzo de' Medici.

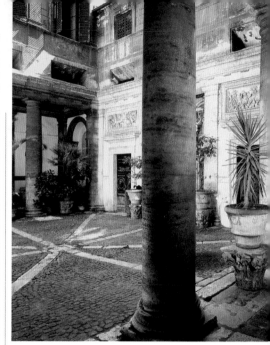

→ The courtyard of the 16th-century Palazzo Massimo alle Colonne, designed by Baldassare Peruzzi

# EAT

### Lo Zozzone

A Roman institution, this cosy place serves delicious *pizza bianca* with an array of fillings from mozzarella to artichoke, plus tasty pasta dishes and crisp Roman-style pizza.

⚑ T3 ⌂ Via del Teatro Pace 32
☎ 06-6880 8575

€€€

───────────

### Osteria del Pegno

This romantic little restaurant with low lighting can be found on the ground floor of a 15th-century palazzo and offers a menu of perfectly executed Italian dishes. Complimentary limoncello and homemade biscuits round off a meal nicely.

⚑ S2 ⌂ Vicolo Montevecchio 8
☎ 06-6880 7025

€€€

───────────

### Casa Bleve

Set in a grand vaulted dining room, this *enoteca* has an impressive wine list and a menu of gourmet offerings such as braised beef cheek served in Nebbiolo wine.

⚑ U3 ⌂ Via del Teatro Valle 48 ✕ Sun
ⓦ casableve.com

€€€

───────────

**❼**

## Palazzo Massimo alle Colonne

⚑ T3 ⌂ Corso Vittorio Emanuele II 141 🚌 40, 46, 62, 64, 70, 81, 87, 116, 186, 492, 628
🕐 16 Mar 7am–1pm only

During the last two years of his life, Baldassarre Peruzzi built this palazzo for the Massimo family, whose home had been destroyed in the 1527 Sack of Rome. Peruzzi displayed great ingenuity in dealing with an awkwardly shaped site. The previous building had stood on the ruined Theatre of Domitian, which created a curve in the great processional Via Papalis. Peruzzi's convex colonnaded façade follows the line of the street. His originality is also evident in the small square upper windows, the courtyard and the stuccoed vestibule. A single column from the theatre has been set up in the piazza.

The Massimo family traced its origins to Quintus Fabius Maximus, conqueror of Hannibal in the 3rd century BC, and their coat of arms is borne by an infant Hercules. Over the years this family dynasty produced many great Humanists, and in the 19th century, it was a Massimo who negotiated peace with Napoleon. On 16 March each year the family chapel opens to the public for a few hours (7am–1pm) to commemorate young Paolo Massimo's resurrection from the dead by San Filippo Neri in 1538.

───────────

**❽**

## Pasquino

⚑ T3 ⌂ Piazza di Pasquino 🚌 40, 46, 62, 64, 70, 81, 87, 116, 492, 628

This rough chunk of marble is all that now remains of a Hellenistic group, probably representing the incident in Homer's *Iliad* in which Menelaus shields the body of the slain Patroclus. For years it lay as a stepping stone in a muddy medieval street until it was erected on this corner in 1501, near the shop of an outspoken cobbler named Pasquino. Freedom of speech was not encouraged in papal Rome, so the cobbler wrote out his satirical comments on current events and attached them to the statue.

Other Romans followed suit, hanging their maxims and verses on the statue by night to escape punishment. Despite the wrath of the authorities, the sayings of the "talking statue" (renamed Pasquino) were part of popular culture up until the 19th century. Anonymous political maxims were hung on other statues, too. Sometimes satirical poems are still stuck onto the Pasquino statue.

---

**9**

## Sant'Ivo alla Sapienza

**U3** **Corso del Rinascimento 40** **06-0608** **40, 46, 64, 70, 81, 87, 116, 186, 492, 628** **9am-noon Sun**

The church's lantern is crowned with a cross on top of a twisted spiral – a highly distinctive landmark from Rome's roof terraces. No other Baroque church is quite like this one, made by Borromini, based on a design of astonishing geometrical complexity. The church stands in the courtyard of the Palazzo della Sapienza, seat of the old University of Rome from the 1400s until 1935.

---

**10**

## Palazzo Braschi

**T3** **Piazza San Pantaleo 10** **06-6710 8303** **40, 46, 62, 64, 70, 81, 87, 116, 186, 492, 628** **10am-7pm Tue-Sun, by appt only**

The last Roman palazzo to be built for the family of a pope, Palazzo Braschi was erected in the late 18th century for Pope Pius VI Braschi's nephews. Architect Cosimo Morelli gave the building its imposing façade overlooking the piazza.

The palazzo now houses the municipal Museo di Roma, with exhibits illustrating life in Rome from medieval times to the 19th century.

---

**11**

## Sant'Andrea della Valle

**U4** **Piazza Sant' Andrea della Valle** **06-686 1339** **H, 40, 46, 62, 64, 70, 81, 87, 116, 186, 492, 628** **8** **7:30am-7:30pm daily**

The church is the scene of the first act of Puccini's opera *Tosca*. Opera fans will not find the Attavanti Chapel a mere poetic invention. The real church still has much to recommend it – the impressive façade shows the flamboyant Baroque style at its best. Inside, a golden light filters through high windows, showing off the gilded interior. Here lie the two popes of the Sienese Piccolomini family: on the left of the central nave is the tomb of Pius II, the first Humanist pope (reigned 1458–64); Pope Pius III lies opposite – he reigned for less than a month in 1503.

The church is famous for its beautiful dome, which is the largest in Rome after St Peter's. It was built by Carlo Maderno in 1622–5 and was painted with splendid frescoes by Domenichino and Giovanni Lanfranco. The latter's extravagant style, to be seen in the dome fresco *Glory of Paradise*, won him most of the commission, and the jealous Domenichino is said to have tried to kill his colleague. He failed, but Domenichino's jealousy was unnecessary, as shown by his two beautiful paintings of scenes from the life of St Andrew around the apse and altar. In the Strozzi Chapel, built in the style of Michelangelo, the altar has copies of the *Leah* and *Rachel* by Michelangelo in San Pietro in Vincoli (*p207*).

↑ The coat of arms of Pope Francis on the portal of Sant'Andrea della Valle

## 12

## Via del Governo Vecchio

📍 S3 🚌 40, 46, 62, 64

The street takes its name from Palazzo del Governo Vecchio, which was the seat of papal government in the 17th and 18th centuries. Once part of the Via Papalis, which led from the Lateran to St Peter's, the street is lined with 15th- and 16th-century houses and small workshops. Particularly interesting are those at No. 104 and No. 106. The small palazzo at No. 123 was once thought to have been the home of the architect Bramante.

Opposite is Palazzo del Governo Vecchio. It is also known as Palazzo Nardini, from the name of its founder, which is inscribed, along with the date 1477, on the first-floor windows.

## 13

## Torre dell'Orologio

📍 S3 📍 Piazza dell'Orologio
🚌 40, 46, 62, 64

Borromini built this clock tower to decorate one corner of the Convent of

↑ *Madonna and Angels* (1606–8), by Peter Paul Rubens, which hangs above the altar in the Chiesa Nuova

the Oratorians of San Filippo Neri in 1647–9. Its front and rear are concave and the sides convex. The mosaic of the Madonna under the clock is by Pietro da Cortona, while on the corner of the building is a small tabernacle to the Madonna flanked by angels in the style of Bernini.

## 14

## Chiesa Nuova

📍 S3 📍 Piazza della Chiesa Nuova 📞 06-687 5289
🚌 40, 46, 62, 64 🕐 7:30am– noon & 4:30–7pm daily

San Filippo Neri (St Philip Neri) is the most appealing

← The magnificent clock tower Torre dell'Orologio

of the Counter-Reformation saints. An unconventional reformer, he required his noble Roman followers to humble themselves in public – for example by setting noblemen to work as labourers on building his church. With the help of Pope Gregory XIII, his church was constructed in place of an old medieval church and it has been known ever since as the Chiesa Nuova (new church).

Begun in 1575 by Matteo da Città di Castello and continued by Martino Longhi the Elder, it was consecrated in 1599 (but the façade, by Fausto Rughesi, was only finished in 1606). Against San Filippo's wishes, the interior was decorated after his death; Pietro da Cortona frescoed the nave, dome and apse, taking nearly 20 years. There are also three paintings by Rubens: *Madonna and Angels*; *Saints Domitilla, Nereus and Achilleus*; and *Saints Gregory, Maurus and Papias*. San Filippo is buried in his own chapel, to the left of the altar.

## 15

### Oratorio dei Filippini

📍 S3 🏛 Piazza della Chiesa Nuova ☎ 06-6710 8100
🚌 46, 62, 64 🔒 To the public

With the adjoining church and convent, the Oratory formed the centre of Filippo Neri's religious order, founded in 1575. Its members are known as Filippini. The musical term "oratorio" (a religious text sung by solo voices and chorus) derives from the services that were held here. Filippo Neri came to Rome aged 18 to work as a tutor at a time of religious strife, an economic slump and an outbreak of the plague after the Sack of Rome in 1527. New-comers like Neri and Ignazio di Loyola set out to revive the spiritual life of the city.

Neri formed a brotherhood of laymen who helped pilgrims and the sick (*see Santissima Trinità dei Pellegrini p167*). He founded the Oratory as a centre for religious discourse. Its conspicuous curving brick façade was built by Borromini.

## 16

### Palazzo del Banco di Santo Spirito

📍 R2 🏛 Via del Banco di Santo Spirito 🚌 40, 46, 62, 64 🕐 Normal banking hours

Formerly the mint of papal Rome, this palazzo is often referred to as the Antica Zecca (old mint). The upper storeys of the façade, built by Antonio da Sangallo the Younger in the 1520s, are in the shape of a Roman triumphal arch. Above it stand two Baroque statues symbolizing Charity and Thrift, and in the centre of the arch above the main entrance an inscription records the founding of the Banco di Santo Spirito by Pope Paul V Borghese in 1605.

Pope Paul was a very shrewd financier and he encouraged Romans to deposit their money at the bank by offering the vast estates of the Hospital of Santo Spirito (*p300*) as security. The building still houses a modern bank.

→
The grand façades of the Oratorio dei Filippini (*left*) and Chiesa Nuova (*right*)

### ⓱

## San Salvatore in Lauro

📍S2 🏛Piazza San Salvatore in Lauro 15 ☎06-687 5187 🚍70, 81, 87, 116, 186, 280, 492 🕐10am–1pm & 4–7pm daily

Named "in Lauro" after the laurel grove that grew here in ancient times, this church was built at the end of the 1500s by Ottaviano Mascherino. The bell tower and sacristy were 18th-century additions by Nicola Salvi, famous for the Trevi Fountain (p184).

The church contains the first great altarpiece by the 17th-century artist Pietro da Cortona, The Birth of Jesus, in the first chapel to the right.

The adjacent convent of San Giorgio includes a frescoed refectory and the monument to Pope Eugenius IV (reigned 1431–47), moved here when the old St Peter's was pulled down. An extravagant Venetian, Eugenius would willingly spend thousands of ducats on his gold tiara, but requested a "simple, lowly burial place" near his predecessor Pope Eugenius III.

In 1669 San Salvatore in Lauro became the seat of a pious association, the Confraternity of the Piceni, who were inhabitants of the Marche region. Fanatically loyal to the pope, the Piceni were employed as papal soldiers and tax collectors.

### ⓲

## Museo Napoleonico

📍T2 🏛Piazza di Ponte Umberto 1 🚍70, 81, 87, 116, 186, 280, 492 🕐10am–6pm Tue–Sun, by appt only 🚫1 Jan, 1 May, 25 Dec 🌐museonapoleonico.it

This free museum is dedicated to Napoleon Bonaparte and his family. Items that belonged to Napoleon himself include an Indian shawl he wore during his exile on St Helena.

After Napoleon's death in 1821 the pope allowed many of the Bonaparte family to settle in Rome, including his sister Pauline who married the Roman Prince Camillo Borghese. The museum has a cast of her right breast, made by Canova in 1805 as a study for his statue of her as a reclining Venus, now in the Galleria Borghese (p146). Portraits and personal effects of other members of the family are on display, including uniforms, court dresses and a penny-farthing bicycle that belonged to Prince Eugène, the son of Emperor Napoleon III.

The collection was assembled in 1927 by the Counts Primoli, the sons of Napoleon Charles's sister, Carlotta.

The palace next door, in Via Zanardelli, houses the Racolta Praz (open Thu & Fri), a huge selection of objets d'art, paintings and furniture. Dating from the 17th and 18th centuries, they were collected by the art historian and literary critic Mario Praz.

← A bust of Napoleon on display in the Museo Napoleonico

↑ A bustling street corner at the top of the historic Via dei Coronari

### ⓳

## Via dei Coronari

📍S2 🚍40, 46, 62, 64, 70, 81, 87, 116, 186, 280, 492

Large numbers of medieval pilgrims making their way to St Peter's walked along this street to cross over the Tiber at Ponte Sant'Angelo. Of the businesses that sprang up, the most enduring was the selling of rosaries. The street is still named after the rosary sellers (coronari) who had their shops along it in medieval times. It followed the course of the ancient Roman Via Recta (straight street), which ran from today's Piazza Colonna to the Tiber.

Making one's way through the vast throng of people in Via dei Coronari could be extremely hazardous. In the Holy Year of 1450, some 200 pilgrims died, crushed by the crowds or drowned in the Tiber. Although the rosary sellers have been replaced by antiques dealers, the street still has many original buildings from the 15th and 16th centuries. One of the earliest, at Nos. 156–7, is known as the House of Fiammetta, the mistress of Cesare Borgia.

### Palazzo Altemps

📍 T2  🏛 Via di Sant' Apollinare 46  🚌 70, 81, 87, 116, 280, 492, 628  🕐 2-7:45pm Tue-Fri, 10:30am-7:45pm Sat & Sun (last adm: 1 hour before closing)  📅 1 Jan, 25 Dec  🌐 coopculture.it

An extraordinary collection of Classical sculpture is housed in this branch of the Museo Nazionale Romano. The palazzo was originally built for Girolamo Riario, nephew of Pope Sixtus IV, in 1480 and was restored as a museum in the 1990s. The Riario coat of arms can still be seen in the janitor's room. In the popular uprising that followed the pope's death in 1484, the building was sacked and Girolamo fled the city.

In 1568 the palazzo was bought by Cardinal Marco Sittico Altemps, and it was renovated by Martino Longhi the Elder in the 1570s. He added the great belvedere, crowned with obelisks and a marble unicorn.

The Altemps family were ostentatious collectors; the courtyard and its staircase are lined with ancient sculptures. These form part of the museum's collection, together with the Ludovisi collection of ancient sculptures, which was previously housed in the Museo Nazionale Romano in the Baths of Diocletian (p189). On the first floor, at the far end of the courtyard, visitors can admire the Painted Loggia, dating from 1595. The Ludovisi throne, a Greek original carved in the 5th century BC, is on the same floor. In the Salone del Camino is the powerful statue *Galatian's Suicide*, a marble Roman replica of a group originally made in bronze in ancient Greece. Nearby is the Ludovisi Sarcophagus, dating from the 3rd century AD.

# A SHORT WALK
# PIAZZA NAVONA

**Distance** 0.8 km (0.5 mile) **Nearest bus** 46, 62, 64, 70, 81, 87, 116, 492, 628 **Time** 20 minutes

To discover an older Rome, walk along Via del Governo Vecchio to admire the façades of its Renaissance buildings and browse in the fascinating antiques shops. Piazza Navona is one of Rome's most beautiful squares. Day and night there is always something going on in the pedestrian area around its three flamboyant fountains. The Baroque is also represented in many of the area's churches.

*The Torre dell' Orologio clock tower by Borromini (1648) is part of the Convent of the Filippini (p131).*

**START**

*The musical term "oratorio" comes from the Oratorio di Filippini, a place of informal worship (p131).*

*The Chiesa Nuova was rebuilt in the late 16th century for the order founded by San Filippo Neri (p130).*

VIA DEL CORALLO

VIA DEL GOVERNO VECCHIO

*The Via del Governo Vecchio preserves a large number of fine Renaissance houses (p130).*

CORSO VITTORIO EMANUELE II

DI PASQ

*Romans hung satirical verses and dialogues on the weather-beaten Pasquino statue (p128).*

*The late 18th-century Palazzo Braschi has a splendid balcony and houses the Museo di Roma.*

PIA DI S PANTALE

← The Fontana del Moro and Sant' Agnese in Agone on Piazza Navona

| 0 metres | | 50 |
| --- | --- | --- |
| 0 yards | | 50 |

N ↗

**Locator Map**
*For more detail see p122*

*Santa Maria della Pace*

*Santa Maria dell'Anima has been the German church in Rome for four centuries.*

*Borromini's startling concave façade of Sant'Agnese in Agone (1657) dominates one side of Piazza Navona (p125).*

*The unique Piazza Navona owes its shape to a Roman race-track and its stunning decor to the genius of the Roman Baroque.*

*The Fontana dei Quattro Fiumi supporting an obelisk was designed by Bernini (p125).*

*An 18th-century statue of St Louis stands in a niche in the façade of San Luigi dei Francesi (p127).*

*A spread-eagled stone lion skin decorates the central doorway of the Palazzo Madama, now the Italian Senate (p126).*

*The tiny domed church of Sant'Ivo alla Sapienza is one of Borromini's most original creations. He worked on it between 1642 and 1650 (p129).*

*Fontana del Moro was remodelled in 1653 by Bernini, who designed the central sea god (p125).*

*The grand Palazzo Pamphilj was built for Pope Innocent X and his family in the mid-17th century.*

*The magnificent curving colonnade of the Palazzo Massimo alle Colonne (1536) is by Baldassarre Peruzzi (p128).*

**FINISH**

*Sant'Andrea della Valle, with its grandiose façade by Carlo Rainaldi (1665), has gained fame as the setting of the first act of Puccini's Tosca (p129).*

VIA DI SANTA MARIA DELL' ANIMA

NAVONA

CORSIA AGONALE

PIAZZA

VIA DEL SALVATORE

CORSO DEL RINASCIMENTO

VIA DEGLI STADERARI

VIA DEI SEDIARI

PIAZZA DI SANT'ANDREA DELLA VALLE

A view of the Spanish Steps and church of Trinità dei Monti from Via dei Condotti

# PIAZZA DI SPAGNA AND VILLA BORGHESE

By the 16th century, the increase in the numbers of visiting pilgrims and ecclesiasts was making life in Rome's already congested medieval centre unbearable. A new triangle of roads was built, still in place today, designed to channel pilgrims as swiftly as possible from the city's north gate, Porta del Popolo, to the Vatican. By the 18th century hotels had sprung up all over the district. With Piazza di Spagna at its heart, this area remains busy day and night, the target of visitors from all over the world. Beyond the still visible traces of the old city walls lie the extensive grounds of Villa Borghese, now Rome's most popular public park. The villa and gardens were designed in the early 17th century by Cardinal Scipione Borghese as a recreational retreat at the edge of Rome and to house his private art collection. The present gardens were redeveloped in the early 19th century and have a boating lake, a replica of Shakespeare's Globe Theatre, a zoo, a few cafés and several of Rome's finest museums.

## F

**1**

VIALE DELLE BELLE ARTI

VIA DI VILLA GIULIA

V. ENRICO PESSINA

VIA GIOVANNI GRAVINA

VIA G. FILANGERI

LUNGOTEVERE DELLE NAVI

VIA FLAMINIA

PIAZZA DELLA MARINA

VIA DOMENICO ALBERTO AZUNI

**4** Villa Giulia

VIALE DELLE BELLE ARTI

PIAZZA THORWALDSEN

Galleria Nazionale D'Arte Moderna

PIAZZALE FIRDUSI

PIAZZALE FERDOWSI

VIALE MADA MA LETIZIA

Tempio d'Esculapio

VIA LE F. BERNADOTTE

Boating Lake

VIALE ESCULAPIO

VIALE D. ARANCIERA

**2**

Museo Carlo Bilotti

## G

VIALE BRUNO BUOZZI

VIA ANTONIO GRAMSCI

Ponte G. Matteotti

LUNGOTEVERE MICHELANGELO

Ponte P. Nenni

Villa Ruffo

VIA M. FORTUNY

VIA P. PISANELLI

VIA C. ROMAGNOSI

VIA G.D. ROMAGNOSI

VIA G. B. VICO

BECCARIA

LUNGOTEVERE ARNALDO DI BRESCIA

VIA P. S. MANCINI

S. MANCINI

VIA GIANTURCO

VIA FLAMINIA

V. M. CRISTINA

VIA P. CLOTILDE

Stazione Roma Nord

Flaminio

P.LE DEL FIOCCO

VIALE D. ORTI GIUSTINIANI

VIALE D. LUBIN

VIALE WASHINGTON

V.LE DEL MURO TORTO

VLE F. LA GUARDIA

**2**

Teatro San Carlino

VIALE DELLE MAGNOLIE

VIALE DEL GALOPPATOIO

**2** Santa Maria del Popolo

**13** Pincio Gardens

VIALE DEL MURO TORTO

## H

VIALE DEL

**1**

Ponte Regina Margherita

LUNGOTEVERE ARNALDO DI BRESCIA

V. LUISA DI SAVOIA

Porta del Popolo

PIAZZALE FLAMINIO

VIA M. CRISTINA

Ponte Regina Margherita

VIA D. PENNA

VIA FERDINANDO DI SAVOIA

**11** Piazza del Popolo

**12** Santa Maria dei Miracoli

Santa Maria in Montesanto

VIALE G. D'ANNUNZIO

VIALE TRINITA DEI

Villa Medici **8**

VIALE DEL MURO TORTO

**3**

VATICAN
p282

VIA FEDERICO CESI

VIA A. BRUNETTI

VIA DEL VANTAGGIO

Casa di Goethe **17**

VIA DEL CORSO

VIA LAURINA

VIA DI GESU E MARIA

All Saints' **9**

VIA MARGUTTA

VIA DEL BABUINO

VIA SAN GIACOMO

VIA DEI GRECI

VIA ALIBERT

CAMPO MARZIO

VIA VITTORIA

Spagna **1**

M

Trinità dei Monti

LUNGOTEVERE IN AUGUSTA

VIA DI RIPETTA

VIA ANTONIO CANOVA

VIA DELLA FREZZA

Mausoleum of Augustus **15**

PIAZZA AUGUSTO IMPERATORE

VIC. DEL LUPO

V. C. BELSIANA

VIA DELLA CROCE

VIA MARIO DE' FIORI

Piazza di Spagna **1**

Spanish Steps **1**

**3**

Colonna dell' Immacolata

PIAZZA MIGNANELLI

Ara Pacis **10**

San Rocco **16**

Santi Ambrogio e Carlo al Corso **14**

VIA TOMACELLI

Ponte Cavour

Palazzo di Giustizia

Palazzo di Giustizia

LUNGOT. PRATI

VIA V. COLONNA

Ponte Umberto

**4**

PIAZZA DELLA ROTONDA
p102

PIAZZA D. PARLAMENTO

Palazzo Chigi

Via Condotti **7**

VIA BORGOGNONA

VIA CONDOTTI

VIA DI PROPAGANDA FIDE

Palazzo di Propaganda Fide **6**

VIA DEI DUE MACEL

TREVI

VIA FRATTINA

VIA DELLA VITE

VIA DELLA MERCEDE

Sant'Andrea delle Fratte **5**

V. DEL POZZETTO

PIAZZA DI SAN SILVESTRO

VIA CLAUDIO

LARGO CHIGI

VIA DE

QUIRINAL AND MONT
p180

0 metres 200
0 yards 200

N

## F

## G

## H

## PIAZZA DI SPAGNA AND VILLA BORGHESE

### Must Sees
1. Piazza di Spagna
2. Santa Maria del Popolo
3. Villa Borghese
4. Villa Giulia

### Experience More
5. Sant'Andrea delle Fratte
6. Palazzo di Propaganda Fide
7. Via Condotti
8. Villa Medici
9. All Saints'
10. Ara Pacis
11. Piazza del Popolo
12. Santa Maria dei Miracoli and Santa Maria in Montesanto
13. Pincio Gardens
14. Santi Ambrogio e Carlo al Corso
15. Mausoleum of Augustus
16. San Rocco
17. Casa di Goethe

### Eat & Drink
1. Babington's Tea Rooms
2. Casina del Lago Café
3. Antico Caffè Greco

# PIAZZA DI SPAGNA

**Q** H3 🚌 116, 117, 119 Ⓜ Spagna

Shaped like a crooked bow tie and surrounded by tall, shuttered houses painted in muted shades of ochre, pink and cream, Piazza di Spagna is the most famous square in Rome.

The square was long the haunt of expatriates and foreign visitors. In the 17th century the Spanish embassy was here, and the area around it was deemed to be Spanish territory – anyone who unwittingly trespassed was in danger of being dragooned into the Spanish army. In the 18th and 19th centuries the square stood at the heart of the main hotel district, attracting visitors from all over the world. Today the piazza is thronged with people all day and, in summer, most of the night. The church at the top of the steps, Trinità dei Monti, founded by the French in 1485, is famous for its breathtaking views.

## Fontana della Barcaccia

Designed either by Gian Lorenzo Bernini or his father, Pietro, this fountain was an ingenious solution to the fact that the

water pressure on the square was so low that spectacular cascades were not possible. Instead, the fountain represents a sinking boat, lying half submerged in a shallow pool. Pope Urban VIII Barberini commissioned the fountain in 1627.

←

Fontana della Barcaccia, the least showy of Rome's Baroque fountains

# EAT

**Babington's Tea Rooms**

These old-fashioned tea rooms were opened in 1896 by Englishwoman Anna Maria Babington to serve homesick British travellers with scones and tea. The menu today also includes burgers, salads, scrambled eggs, muffins and cakes. It is open for breakfast, lunch and dinner.

**Q** H3 **🅐** Piazza di Spagna 23
**Ⓦ** babingtons.com

€€€

## KEATS-SHELLEY MEMORIAL HOUSE

**◎ Q** H3 **🅐** Piazza di Spagna 26
**🕐** 10am-1pm & 2-6pm Mon-Sat
**Ⓦ** keats-shelley-house.org

This is where the poet John Keats stayed with his friend, the painter Joseph Severn, in 1820. Suffering from consumption, Keats had been sent to Rome by his doctor, in the hope that it would help him recuperate. Depressed because of scathing criticism of his poetry, and unrequited love, Keats died a few months later aged 25. His death inspired poet Percy Bysshe Shelley to write the poem *Mourn not for Adonaïs*. Shelley died the following year in a boating accident; both poets are buried in the Protestant cemetery (p250). The house is now a museum dedicated to the Romantic poets.

↑ The Spanish Steps with azaleas in full bloom and the church of Trinità dei Monti

❷

# SANTA MARIA DEL POPOLO

📍G2 ⌂ Piazza del Popolo 12 🚌 117, 119, 490, 495, 926 🚊2 Ⓜ Flaminio
🕐 8:30am-noon & 4-6pm Mon-Fri, 4:30-6pm Sat & Sun 🚫No visits during Mass 🌐 smariadelpopolo.com

**Occupying the site where, according to legend, Nero was buried, this early Renaissance church was commissioned by Pope Sixtus IV della Rovere in 1472. It is one of Rome's greatest stores of artistic treasures.**

Among the artists who worked on the building were Andrea Bregno and Pinturicchio. Later additions were made by Bramante and Bernini. Many illustrious families have chapels here, all decorated with appropriate splendour. The Della Rovere Chapel has delightful frescoes by Pinturicchio, the Cerasi Chapel has two Caravaggio masterpieces, but the finest of all is the Chigi Chapel designed by Raphael in 1513–16 for his patron, the banker Agostino Chigi. The most striking of the church's many Renaissance tombs are the two by Andrea Sansovino behind the main altar.

↑ One of two Caravaggios in the Cerasi Chapel, *The Crucifixion of St Peter* uses dramatic foreshortening to highlight the sheer effort involved in turning the saint's crucifix upside down.

↑ Behind the altar, the stained-glass windows by the French artist Guillaume de Marcillat were the first in Rome.

*1099*

△ Paschal II builds chapel over tombs of the Domitia family (which included Nero) in honour of the Madonna.

*1213–27*

▽ Chapel enlarged under Gregory IX.

*1472–8*

△ Sixtus IV builds church (one of the first Renaissance churches in Rome).

*1485–9*

▽ Della Rovere Chapel painted by Pinturicchio.

↑ The dome of Raphael's Chigi Chapel, with mosaics showing God as creator of the seven heavenly bodies

VIRGINI LAVRETANAE S

**3** 🖥

# VILLA BORGHESE

📍 J1  🏛 Entrances at Piazzale Flaminio,
Porta Pinciana & Pincio Gardens  🚌 52, 53, 88,
116, 490, 495  🚊 3, 19

**One of Rome's largest parks, Villa Borghese was laid
out in the early 17th century by Cardinal Scipione
Borghese, the pleasure-loving nephew of Pope Paul V.**

A keen art collector, Scipione Borghese amassed one of
Europe's finest collections of paintings, sculptures and
antiquities. The young Bernini created many of his loveliest
sculptures for Scipione, many of which are still displayed in
the Galleria Borghese (formerly called Casino Borghese),
created specifically to house the collection. Borghese was
also a patron of Caravaggio. The park was redesigned in the
18th century by Scottish landscape artist Jacob More, with
artificial lakes and Neo-Classical temples. In 1903 the park
became the property of the Italian state and was opened
to the general public. A replica of Shakespeare's Globe
Theatre was added in 2003.

## EAT

**Casina del Lago**
This charming little
café next to the Museo
Carlo Bilotti has great
outdoor seating on
a terrace (heated in
winter), overlooking
the lake. Open from 9am
until sunset, it offers
simple pizzas, pasta and
rice dishes, salads and
sandwiches, along with
coffees, wine, cakes
and pastries.

📍 H2  🏛 Viale
dell'Aranciera 2
📞 06-8535 2623
🕐 Mon in winter

€€€

Rowing on the lake in the Villa Borghese gardens ↓

## Did You Know?

Bikes, rollerskates, go-karts and boats are all for hire in the park.

① ⊘

### Casina di Raffaello

📍J2 🏛 Piazza di Siena ⏰9am-7pm Tue-Sun (till 3:30pm in winter) 🌐casinadiraffaello.it

This diminutive house – said to have once been owned by the painter Raphael – is now dedicated to young children between the ages of three and ten. It has both indoor and outdoor play areas, a reading corner, wooden toys, as well as a fun-packed programme of activities designed for children and for the whole family to enjoy together.

② 

### Museo Carlo Bilotti

📍H2 🏛 Viale Fiorello La Guardia 📞06-0608 🚍116 Ⓜ Flaminio-Piazza del Popolo (Line A) ⏰1-7pm Tue-Fri (winter: 10am-4pm), 10am-7pm Sat & Sun 🌐museocarlobilotti.it

Housing the art collection of perfume baron and art collector Carlo Bilotti, this free bijou museum has a permanent collection of 22 works by Giorgio de Chirico, along with works by Gino Severini and Giacomo Manzù and a portrait of Bilotti's wife and daughter by Andy Warhol. It also hosts frequent contemporary art and photography exhibitions.

③ ⊘

### Bioparco

📍J1 🏛 Piazzale Giardino Zoologico 🚍3, 52, 53, 217, 360, 910 & 926 🚊3, 19 Ⓜ Flaminio-Piazza del Popolo & Spagna (Line A) ⏰Late Oct-late Mar: 9:30am-5pm daily; late Mar-late Oct: 9:30am-6pm daily (till 7pm Sat & Sun in Apr-Sep) 🌐bioparco.it

Rome's zoo is devoted to research, the preservation of animals in danger of extinction and the education of the public. It houses more than 1,300 animals, ranging from lions, hippos and elephants to snakes and crocodiles, and has excellent information boards.

### A BAROQUE THEME PARK

The gardens were the Baroque equivalent of a theme park, with joke fountains - designed to squirt unwitting passersby - exotic birds, a grotto with artificial rain and a mechanical talking satyr. Scipione originally opened the park to the public, but after a visitor was outraged by the erotic paintings in a summerhouse, Paul V decided it would be more circumspect to keep it private.

④ Ⓜ

### Globe Theatre

📍J1 📌Largo Aqua Felix
🕐Jul & Aug: 7:30pm Sat &
Sun 🌐Peformances:
ticketone.it; tours:
globetheatreroma.com

London's Globe Theatre was
reconstructed here in just
three months in 2003. Every
summer the open-air theatre
showcases Shakespeare's
plays. Most performances are
in Italian though there are
sometimes English language
productions. Tickets include
a tour of the theatre.

⑤ ⊘ ⊡ 🏛

### Galleria Nazionale
d'Arte Moderna

📍H1 📌Viale delle Belli
Arti131 🚌3 🚋19 🕐10am-
6:30pm Tue-Sun 🌐galleria
artemodernaroma.it

Founded in 1833, Rome's
museum of 19th- and 20th-
century art makes its first
impact with a stunning
cracked-mirror floor designed
by the contemporary Italian
artist Alfredo Pirri. The
exhibits are spread over
two floors and the displays
change regularly. The collection includes a section called
"Excuse me, is this art?", which
features several pieces by
French artist Marcel Duchamp
along with slashed and
pierced canvasses created
by Lucio Fontana in the
1950s. There are also works
by Italian Futurists such as
Gino Severini, Mario Sironi
and Giacomo Balla, as well
as Giorgio de Chirico and
Sicilian artist Renato Guttoso.
Other highlights include
works by Cy Twombly, Jean
Arp, Alberto Giacometti and
Henry Moore.

→

Villa Borghese, built by
architect Flaminio Ponzio to
designs by Scipione Borghese

⑥ ⊘ Ⓜ ⊡ 🏛

### Galleria Borghese

📍K1 📌Piazzale del Museo
Borghese 5 🚌52, 53, 116,
910 to Via Pinciana
🚋3, 19 to Viale delle Belle
Arti 🕐9am-7pm Tue-Sun;
advance booking essential;
limited time slots for entry
🌐galleria borghese.beni
culturali.it

Cardinal Scipione Borghese
built Villa Borghese in the
17th century as a country
villa for elaborate parties,
its three wings embracing
the surrounding gardens.
Scipione Borghese was an
extravagant patron of the
arts and filled the villa with
exotic antique statues and
many virtuoso sculptures.

The museum is divided into
two sections: the sculpture
collection occupies the
ground floor while the picture

> **Scipione Borghese
> was an extravagant
> patron of the arts
> and filled the villa
> with exotic antique
> statues and virtuoso
> sculptures.**

gallery is situated on the
upper floor. The highlights of
the sculpture collection are
the superb pieces by Bernini
inspired by Greek mythology.
The sculpture of *David* shows
him with brows furrowed, lips
gripped and catapult held
taut, about to swing the full
weight of his body to launch a
stone to kill the giant Goliath.
The virtuoso life-sized *Apollo
and Daphne* shows Daphne in
the process of metamor-
phosing into a laurel tree to
escape the sun god Apollo.
The gallery's fine art collection

includes Titian's evocation of the difference between chaste and sexual love, *Sacred and Profane Love*, as well as several works by Caravaggio – notably the *Madonna dei Palafranieri*, removed from St Peter's basilica because it was felt to be inappropriately realistic. The gallery also includes a feverish *Self-Portrait of the Artist as Bacchus*, reputedly painted while the artist was ill, as well as the decadent *Boy with a Basket of Fruit* in which flecked vine leaves and over-ripe fruit exude a decaying fecundity.

↑ *Sacred and Profane Love* (1514) by Titian

Another major piece of work is Raphael's *Deposition* (1507), which was commissioned by Perugian matriarch Atalanta Baglioni to honour her assassinated son, who is depicted as a red-shirted pall-bearer.

↑ The mighty *David* (1624) by Bernini - the face was modelled on the artist's own

④ 🖾 🖾 🖵 🖹

# VILLA GIULIA

**📍 G1** **🏛 Piazzale di Villa Giulia 9** **🚌 52, 926 to Viale Bruno Buozzi; 88, 490, 495 to Viale Washington** **🚊 3, 19 to Piazza Thorvaldsen** **🕐 9am–8pm Tue–Sun (last adm: 6:30pm)** **🌐 museoetru.it**

Since 1889 Villa Giulia has housed the ETRU – Museo Nazionale di Villa Giulia, with its collection of pre-Roman antiquities from central Italy. It holds the most important collection of Etruscan art in Italy.

Built as a country retreat for Pope Julius III in the 16th century, Villa Giulia was designed by exceptional architects: Vignola (designer of the Gesù), Vasari and the sculptor Ammannati. Michelangelo also contributed. The villa's main features are its façade, the courtyard and garden and the *nymphaeum*.

### Etruscan Finds

Etruria was not a nation, but a federation of politically and economically independent cities in central Italy. The Etruscans were energetic traders – their wealth was based on prodigious natural resources of metals. If the finds from the tombs of the wealthy are any indication, they had a voracious appetite for the beautiful artifacts produced by their Greek and Phoenician trading partners. Tomb finds include the elaborately decorated chalices, wine jugs and kraters that may have graced Etruscan banqueting tables; mirrors and jewellery; and some extraordinary home accessories including a lion-foot candelabra.

Artifacts on display come from most of the major excavations in Tuscany and Lazio. Rooms 1–13b and 30–40 are arranged by site and include Vulci, Todi, Veio and Cerveteri, while the remaining rooms are devoted to important objects that have been returned after being illegally excavated and sold, as well as private collections that have been donated to the museum.

↑ A beautiful black Etruscan figure vase at the Museum of Villa Giulia.

← Façade of the Renaissance Villa Giulia, designed by several leading architects

---

### VILLA PONIATOWSKI

**📍 G1** **🏛 Piazzale di Villa Giulia 3** **📞 06-3226 571** **🔒 Closed due to COVID-19 with no date for reopening**

The museum's additional collections are at the nearby Villa Poniatowski, which has beautifully restored frescoed rooms. Exhibits include fine gold jewellery, a tomb carved from a tree trunk and decorated make-up containers, along with other finds.

---

←

Sarcophagus of the Spouses (room 12), a 6th-century BC terracotta masterpiece from Cerveteri, showing a dead couple at the eternal banquet

↑ The beautiful portico of Villa Giulia with fresoces by Pietro Venale, leading to the courtyard

# EXPERIENCE MORE

### 5

## Sant'Andrea delle Fratte

📍 H4 🏛 Via Sant'Andrea delle Fratte 1 ☎ 06-679 3191 🚌 116, 117 Ⓜ Spagna 🕐 Summer: 6:30am–12:30pm & 4:30–8pm; winter: 6:15am–1pm & 4–7pm

When Sant'Andrea delle Fratte was built in the 1100s, this was the northernmost edge of Rome. Though the church is now firmly within the city, its name (*fratte* means "thickets") recalls its original setting.

The church was completely rebuilt in the 17th century, partly by Borromini. His bell tower and dome are notable for the complex concave and convex surfaces. The bell tower is particularly fanciful, with angel caryatids, flaming torches, and exaggerated scrolls like semi-folded hearts supporting a spiky crown.

In 1842, the Virgin Mary appeared in the church to a Jewish banker, who promptly converted to Christianity and became a missionary. Inside, the chapel of the Miraculous Madonna is the first thing you notice. The church is better known, however, for the angels that Borromini's rival, Bernini, carved for the Ponte Sant' Angelo. Pope Clement IX declared they were too lovely to be exposed to the weather, so they remained with Bernini's family until 1729, when they were moved to the church.

### 6

## Palazzo di Propaganda Fide

📍 H4 🏛 Via di Propaganda 1 ☎ 06-6988 0266 🚌 116, 117 Ⓜ Spagna 🕐 By appointment only

The Jesuit Congregation for the Propagation of the Faith was founded in 1622. Though Bernini had originally been commissioned to create their headquarters, Innocent X, who became pope in 1644, preferred the style of Borromini, who was asked to continue. His extraordinary west façade, completed in 1662, is striped with broad pilasters, between which the first-floor windows bend in and the central bay bulges. A rigid band divides its floors, and the cornice above the convex central bay swerves inwards. The more you look at it, the more restless it seems; a sign perhaps of the increasing unhappiness of the architect who committed suicide in 1667.

### 7

## Via Condotti

📍 G3 🚌 81, 116, 117, 119, 492 and many routes along via del Corso or stopping at Piazza San Silvestro Ⓜ Spagna

Named after the conduits that carried water to the Baths of Agrippa near the Pantheon, Via Condotti is now home to the

←

Via Condotti, the famous shopping street leading to the Spanish Steps

most traditional of Rome's designer clothes shops. Stores selling shoes and other leather goods are also well represented. The street is popular for early evening strolls, when elegant Italians mingle with casually dressed tourists.

The street is home to Gucci, Louis Vuitton, Dolce e Gabbana, Bulgari, Salvatore Ferragamo, Burberry, Prada and Trussardi, among other designer boutiques.

---

**8**

## Villa Medici

**H3** **Accademia di Francia a Roma, Viale Trinità dei Monti 1** **117, 119** **Spagna** **9:30am-6:30pm Tue-Sun (booking recommended)** **villamedici.it**

Superbly positioned on the Pincio hill above Piazza di Spagna, this 16th-century villa has kept the name it assumed

→

A stained-glass window featuring English text at the All Saints' church

when Cardinal Ferdinando de' Medici bought it in 1576. From the terrace you can look across the city to Castel Sant'Angelo, from where Queen Christina of Sweden is said to have fired the large cannon ball which now sits in the basin of the fountain. The villa's most famous resident was Galileo, who was imprisoned here for falling foul of the Inquisition in 1630–33.

The villa is home to the French Academy, which was founded by Louis XIV in 1666 with the aim of giving a few select painters the chance to study in Rome. Nicolas Poussin was one of the first advisers to the Academy, Ingres was a director, and former students include Jean-Honoré Fragonard and François Boucher.

It is now used for concerts and exhibitions. Guided tours take in the landscaped gardens and frescoed rooms. A highlight is the Stanza degli Uccelli.

---

**9**

## All Saints'

**G3** **Via del Babuino 153B** **06-3600 1881** **117, 119** **9am-5pm Mon-Fri**

In 1816 the pope gave English residents and visitors the right

to hold Anglican services in Rome, but it was not until the early 1880s that they acquired a site to build their own church. The architect was G E Street, who is best known in Britain for his Neo-Gothic churches and the Royal Courts of Justice in London. The style of All Saints' is Victorian Neo-Gothic, and although the interior is splendidly decorated with different coloured Italian marbles, it has a very English air. Street also designed St-Paul's-within-the-Walls in Via Nazionale, whose interior is a jewel of British Pre-Raphaelite art.

The street on which All Saints stands got its name from the Fontana del Sileno, notorious for its ugliness, and nicknamed "baboon".

## Ara Pacis

📍G3 🏛Lungotevere in Augusta 🚌70, 81, 117, 119, 186, 628 🕐9:30am–7:30pm daily (last adm: 6:30pm) 🚫1 Jan, 1 May, 25 Dec 🌐arapacis.it

Reconstructed at considerable expense over the course of many years, the Ara Pacis (Altar of Peace) is one of the most significant monuments of ancient Rome. It celebrates the peace created throughout the Mediterranean area by Emperor Augustus following his victorious campaigns in Gaul and Spain. The monument was commissioned by the Senate in 13 BC and completed four years later. It was positioned in such a way that the shadow of the huge obelisk sundial on Campus Martius (p114) would fall upon it on Augustus's birthday.

Forming a square enclosure on a low platform with the altar in the centre, the Ara Pacis is decorated with magnificent friezes and reliefs carved in Carrara marble. The reliefs on the north and south walls depict a procession that took place on 4 July 13 BC, in which the members of the emperor's family can be identified, ranked by their position in the succession. At the time, the heir apparent was Marcus Agrippa, husband of Augustus's daughter Julia. All the portraits in the relief are carved with extraordinary realism, even the innocent toddler clinging to his mother's skirts.

The history of the rediscovery of the Ara Pacis dates back to the 16th century, when the first panels were unearthed at nearby Via in Lucina. One of the sections ended up in Paris, while another found its way to Florence. Further discoveries were made in the late 19th century, when archaeologists finally realized just what they had found. The monument as it appears today has all been pieced together since 1938, with some parts original and other parts reproductions. The American architect Richard Meier designed a dedicated glass building to house the entire structure, which opened in 2006.

The Ara Pacis monument and (inset) a detail of one of the many intricate reliefs ↓

## Piazza del Popolo

📍G2 🚌117, 119, 490, 495, 926 🚋2 ⓂFlaminio

A vast cobbled oval standing at the apex of the triangle of roads known as the Trident, Piazza del Popolo forms a grand symmetrical ante-chamber to the heart of Rome. Twin Neo-Classical façades stand on either side of the Porta del Popolo; an Egyptian obelisk rises in the centre; and the matching domes and porticoes of Santa Maria dei Miracoli and Santa Maria in Montesanto flank the beginning of Via del Corso.

Although it is now one of the most unified squares in Rome, Piazza del Popolo evolved gradually over the centuries. In 1589 the great town-planning pope, Sixtus V, had the obelisk erected in the centre by Domenico Fontana. Over 3,000 years old, the obelisk in

Piazza del Popolo, with Santa Maria dei Miracoli, Santa Maria in Montesanto and the Egyptian obelisk ↓

Piazza del Popolo was originally brought to Rome by Augustus to adorn the Circus Maximus after the conquest of Egypt. Almost a century later Pope Alexander VII commissioned Carlo Rainaldi to build the twin Santa Marias. In the 19th century the piazza was turned into a grandiose oval by Giuseppe Valadier, the designer of the Pincio Gardens.

In contrast to the piazza's air of ordered rationalism, many of the events staged here were barbaric. In the 18th and 19th centuries, public executions were held. Condemned men were sometimes hammered to death by repeated blows to the temples. The last time a criminal was executed in this way was in 1826, even though the guillotine had by then been adopted as a more scientific means of execution. The riderless horse races from the piazza down Via del Corso were scarcely more humane: the performance of the runners was enhanced by feeding the horses stimulants, wrapping them in nail-studded ropes and letting off fireworks at their heels.

To the north of the piazza, Via Flaminia, built in 220 BC to connect Rome with Italy's Adriatic coast, enters the city at Porta del Popolo, a grand 16th-century gate built on the orders of Pope Pius IV de' Medici. The architect, Nanni di Baccio Bigio, modelled it on a Roman triumphal arch. The outer face has statues of St Peter and St Paul on either side and a Medici coat of arms.

A century later, Pope Alexander VII commissioned Bernini to decorate the inner face to celebrate the arrival in Rome in 1655 of Queen Christina of Sweden after abdicating her throne and converting to Roman Catholicism the previous year. Lesser visitors were often delayed while customs officers rifled their luggage. The only way to speed things up was with a bribe.

**Over 3,000 years old, the obelisk in Piazza del Popolo was originally brought to Rome by Augustus to adorn the Circus Maximus after the conquest of Egypt.**

**⑫**

## Santa Maria dei Miracoli and Santa Maria in Montesanto

📍 G2 🏛 Piazza del Popolo 🚌 117, 119, 490, 495, 628, 926 🚊 2 Ⓜ Flaminio
Santa Maria dei Miracoli:
☎ 06-361 0250 🕐 7am-12:30pm & 4-7:30pm daily
Santa Maria in Montesanto:
☎ 06-361 0594 🕐 5:30-8pm Mon-Fri, 11am-1:30pm Sun

The two churches at the south end of Piazza del Popolo were designed by the architect Carlo Rainaldi (1611–91), the plans were revised by Bernini and it was Carlo Fontana who eventually completed the project. To provide a focal point for the piazza, the churches had to appear symmetrical. Although the two churches appear identical at first glance, there are differences if you look carefully. The site on the left was narrower. Hence, Rainaldi gave Santa Maria dei Miracoli (on the right) a circular dome and Santa Maria in Montesanto an oval one to squeeze it into the narrower site, while keeping the sides of the supporting drums that face the piazza identical.

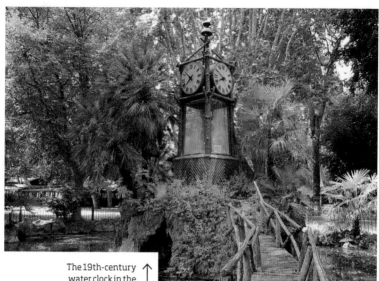

The 19th-century water clock in the Pincio Gardens

# ⑬ Pincio Gardens

📍 G2 🚩 Il Pincio 🚌 117, 119, 490, 495, 628, 926 🚋 2 Ⓜ Flaminio

The Pincio Gardens lie above Piazza del Popolo on a hillside that has been so skilfully terraced and richly planted with trees that, from below, the zig-zagging road climbing to the gardens is virtually invisible. In ancient Roman times, there were magnificent gardens on the Pincio Hill. The present gardens were designed in the early 19th century by Giuseppe Valadier (who also redesigned the Piazza del Popolo). The broad avenues, lined with umbrella pines, palm trees and evergreen oaks soon became a fashionable place to stroll, and even in the 20th century such diverse characters as Gandhi and Mussolini, Richard Strauss and King Farouk of Egypt patronized the Casina Valadier, an exclusive café and restaurant in the grounds.

From the Pincio's main square, Piazzale Napoleone I, the panoramic views of Rome stretch from the Monte Mario to the Janiculum.

One of the most striking features of the park itself is an Egyptian-style obelisk which Emperor Hadrian erected on the tomb of his favourite, Antinous, an enslaved man. After Antinous's premature death (according to some accounts he died saving the emperor's life), Hadrian deified him.

Marble busts of many historical Italian and other European figures line the paths of the gardens.

The 19th-century water clock on Via dell'Orologio was designed by a Dominican monk. It was displayed at the Paris Exhibition of 1889.

---

GREAT VIEW
**Pincio Gardens**

Approach the Pincio Gardens from the grounds of Villa Borghese (p144), or along Viale della Trinità dei Monti. The panoramic views of Rome, including the historic centre and the Vatican, are beautiful at sunset.

---

# ⑭ Santi Ambrogio e Carlo al Corso

📍 G3 🚩 Via del Corso 437 ☎ 06-682 8101 🚌 81, 117, 492, 628, 926 🕐 7am–7pm daily

This church belonged to the Lombard community in Rome, and is dedicated to two canonized bishops of Milan, Lombardy's capital. In 1471 Pope Sixtus IV gave the Lombards a church, and they dedicated it to Sant' Ambrogio, who died in 397. Then in 1610, when Carlo Borromeo was canonized, the church was rebuilt in his honour. Most of the work on the new church was carried out by father and son Onorio and Martino Longhi, but the fine dome is by Pietro da Cortona. The altarpiece by Carlo Maratta (1625–1713) is the Gloria dei Santi Ambrogio e Carlo. An ambulatory leads behind the altar to a chapel housing the heart of San Carlo, which is held in a richly decorated reliquary.

## ⑮ Mausoleum of Augustus

**⑨ G3 ⑩ Piazza Augusto Imperatore ⓒ 06-0608
🚌 81, 117, 492, 628, 926**

Only the brick core, which is overgrown with plants, is left today of what was once the most prestigious burial place in Rome. It is currently being restored after many years of neglect. Augustus had the mausoleum built in 28 BC, the year he became sole ruler, as a tomb for himself and his descendants. The circular building was 87 m (285 ft) in diameter.

Inside were four concentric passageways linked by corridors where the urns containing the ashes of the Imperial family were placed. The first to be buried here was Augustus's favourite nephew, Marcellus, who had married Julia, the emperor's daughter. He died in 23 BC, possibly poisoned by Augustus's second wife Livia, who felt that her son, Tiberius, would make a more reliable emperor. When Augustus died in AD 14, his ashes were placed in the mausoleum, Tiberius duly became emperor, and dynastic poisonings continued to fill the family vault with urns.

This sinister monument was later used as a medieval fortress, a vineyard, a private garden, and even, in the 18th century, as an auditorium and theatre. It can now only be admired from the outside, but after restoration is complete (estimated by spring 2019) it will open to the public.

---

## ⑯ San Rocco

**⑨ G3 ⑩ Largo San Rocco 1
ⓒ 06-689 6416 🚌 81, 117, 492, 628, 926 ⏰ 7-9am & 4:30-8pm Mon-Sat, 8:30am-1pm & 4:30-8pm Sun
⏳ Closed 2 weeks in Aug**

This church, with a restrained Neo-Classical façade by Giuseppe Valadier, the designer of Piazza del Popolo, began life as the chapel of a 16th-century hospital with beds for 50 men – San Rocco was a healer of the plague-stricken. A maternity wing was added for the wives of Tiber bargees to save them from having to give birth in the insanitary conditions of a boat. The hospital came to be used by unmarried mothers, and one section was set aside for women who wished to be unknown. They were even permitted to wear a veil for the duration of their stay.

Unwanted children were sent to an orphanage, and if any mothers or children died they were buried in anonymous graves. The hospital was abandoned in the early 20th century, and demolished in the 1930s during the excavation of the Mausoleum of Augustus.

The church sacristy contains an interesting Baroque altar-piece (c 1660) by Il Baciccia, the artist who decorated the ceiling of the Gesù (p108).

---

## ⑰ Casa di Goethe

**⑨ G3 ⑩ Via del Corso 18
🚌 117, 119, 490, 495, 628, 926 🚊 2 Ⓜ Flaminio
⏰ 10am-6pm daily
🌐 casadigoethe.it**

The German poet, dramatist and novelist Johann Wolfgang von Goethe (1749–1832) lived in this house from 1786 until 1788 and worked on a journal that eventually formed part of his travel book *The Italian Journey*. Rome's noisy street life irritated him, especially during Carnival time. He was a little perturbed by the number of murders in his neighbourhood, but Rome energized him and his book became one of the most influential ever written about Italy.

The elegant Neo-Classical church of San Rocco, with a façade by Giuseppe Valadier ↓

# A SHORT WALK
# PIAZZA DI SPAGNA

**Distance** 1.5 km (1 mile) **Nearest metro** Spagna **Time** 30 minutes

Wandering around the network of narrow streets between Piazza di Spagna and Via del Corso gives you a feel for one of the liveliest areas in Rome, which draws throngs of tourists and Romans to its discreet and elegant shops. Since the 18th century the area has been popular with visitors, including famous writers and composers.

↑ Via Condotti, one of Rome's busiest shopping streets

For almost three centuries the Piazza di Spagna with its curious Barcaccia fountain in the centre has been the chief meeting place for visitors to Rome (p140).

Antico Caffè Greco has busts and portraits recalling the café's former artistic patrons (p151).

Via delle Carrozze took its name from the carriages of wealthy tourists that used to queue up here for repairs.

The shady, narrow Via Condotti has the smartest shops in one of the chicest shopping areas in the world (p150).

VIA VITTORIA

VIA DELLA CROCE

VIA BOCCA DI LEONE

VIA DELLA CARROZZE

VIA DEL CORSO

VIA CONDOTTI

VIA BORGONONA

PIAZZA DI SPAGNA

START

FINISH

← Fontana della Barcaccia in Piazza di Spagna, with Trinità dei Monti in the distance

Spagna station

At Babington's Tea Rooms visitors are catered for in the style of the 1890s.

The 16th-century Trinità dei Monti has a spectacular setting and some of the finest views in Rome.

**Locator Map**
For more detail see p138

PIAZZA DI SPAGNA AND VILLA BORGHESE

Even when obscured by crowds, the Spanish Steps are one of the glories of late Baroque Rome.

The Keats-Shelley Memorial House is a small museum where the English poet Keats died in 1821 (p140).

The Colonna dell'Immacolata Roman column supports a statue of the Virgin Mary.

In Sant'Andrea delle Fratte Pasquale Marini painted The Redemption in 1691 to decorate the interior of Borromini's high dome (p150).

VIA DI PROPAGANDA

VIA FRATTINA

VIA DELLA VITE

Bulgari sells beautiful (though expensive) jewellery in Via Condotti.

Palazzo di Propaganda Fide's façade (1665) was one of the last works of the great Francesco Borromini.

## Did You Know?

The area was full of hotels for English aristocrats taking the Grand Tour in the 18th century.

0 metres 75
0 yards 75

N

# A LONG WALK
# ROMAN TOMBS, LEGENDS AND ARTISTS

**Distance** 3.5 km (2 miles) **Walking time** 1.5 hours
**Nearest metro** Lepanto

The northern half of central Rome with its air of mystery is a great place for families to explore. Following this trail of places and famous deaths, interspersed with glimpses of the city's historic artists' centre, visitors can see Imperial mausoleums, a death mask and a crypt decorated with monks' bones. Here, art is everywhere – you will see working art studios, pass Rome's Gallery of Fine Arts and wander down the famous Via Margutta, known as "artists' row".

*Piazza del Popolo is named after the church* **Santa Maria del Popolo** (p142).

*Rome's* **Via del Corso** *consists of 1.5 km (a mile) of palazzi and shops.*

**Via Canova** *is named after the sculptor Antonio Canova.*

*Rome's fine art academy, the* **Accademia di Belle Arti**, *was designed in 1845 by Pietro Camporese.*

*Start the walk at* **Castel Sant'Angelo** (p298), *the site of Emperor Hadrian's tomb.*

*The ancient altar of* **Ara Pacis** (p152) *shows the family of the emperor Augustus.*

*Church of* **San Rocco** (p155)

*Carlo Rinaldi's Baroque church,* **Chiesa di Gesù e Maria**, *was built in 1675.*

Porta del Popolo
Santa Maria del Popolo
PIAZZA DEL POPOLO
VIA L. DI SAVOA
VIA A. BRUNETTI
LUNGOTEVERE IN AUGUSTA
VIA DI RIPETTA
VIA DEL CORSO
VIA A. CANOVA
Chie... da... Ges... Ma...
V. DELLA FREZZA
Accademia di Belle Arti
Mausoleum of Augustus
Ara Pacis
Chiesa di San Rocco
VIA TOMACELLI
VIA V. COLONNA
Ponte Cavour
VIA DELLA SCROFA
Palazzo Borghese
CRESCENZIO
PIAZZA CAVOUR
VIA TRIBONIANO
VIA ULPIANO
Palazzo di Giustizia
LUNGOT. PRATI
LUNGOTEVERE MARZIO
Ponte Umberto
VIA M. TE BRIANZO
PIAZZA ADRIANA
Castel Sant'Angelo
PIAZZA PIA **START**
LUNGOTEVERE CASTELLO
Ponte Sant'Angelo
Fiume Tevere

PIAZZA DI SPAGNA
AND VILLA BORGHESE

*Roman Tombs,
Legends and Artists*

**Locator Map**
*For more detail see p138*

**Via Margutta**
is the home of
artists' studios
and galleries.

Locals declare that
the ravens' screams
at the **Pincio
Gardens** (p154),
are those of the
dead emperor.

↑ Visitors inside Castel Sant'Angelo's
magnificent Paolina room

**Via del Babuino**, which ends in Piazza di Spagna,
is lined with art galleries hawking everything
from Old Master Madonnas to Modernist abstracts.

Rome's **Piazza di
Spagna** (p140) is
usually thronged
with tourists.

Head up the Spanish Steps to
find magnificent views at the
**Trinità dei Monti**.

*Pincio
Gardens*

VIALE DEL MURO TORTO

LARGO
FEDERICO
FELLINI

VIALE TRINITÀ
DEI MONTI

Villa Medici

VIA PORTA PINCIANA

VIA LAZIO

VIA VITTORIO VENETO

VIA
MARGUTTA

VIA LOMBARDIA

VIA
DEL BABUINO

CAMPO
MARZIO

Spagna Ⓜ

Casino
dell'Aurora

VIA AURORA

VIA LUDOVISI

VIA VITTORIO VENETO

LIGURIA

IA VITTORIA

VIA MARIO
DE' FIORI

PIAZZA DI
SPAGNA

SPANISH
STEPS

Trinità dei
Monti

VIA DELLA CROCE

Palazzetto
Zuccari

BELSIANA

Keats-Shelley
Memorial House

V. D. ARTISTI

Santa Maria
della Concezione

CONDOTTI

PIAZZA
MIGNANELLI

VIA
GREGORIANA

VIA FRANCESCO CRISPI

VIA
SISTINA

Capuchin Museum

**FINISH** ⓠ

Barberini Ⓜ

*The **Keats-Shelley
Memorial House**
(p140) features
Keats' death mask.*

VIA
ZUCCHELLI

PIAZZA
BARBERINI

*Find chapels decorated
with skeletal displays at
the **Capuchin Museum**.*

*Painter Federico
Zuccari turned the door
and window frames of
his **Palazzetto Zuccari**
into monsters.*

0 metres     300
0 yards      300

N ↑

# CAMPO DE' FIORI

Between Corso Vittorio Emanuele II and the Tiber, the city displays many distinct personalities. The open-air market in Campo de' Fiori preserves the lively, bohemian atmosphere of the medieval inns that once flourished here, while the area also contains grand Renaissance palazzi, such as Palazzo Farnese and Palazzo Spada, where powerful Roman families built their fortress-like houses near the route of papal processions. Close by, overlooking the picturesque Tiber Island, lies the Jewish Ghetto, the oldest Jewish settlement in Europe, where many traces of daily life from past centuries can still be seen. The Portico of Octavia and the Theatre of Marcellus are spectacular examples of the city's many-layered history, built over the half-ruined remains of ancient Rome.

## Map Labels

**R** · **S** · **T**

**2** · **3** · **4** · **5**

Castel Sant' Angelo

LARGO MUTILATI E INVALIDI DI GUERRA

PIAZZA DEI TRIBUNALI

LUNGOTEVERE CASTELLO

Fiume

Ponte S. Angelo

Ponte Umberto

Tevere

Ponte Vittorio Emanuele II

LUNGOT. DEGLI ALTOVITI

LUNGOTEVERE TOR DI NONA

V. DI PANICO

V. DEI VECCHIARELLI

San Salvatore in Lauro

V. DEI CORONARI

V. D. MASCHERA D'ORO

V. G. ZANARDELLI

Ponte Principe

PIAZZA DELL'ORO

CORSO

VITTORIO

V. D. CONSOLATO

V. D. CIMATORI

Palazzo dei Banco di Santo Spirito

PONTE

**26** San Giovanni dei Fiorentini

LUNGOT. DEI FIORENTINI

VIC. ORBITELLI

VIC. D. PALLE

VIA

VICOLO DEL CEFALO

VIA DEI BRESCIANI

VIC. SUGARELLI

VIA GIULIA

VIA DEI BANCHI VECCHI

EMANUELE

Palazzo del Governo Vecchio

V. DEL TEATRO PACE

V. DI SANTA MARIA DELL'ANIMA

PIAZZA NAVONA
*p120*

LUNGOT. D. SANGALLO

Museo Criminologico

**4**

VIC. D. GONFALONE

VICOLO D. SCIMMIA

VICOLO D. PRIGIONI

II

VIC. CELLINI

VIA DEI CARCERI

VIA DEI CARTARI

VIA LARGA

VIA CERRI

VIA DEL

CORSO

VITTORIO EMANUELE

Pasquino

Palazzo Braschi

LUNGOTEVERE GIANICOLENSE

Ponte Giuseppe Mazzini

VIA D. MORETTA

PARIONE

VIC. D. MALPASSO

PELLEGRINO

VIA DEI CAPPELLARI

**7** Palazzo della Cancelleria

**14**

**13** Piccola Farnesi

Carcere di Regina Coeli

JANICULUM
*p270*

VIA SAN FRANCESCO DI SALES

VIA DELLA

VIA DEI RIARI

Ponte Sisto

VIA DI S. AUREA

Palazzo Ricci **9**

VIA DELLA BARCHETTA

Sant'Eligio degli Orefici **11**

Santa Maria In Monserrato **7**

VIA DI MONSERRATO

VIA DI MONTORO

LUNGOTEVERE DEI TEBALDI

VIA DI SANT'ELIGIO

VIA IN CATERINA

VIA DI SAN GIROLAMO D. CARITÀ

San Girolamo della Carità

VIA DI MASCHERONE

V. DEI FARNESI

VIA GIULIA

VICOLO D. POLVERONE

**10**

PIAZZA FARNESE

**12** Palazzo Farnese

Campo de' Fiori **1**

**1**

Teatro di Pompeo

PIAZZA DEL BISCIONE

V. DEI BAULLARI

V. DEI BAULLARI

V. DEI BALESTRARI

VIA CORDA

VIC. D. GROTTE

VIA CAPO DI FERRO

V. DEI PETTINARI

Fiume

LUNGOTEVERE FARNESINA

Casa della Fornarina

Porta Settimiana

V. DI S. DOROTEA

VIA DELLA SCALA

VIA BENEDETTA

LUNGOT. R. SANZIO

Tevere

Santa Maria dell'Orazione e Morte **8**

Palazzo Spada **6**

Santissima Trinità dei Pellegrini **5**

V. D. TRINITÀ D. PELLEGRINI

REGOLA

LUNGOTEVERE D. VALLATI

LUNGOTEVERE D. VALLATI

TRASTEVERE
*p256*

CAMPO DE' FIORI

0 metres — 200

0 yards — 200

N

# CAMPO DE' FIORI

## Must See
1. Campo de' Fiori

## Experience More
2. Teatro di Pompeo
3. Palazzo del Monte di Pietà
4. Sotterranei di San Paolo alla Regola
5. Santissima Trinità dei Pellegrini
6. Palazzo Spada
7. Santa Maria in Monserrato
8. Santa Maria dell'Orazione e Morte
9. Palazzo Ricci
10. San Girolamo della Carità
11. Sant'Eligio degli Orefici
12. Palazzo Farnese
13. Piccola Farnesina
14. Palazzo della Cancelleria
15. Teatro Argentina
16. Area Sacra di Largo Argentina
17. San Carlo ai Catinari
18. Fontana delle Tartarughe
19. Crypta Balbi
20. Santa Maria in Campitelli
21. San Nicola in Carcere
22. Theatre of Marcellus
23. Portico of Octavia
24. Tiber Island
25. Ghetto and Synagogue
26. San Giovanni dei Fiorentini
27. Casa di Lorenzo Manilio
28. Palazzo Cenci

## Eat
1. Il Forno di Campo de' Fiori
2. Roscioli
3. Piperno

## Stay
4. DOM Hotel
5. Hotel Teatro di Pompeo

## Shop
6. Beppe e i suoi Formaggi
7. Atelier Patrizia Pieroni
8. Ibiz

**①**

# CAMPO DE' FIORI

**◉ T4 🚌 116** and routes to Largo di Torre Argentina or Corso Vittorio Emanuele II

A lively square since medieval times, Campo de' Fiori bursts with colour during the morning market, and again after dark when its restaurants and bars make it a centre of Roman nightlife.

Occupying the site of a meadow in ancient times behind the vast structure of the Teatro di Pompeo (p166), Campo de' Fiori became the bustling, raffish – and at times rough – heart of Renaissance Rome, populated by artists, craftsmen and courtesans, and packed with cheap inns. Murders were not uncommon – Caravaggio killed his opponent on the piazza after losing a game of tennis, and the goldsmith Benvenuto Cellini murdered a business rival on nearby Via della Moretta. Today the square is home to Rome's most central fresh produce market between 7am and 1:30pm Monday to Saturday (p50).

## Giordano Bruno Monument

In the centre of Campo de' Fiori is a statue of the philosopher Giordano Bruno. A former Catholic priest who dabbled in Calvinism and Lutheranism before being excommunicated by both, Bruno eventually concluded that philosophy and magic were superior to religion. He was tried for heresy and burned at the stake in 1600. His hooded statue is a grim reminder of the executions by the Inquisition that took place in the piazza.

> 💬 INSIDER TIP
> **Shopping**
>
> The streets around the piazza, named for the medieval artisans who traded there, are lined with boutiques. One of the best is Via de' Giubbonari ("jerkin-makers"), which has many chic clothes shops.

### VANOZZA DEI CATANEI'S SHIELD

In the 15th century the area around Campo de' Fiori was full of inns, many of them owned by the successful courtesan Vanozza dei Catanei, mistress of Pope Alexander VI Borgia. On the corner of Campo de' Fiori and Via del Pellegrino you can see Catanei's shield, which she had decorated with her own coat of arms, along with those of both her husband and Borgia.

↑ Fresh artichokes on sale at the market on Campo de' Fiori

The market in Campo de' Fiori and *(inset)* a statue of Giordano Bruno ↓

# EXPERIENCE MORE

## ② Teatro di Pompeo

📍T4 🏛Da Pancrazio, Piazza del Biscione 92 🚌116 and routes to Largo Torre Argentina or Corso Vittorio Emanuele II

A hint of Pompey's 55 BC theatre is evident in the curve of medieval Largo del Pollaro. The theatre could seat 17,000 people. Traces of it are visible in the ancient travertine corridors of the Pancrazio restaurant where you can see early examples of *opus reticulatum* – small square blocks of tufa (porous rock) set diagonally as a facing for a concrete wall.

## ③ Palazzo del Monte di Pietà

📍T5 🏛Piazza del Monte di Pietà 33 ☎06-684 42001 🚌116 and routes to Largo di Torre Argentina or Corso Vittorio Emanuele II 🚊8

The Monte, as it is known, is a public institution, founded in 1539 by Pope Paul III Farnese as a pawnshop to staunch the usury then rampant in the city. The building still has offices and auction rooms for the sale of unredeemed goods.

The stars with diagonal bands on the huge central plaque decorating the façade are the coat of arms of Pope Clement VIII Aldobrandini, added when Carlo Maderno enlarged the palace in the 17th century. The clock under the bell tower on the left was added towards the end of the 18th century.

Within, the chapel (which is open only for accredited groups; phone ahead) is a jewel of Baroque architecture, adorned with gilded stucco, marble panelling and reliefs. It is a perfect setting for the sculptures by Domenico Guidi – a bust of San Carlo Borromeo and a relief of the *Pietà*. There are also splendid reliefs by Giovanni Battista Théudon and Pierre Legros of biblical scenes illustrating the charitable nature of the institution.

## ④ 🏛 Sotterranei di San Paolo alla Regola

📍T5 🏛Via di San Paolo alla Regola ☎06-0608 🚌23, 116, 280 and routes to Largo di Torre Argentina 🚊8 🕐By appt only

The 16th-century Palazzo Specchi and the 18th-century church of San Paolo alla Regola hide the perfectly preserved underground remains of an ancient Roman house, dating from the 2nd to 3rd centuries. At present the site can only be visited by groups as part of a guided tour by prior arrangement (phone ahead).

A ramp leads down well below today's street level, to reveal the locations of residential buildings, warehouses and shops of the time with remains of amphorae. One level above is the Stanza della Colonna, at one time an open courtyard, with traces of frescoes and mosaics on its walls. The structures were reused in medieval times.

↑ The 17th-century altarpiece depicting the *Holy Trinity* by Guido Reni in Santissima Trinità dei Pellegrini

↑ Borromini's forced-perspective colonnaded gallery at Palazzo Spada

## 5

### Santissima Trinità dei Pellegrini

📍 T5 🏠 Via dei Pettinari 36A
📞 06-686 8451 🚌 23, 116, 280 and routes to Largo di Torre Argentina 🚋 8
🕐 4–8pm Mon-Sat, 8am–1pm & 4–8pm Sun

The church was donated in the 16th century to a charitable organization founded by San Filippo Neri to care for the poor and sick. The 18th-century façade has niches with statues of the Evangelists by Bernardino Ludovisi. The interior, with Corinthian columns, ends in a horseshoe vault and apse, dominated by Guido Reni's striking altarpiece of the Holy Trinity (1625). The frescoes in the lantern are also by Reni. Other interesting paintings include *St Gregory the Great Freeing Souls from Purgatory* by Baldassarre Croce (third chapel to the left); Cavalier d'Arpino's *Virgin and Saints* (second chapel to the left); and a painting by Borgognone (1677) of the Virgin and recently canonized saints. In the sacristy are depictions of the nobility washing the feet of pilgrims, a custom started by San Filippo.

---

## 6

### Palazzo Spada

📍 T5 🏠 Piazza Capo di Ferro 13 📞 06-683 2409 🚌 23, 116, 280 and routes to Largo di Torre Argentina 🚋 8
🕐 8:30am–7:30pm Wed-Mon (last adm: 7pm)

This majestic palazzo, built around 1550 for Cardinal Capo di Ferro, has an elegant stuccoed courtyard and façade decorated with reliefs evoking Rome's glorious past.

Cardinal Bernardino Spada, who lived here in the 17th century with his brother Virginio (also a cardinal), hired architects Bernini and Borromini to work on the building. The brothers' whimsical delight in false perspectives resulted in a colonnaded gallery by Borromini that appears four times longer than it really is.

The cardinals also amassed a superb private collection of paintings, which is now on display in the Galleria Spada. The collection, housed in four rooms, features 16th- and 17th-century pieces by a wide range of artists, including Rubens, Dürer, Guercino, Guido Reni and Artemesia Gentileschi. The most significant of the artworks on display include *The Visitation* by Andrea del Sarto (1486–1530), *Cain and Abel* by Giovanni Lanfranco (1582–1647) and *The Death of Dido* by Guercino (1591–1666).

The palace is also the seat of government offices.

> **The brothers' whimsical delight in false perspectives resulted in a colonnaded gallery by Borromini that appears four times longer than it really is.**

Interior view of the Church of Santa Maria in Monserrato ↑

**7**

## Santa Maria in Monserrato

📍 S4 🏛 Via di Monserrato 115 📞 06-688 9651 🚌 23, 40, 46, 62, 64, 116, 280 🕐 8:30am-1pm & 3-7pm Mon-Sat, 10am-12:30pm & 3:30-7:30pm Sun (call ahead as times may vary)

The origins of the Spanish national church in Rome go back to 1506, when a hospice for Spanish pilgrims was begun by a brotherhood of the Virgin of Montserrat in Catalonia. Inside is Annibale Carracci's painting *San Diego de Alcalà* and a copy of a Sansovino statue of St James. Some 15th-century tombs are in the courtyard and side chapels. Do not miss Bernini's bust of church benefactor Pedro Foix de Montoya.

> The doors and windows of Ferdinando Fuga's dramatic Baroque façade are decorated with unnerving winged skulls.

**8**

## Santa Maria dell'Orazione e Morte

📍 S4 🏛 Via Giulia 262 📞 06-6880 6862 🚌 23, 116, 280 🕐 For restoration

A pious confraternity was formed here in the 16th century to collect the bodies of the unknown dead and give them a Christian burial. The theme of death is stressed in this church, dedicated to St Mary of Prayer and Death. The doors and windows of Ferdinando Fuga's dramatic Baroque façade are decorated with unnerving winged skulls. Above the central entrance is a *clepsydra* (an ancient hour-glass) – symbolic of death.

**9**

## Palazzo Ricci

📍 S4 🏛 Piazza de' Ricci 🚌 23, 40, 46, 62, 64, 116, 280, 870 🕐 To the public

Palazzo Ricci was famous for its frescoed façade – now rather faded – originally painted in the 16th century

by Polidoro da Caravaggio, one of Raphael's most influential followers.

In Renaissance Rome it was common to commission artists to decorate the outsides of houses with heroes of Classical antiquity. A fresco by a leading artist such as Polidoro, reputedly the inventor of this style of painting, was a conspicuous status symbol, in the nobility's attempts to outshine each other with their palazzi.

---

**10**

## San Girolamo della Carità

📍 S4 🏛 Via di Monserrato 62A 📞 06-687 9786 🚌 23, 40, 46, 62, 64, 116, 280 🕐 5-7pm Tue-Fri, 10am-1pm Sun

The church was built on a site incorporating the home of San Filippo Neri, the 16th-century saint from Tuscany who renewed Rome's spiritual and cultural life by his friendly, open approach to religion. He would have loved the frolicking putti shown around his statue in the Antamoro chapel they would have reminded him of the Roman urchins he had cared for during his lifetime.

The breathtaking Spada Chapel, designed by Borromini, is unique both as a work of art and as an illustration of the spirit of the Baroque age. All architectural elements are concealed so that the space of the chapel's interior is defined solely by decorative marble-work and statues. Veined jasper and precious multi-coloured marbles are sculpted to imitate flowery damask and velvet hangings. Even the altar rail is a long swag of jasper drapery held up by a pair of kneeling angels with wooden wings.

Although there are memorials to former members of the Spada family, oddly there is no indication as to which of the Spadas was responsible for endowing the chapel. It is thought that it was probably the art-lover Virgilio Spada, who was a follower of San Filippo Neri.

---

**11**

## Sant'Eligio degli Orefici

📍 S4 📌 Via di Sant'Eligio 8A 📞 06-686 8260 🚌 23, 40, 46, 62, 64, 116, 280 🕐 9:30am–1pm Mon–Fri (ring bell first at Via di Sant'Eligio 7) 🚫 Aug

The name of the church marks the fact that it was commissioned by a rich corporation of goldsmiths (orefici) in the early 16th century. The original design was by Raphael, who, like his master Bramante, had acquired a sense of the grandiose from the remains of Roman antiquity. The influence of some of Bramante's works, such as the choir of Santa Maria del Popolo (p142), is evident in the simple way the arches and pilasters define the structure of the walls. The cupola of Sant' Eligio is attributed to Baldassarre Peruzzi, while the façade was added in the early 17th century by Flaminio Ponzio.

---

**12** 🔧

## Palazzo Farnese

📍 T4 📌 Piazza Farnese 🚌 23, 116, 280 and routes to Corso Vittorio Emanuele II 🕐 For guided tours only (Mon, Wed & Fri, times may vary); book online at least one week ahead 🌐 inventerrome.com

The prototype for numerous palaces, Palazzo Farnese was originally built for Cardinal Alessandro Farnese (who became Pope Paul III in 1534). He commissioned the greatest artists to work on it, starting with Antonio da Sangallo the Younger as architect in 1517.

Michelangelo, who took over after him, created the great cornice and central window of the main façade, and the third level of the courtyard. The interior is decorated with frescoes by Annibale Carracci and Daniele da Volterra.

Michelangelo had a plan for the Farnese gardens to be connected by a bridge to the Farnese home in Trastevere, Villa Farnesina (p274), but the scheme was unrealized. The palazzo was completed in 1589, on a less ambitious scale, by Giacomo della Porta. It is has housed the French Embassy since 1635.

### Did You Know?

Charles Barry used Palazzo Farnese as the model for London's Reform Club in 1841.

↑ The Farnese arch on Via Giulia, with Palazzo Farnese in the background

↑ The courtyard of the Renaissance Palazzo della Cancelleria

## ⑬ Piccola Farnesina

**◊ T4 ⚑ Corso Vittorio Emanuele II 168 🚌 40, 46, 62, 64, 70, 81, 87, 116, 492 ⏰ Oct-May: 10am-4pm Tue-Sun; Jun-Sep: 1-7pm Tue-Sun 🌐 museobarracco.it**

This miniature palazzo acquired its name from the lilies decorating its cornices that were mistakenly identified as part of the Farnese family crest. In fact they were part of the coat of arms of a French clergyman, Thomas Le Roy, for whom the palazzo was built in 1523.

The entrance is in a façade built to overlook Corso Vittorio Emanuele II when the road was built at the start of the 1900s. The original façade on the left of today's entrance is attributed to Antonio da Sangallo the Younger.

The Piccola Farnesina now houses the Museo Barracco, a sculpture collection assembled during the 19th century by the politician Baron Giovanni Barracco. A bust of the baron is in the courtyard. The collection includes an ancient Egyptian relief of the scribe Nofer, some Assyrian artifacts and, among the Etruscan exhibits, a delicate ceramic female head. On the first floor is the Greek collection with a head of Apollo.

## ⑭ Palazzo della Cancelleria

**◊ T4 ⚑ Piazza della Cancelleria 📞 06-6988 7566 🚌 40, 46, 62, 64, 70, 81, 87, 116, 492 Courtyard: ⏰ 7:30am-8pm Mon-Sat, 9:30am-7pm Sun Sala Riaria and Salone dei Cento Giorni: ⏰ Tue pm & Sat am (call 06-6988 7566 at least a month in advance)**

The palazzo, a prime example of Early Renaissance architecture, was begun in 1485. It was financed partly with the gambling winnings of Cardinal Raffaele Riario, who was in charge of the Papal Chancellery. Roses, the emblem of the Riario family, adorn the vaults and capitals of the beautiful Doric courtyard. The palazzo's interior was decorated after the Sack of Rome in 1527. Giorgio Vasari boasted that he had completed work on one enormous room in just 100 days (thus it was named Salone dei Cento Giorni); Michelangelo allegedly retorted: "It looks like it." Mannerist artists Perin del Vaga and Francesco Salviati frescoed the cardinal's rooms. The splendid Sala Riaria has a clock face painted by Baciccia.

On the right of the palazzo's main entrance is the church of San Lorenzo in Damaso, founded by Pope Damasus (reigned 366–84). It was reconstructed in 1495.

## ⑮  Teatro Argentina

**◊ U4 ⚑ Largo di Torre Argentina 52 🚌 40, 46, 62, 64, 70, 81, 87, 186, 492, 810 🚋 8 ⏰ Museum by appt only (call 06-0608) 🌐 teatrodiroma.net**

One of Rome's most influential theatres was founded by the Sforza Cesarini family in 1732, though the façade dates from

# SHOP

### Beppe e i suoi Formaggi
This *enoteca* and gourmet cheese shop is a wonderful place for special wine and foodie souvenirs, particularly cheeses, all made from the milk of Alpine cows, sheep and goats.

**◊ U5 ⚑ Via Santa Maria del Pianto 9A 🌐 beppeeisuoi formaggi.it**

### Atelier Patrizia Pieroni
Roman designer Patrizia Pieroni creates chic womenswear. Her boutique holds rails full of colourful offerings and stunning accessories to lift any outfit. The second floor is an art gallery hosting exhibitions and events.

**◊ S3 ⚑ Via del Pellegrino 172 🌐 patriziapieroni.it**

### Ibiz
If you're in the market for a unique bag to take home, look no further: this little shop is brimming with colourful bags and purses handcrafted in leather on the premises.

**◊ U4 ⚑ Via dei Chiavari 39 🌐 ibizroma.it**

a century later. Many famous operas, including those of Verdi, were first performed here. In 1816 the theatre saw the ill-fated debut of Rossini's *Barber of Seville*, during which the composer insulted the unappreciative audience, who then pursued him hissing and jeering through the streets.

**16**

## Area Sacra di Largo Argentina

**U4** ◫ Largo di Torre Argentina ⊞ 40, 46, 62, 64, 70, 81, 87, 186, 492, 810 ⊞ 8 ⊙ To the public, but ruins clearly visible from street

The remains of four temples were discovered here in the 1920s, the oldest (temple C) dating from the early 3rd century BC. It was placed on a high platform preceded by an altar. In medieval times the church of San Nicola de' Cesarini was built over temple A's podium. The north column stumps belonged to a great portico, the Hecatostylum (portico of 100 columns). In Imperial times two marble lavatories were built here – the remains of one is visible behind temple A. Behind temples B and C are remains of a great platform of tufa blocks identified as part of

The Baroque interior of the basilica of San Carlo ai Catinari ↓

the Curia of Pompey – a rectangular building with a statue of Pompey. It was here that the Senate met and Julius Caesar was murdered on 15 March 44 BC. At the southwest corner of the site is a cat sanctuary for Rome's abandoned felines.

---

**17**

## San Carlo ai Catinari

**U4** ◫ Piazza B. Cairoli ☎ 06-6830 7070 ⊞ 40, 46, 62, 64, 70, 81, 87, 186, 492, 810 ⊞ 8 ⊙ For restoration

In 1620 Rome's Milanese congregation decided to honour Cardinal Carlo Borromeo, who was made a saint, with this great church. It was called "ai Catinari" on account of the many bowl-makers' *(catinari)* shops in the area surrounding the church. The solemn travertine façade was completed in 1638 by the Roman architect Soria. The 16th-century basilican plan is flanked by chapels. The St Cecilia Chapel was designed and decorated by Antonio Gherardi. The church's paintings and frescoes by Pietro da Cortona and Guido Reni depict the life and acts of San Carlo.

The ornate crucifix on the sacristy altar is inlaid with marble and mother-of-pearl and is by the 16th-century sculptor Algardi.

---

### ASSASSINATION OF JULIUS CAESAR

According to legend, the night before Caesar was killed, his wife Calpurnia dreamed she was holding his dead body, and she tried to persuade him to stay at home. Refusing to listen, he went to a meeting at the Curia of Pompey, as scheduled. He was attacked by a group of senators, including his former ally Brutus, who were opposed to his growing megalomania. His dying words were allegedly, "Tu quoque, Brute?" ("You too, Brutus?")

## 18

### Fontana delle Tartarughe

📍 V5 🏛 Piazza Mattei
🚌 46, 62, 63, 64, 70, 87, 186, 492, 810 🚊 8

The delightful Fontana delle Tartarughe (*tartarughe* means "tortoises") was commissioned by the Mattei family between 1581 and 1588 to decorate "their" piazza. The design was by Giacomo della Porta, but the fountain owes much of its charm to the four bronze youths each resting one foot on the head of a dolphin, sculpted by Taddeo Landini. Nearly a century after the fountain was built an unknown sculptor, possibly Bernini, added the tortoises to complete the composition.

## 19 ♿

### Crypta Balbi

📍 V4 🏛 Via delle Botteghe Oscure 🕐 9am–7:45pm Sat & Sun, by appt only
🌐 coopculture.it

Part of the Museo Nazionale Romano, Crypta Balbi is an inventive museum devoted to urban archaeology, and illustrates how a piece of land in central Rome has been used over the centuries. It stands on the remains of a

↑ An ancient jug – one of the finds on display at the Crypta Balbi museum

theatre built in 13 BC, the ruins of which can still be seen. Further excavations revealed that in the 1st century AD the *esedra* (the curved auditorium) had been converted into what appears to have been a smart public lavatory, with marble seats. Then, it seems, the area went downhill, as in the 3rd century blocks of flats (*insulae*) for the poor were constructed, one of them with a Mithraeum in the basement. By the 7th century the area had become a glassworks, evidenced by a huge dump of discarded glass.

## 20

### Santa Maria in Campitelli

📍 V5 🏛 Piazza di Campitelli 9 📞 06-6880 3978 🚌 40, 46, 62, 63, 64, 70, 87, 186, 780, 810 🕐 7am–7pm daily

In 17th-century Rome the plague could still strike fiercely and there were no reliable, effective remedies. Many Romans simply prayed for a cure to a sacred medieval icon of the Virgin, the Madonna del Portico. When a particularly lethal outbreak of plague abated in 1656, popular gratitude was so strong that a new church was built to house the icon.

The church, designed by Bernini's pupil Carlo Rainaldi, was completed in 1667. The main elements of the lively Baroque façade are the graceful columns, symbolizing the supporters of the true faith.

Inside the church stands a fabulously ornate, gilded altar tabernacle with spiral columns, designed by Giovanni Antonio de Rossi to contain the image of the Virgin. The side chapels are decorated by some of Rome's finest Baroque artists: Sebastiano Conca, Giovanni Battista Gaulli (known as Il Baciccia) and Luca Giordano.

↑ Domed ceiling of the church of Santa Maria in Campitelli

# STAY

### DOM Hotel

From the intimate, dimly lit bar area, hung with Warhol prints and stags' heads, to the luxuriously appointed guest rooms decorated with splashy modern art, DOM has an appealingly rock-star feel. There's also a bijou roof terrace for sipping cocktails under the stars.

📍 R3 🏛 Via Giulia 131
🌐 domhotelroma.com

### Hotel Teatro di Pompeo

Built on the site of the ancient Teatro di Pompeo, this friendly three-star hotel offers great value for money. Guest rooms feature beamed ceilings and big windows, while the breakfast room has ancient Roman remains.

📍 T4 🏛 Largo del Pallaro 8
🌐 hotelteatrodi pompeo.it

Aerial view towards the Capitoline Hill, with the Theatre of Marcellus in the foreground ↑

## 21 San Nicola in Carcere

**V5** ⬛ Via del Teatro di Marcello 46 ☎ Church: 06-6830 7198; excavations: 347-381 1874 🚌 44, 63, 81, 160, 170, 628, 780, 781 🕐 10am–5pm daily 🌐 sotterraneidiroma.it

The medieval church of San Nicola in Carcere stands on the site of three Roman temples of the Republican era which were converted into a prison (carcere) in the Middle Ages. The temples of Juno, Spes and Janus faced a city gate leading from the Forum Holitorium, the city's vegetable and oil market, to the road down to the port on the Tiber. The underground excavations are well worth a visit. The columns embedded in the walls of the church belonged to two flanking temples whose platforms are now marked by lawns. The church was rebuilt in 1599, with a new façade by Giacomo della Porta, and restored during the 19th century, but the bell tower and Roman columns, incorporated into the church's façade, are part of the original design.

## 22 Theatre of Marcellus

**V5** ⬛ Via del Teatro di Marcello ☎ 06-0608 🚌 44, 63, 81, 160, 170, 628, 780, 781 🚫 Closed due to COVID-19 with no date for reopening

The curved outer wall of this amphitheatre has supported generations of Roman buildings. It was built by Emperor Augustus (27 BC–AD 14), who dedicated it to Marcellus, his nephew and son-in-law, who had died aged 19 in 23 BC.

The Middle Ages were a turbulent time of invasions and local conflicts and by the 13th century the theatre had been converted into the fortress of the Savelli family. In the 16th century Baldassarre Peruzzi built a great palace on the theatre ruins for the Orsini family. This included a garden that faced the Tiber.

Close to the theatre stand three Corinthian columns and a section of frieze. These are from the Temple of Apollo, which once housed many great works of art that the Romans had plundered from Greece in the 2nd century BC.

## 23 Portico of Octavia

**V5** ⬛ Via del Portico d'Ottavia 🚌 46, 62, 63, 64, 70, 87, 186, 780, 810

Built in honour of Octavia (the sister of Augustus and the abandoned wife of Mark Antony), this is the only surviving portico of what used to be the monumental piazza of Circus Flaminius. The rectangular portico enclosed temples dedicated to Jupiter and Juno, decorated with bronze statues. The part you see today is the great central atrium originally covered by marble facings.

In the Middle Ages a great fish market and a church, Sant'Angelo in Pescheria, were built in the ruins of the portico. As the church was associated with the fishing activities of the nearby river port, aquatic flora and fauna feature in many of its inlays. Links with the Tiber are also apparent in the stucco façade on the adjacent Fishmonger's Oratory, built in 1689. The church has a fresco of the Madonna and angels by the school of Benozzo Gozzoli.

## 24 Tiber Island

**♀ U5 ♙ Isola Tiberina**
**🚌 23, 63, 280, 780  🚋 8**

In ancient times the island, which lay opposite the city's port, had large structures of white travertine at either end, built to resemble the stern and prow of a ship. Since 293 BC, when a temple was dedicated to Aesculapius, the god of healing and protector against the plague, the island has been associated with the sick. San Bartolomeo all'Isola, the church in the island's central piazza, was built on the ruins of the Temple of Aesculapius in the 10th century. Its bell tower is visible from across the river.

From the Ghetto area you can reach the island by a footbridge, the Ponte Fabricio. The oldest original bridge over the Tiber still in use, it was built in 62 BC. In medieval times the Pierleoni and then the Caetani, two powerful families, controlled this strategic point by use of a tower, still *in situ*. The other bridge to the island, the Ponte Cestio, is inscribed with the names of the Byzantine emperors associated with its restoration in AD 370.

## 25 Ghetto and Synagogue

**♀ V5  🚌 23, 63, 280, 780 and routes to Largo di Torre Argentina  🚋 8**

There has been a Jewish community in Rome since the 2nd century BC. Systematic persecution began in the 16th century. From 25 July 1556 all Rome's Jews were forced to live inside a high-walled enclosure erected on the orders of Pope Paul IV. The Ghetto was in a damp, unhealthy part of Rome. Inhabitants were only allowed out during the day, and on Sundays they were driven into the Church of Sant'Angelo in Pescheria to listen to Christian sermons – a practice that was abandoned only in 1848. It wasn't until 1870, the year of the Italian Unification, that the Ghetto was abolished, with Jewish people finally being considered Italian.

Persecution started again in 1943 with the German occupation. Although many Jews were helped to escape or were hidden by Roman citizens, thousands were deported to German concentration camps.

The **Synagogue** on Lungotevere was completed in 1904 and houses a **Jewish Museum** that describes the history of the community, Torahs and other artifacts.

### Synagogue and Jewish Museum

**⊛ ♙ Lungo-tevere dei Cenci**
**☎ 06-6840 0661  🕐 Jewish Museum: Apr-Sep: 10am-6pm Sun-Thu, 10am-4pm Fri; Sep-Mar: 10am-5pm Sun-Thu, 9am-2pm Fri  🕐 Jewish public hols  ⓦ museoebraico. roma.it**

## 26 San Giovanni dei Fiorentini

**♀ R2  ♙ Via Acciaioli 2**
**☎ 06-6889 2059  🚌 23, 40, 46, 62, 64, 116, 280, 870**
**🕐 7:25am-noon & 5-7pm Mon-Sat; 7:30am-1pm & 5-8pm Sun & hols**

The church of St John of the Florentines was built for the large Florentine community in this area. Pope Leo X wanted it to be an expression of the cultural superiority of Florence over Rome. Started in the early 16th century, the church took over a century to build. The principal architect was Antonio da Sangallo the Younger, but many others contributed before Carlo Maderno's elongated cupola was finally completed in 1620. The present façade was added in the 18th century.

The church was decorated mainly by Tuscan artists. One interesting exception is the 15th-century statue of San Giovannino by the Sicilian Mino del Reame in a niche above the sacristy. The spectacular high altar houses a marble group by Antonio

Raggi, *The Baptism of Christ*. The altar itself is by Borromini, who is buried in the church.

The church also has a small museum of sacred art (open 9:30am–noon Mon–Sat).

---

**27**

## Casa di Lorenzo Manilio

🚇 U5 🏠 Via del Portico d'Ottavia 1D 🚌 46, 62, 63, 64, 70, 87, 186, 780, 810 🚫 to the public

Before the Renaissance, most Romans had only vague ideas of their city's past, but the 15th-century revival of interest in the philosophy and arts of antiquity inspired some to build houses recalling the splendour of ancient Rome. In 1468 a certain Lorenzo Manilio built a great house for his family, decorating it with an elegant Classical plaque. The Latin inscription dates the building according to the ancient Roman method – 2,221 years after the foundation of the city – and gives the owner's name. Original reliefs are embedded in the façades. The Piazza Costaguti façade's windows are inscribed *Ave Roma* (Hail Rome).

---

**28**

## Palazzo Cenci

🚇 U5 🏠 Vicolo dei Cenci 🚌 23, 63, 280, 780 and routes to Largo di Torre Argentina 🚫 To the public

Palazzo Cenci belonged to the family of Beatrice Cenci, who was accused, together with her brothers and stepmother, of witchcraft and the murder of her tyrannical father. She was beheaded in 1599.

---

←

The Ponte Fabricio footbridge that links the Ghetto to Tiber Island

---

# EAT

### Il Forno di Campo de' Fiori

This is the best place locally for a takeaway lunch: delicious *pizza bianca* stuffed with anything from mortadella to Nutella. Also try the delicious biscuits and pastries.

🚇 T4 🏠 Vicolo del Gallo 14 🌐 fornocampo defiori.com

€€€

---

### Roscioli

This family-owned restaurant/deli is renowned for its wines, meats and cheeses. The *antipasti* and pasta dishes are particularly delicious.

🚇 U5 🏠 Via dei Giubbonari 21 🌐 salumeriaroscioli.com

€€€

---

### Piperno

Tucked away in the Ghetto, this traditional eatery is a good place to sample Roman cuisine.

🚇 U5 🏠 Via Monte dé Cenci 9 🌐 ristorantepiperno.it

€€€

---

Most of the original medieval palazzo has been demolished, and the building you see today dates back to the 1570s. Heraldic half-moons decorate the main façade on Via del Progresso, while balconies open on the opposite side where a medieval arch joins the palace to Palazzetto Cenci, designed by Martino Longhi the Elder. Many of the rooms retain the decoration that the unfortunate Beatrice would have known as a child.

Tiber Island with Ponte Cestio in the foreground

# A SHORT WALK
# CAMPO DE' FIORI

**Distance** 1.5 km (1 mile)  **Nearest bus** 116
**Time** 30 minutes

A stroll through this fascinating part of Renaissance Rome will take you through some lovely shopping streets, including Via dei Giubbonari with its fashionable clothes shops, past numerous restaurants and bars and to Piazza di Campo de' Fiori, which has a famous morning market. Popular restaurants keep the area alive late into the night. On your walk there will be plenty of great buildings to admire, though few are open to the public. Two exceptions are the Piccola Farnesina, with its collection of Classical statues, and Palazzo Spada, home to many significant paintings.

Palazzo Ricci has painted Classical scenes on its façade, a favourite form of decoration of Renaissance houses (p168).

Sant'Eligio degli Orefici, a small Renaissance church designed by Raphael, is concealed behind a later façade (p169).

## Did You Know?

The market on Campo de' Fiori is one of the oldest in Rome, dating to the 1860s.

Santa Maria in Monserrato has strong connections with Spain, and houses a Bernini bust of Cardinal Pedro Foix de Montoya (p169).

The chief attraction of San Girolamo della Carità is Borromini's fabulous Spada Chapel (p169).

A pair of dramatic winged skulls flank the doorway to Santa Maria dell'Orazione e Morte, dedicated to the burial of the dead (p168).

VIA DI MONSERRATO

VIA GIULIA

LUNGOTEVERE DEI TEBALDI

TEVERE

START

FINISH

← Stalls of fresh produce at the market on Campo de' Fiori

0 metres 75
0 yards 75  N ↑

178

The vast Palazzo della Cancelleria housed the papal administration that ran the affairs of the Church (p170).

The plaque on Piccola Farnesina honours Giovanni Barracco. His sculpture collection is housed in the palazzo (p170).

**Locator Map**
For more detail see p160

The bustling market makes Piazza Campo de' Fiori one of Rome's most entertaining squares (p164).

Heraldic eagles stare down from the pediments of the Palazzo Pio Righetti's windows.

Michelangelo and other great artists helped create the monumental Renaissance Palazzo Farnese (p168).

Palazzo Spada's picture gallery houses a collection started by two wonderfully eccentric 17th-century cardinals (p167).

Palazzo del Monte di Pietà was a papal institution, where the poor pawned their possessions in order to borrow small sums of money (p166).

Santissima Trinità dei Pellegrini's principal role was to look after poor pilgrims arriving in Rome (p167).

Sotterranei di San Paolo alla Regola are the remains of a Roman house in the basement of an old palace (p166).

VIA DEL PELLEGRINO
PIAZZA DELLA CANCELLERIA
VIA DEI BAULLARI
PIAZZA CAMPO DE' FIORI
PIAZZA FARNESE
VIA DEI GIUBBONARI
VIA CAPO DI FERRO
PIAZZA DEL MONTE DI PIETÀ
VIA DEGLI SPECCHI
VIA DEI PETTINARI
PONTE SISTO

# QUIRINAL AND MONTI

One of the original seven hills of Rome, the Quirinal was a largely residential area in Imperial times, once home to the Baths of Constantine. Abandoned in the Middle Ages, the area returned to favour in the 16th century, when the prime site atop the hill was taken by the papacy to create the huge Palazzo del Quirinale, now home to Italy's president, while great aristocratic families such as the Colonna and Aldobrandini built palaces lower down the hill. Following Unification the surrounding area was completely transformed and many old palazzi were replaced by monumental buildings, especially along busy Via Nazionale, now one of the city's main arteries. The small Monti district, hidden behind Trajan's Markets, was a crowded slum teeming with prostitutes in ancient Roman times, separated from the Forum by a long wall. It is now a fashionable bohemian oasis, with trendy shops, bars and cafés clustering around traffic-free Piazza Madonna dei Monti and the hilly streets of Via dei Serpenti and Via del Boschetto.

# QUIRINAL AND MONTI

# ❶
# TREVI FOUNTAIN

📍 H4 🚌 52, 53, 61, 62, 63, 71, 80, 116, 119 and other routes along Via del Corso and Via del Tritone

Tucked away on a tiny piazza, this is the most famous – and the largest – fountain in Rome. Built in 1762 by Italian architect Nicola Salvi, in the flamboyant Rococo style, the Trevi Fountain is a travertine extravaganza of rearing seahorses, conch-blowing Tritons, craggy rocks and palm trees built into the side of the Palazzo Poli.

↑ Relief of Trivia pointing to the spring from which the water flows

The fountain's waters come from the Acqua Vergine, a Roman aqueduct built in 19 BC and fed by springs 22 km (14 miles) from the city. Legend has it that the Acqua Vergine is named after a young virgin called Trivia who showed Roman engineers the location of a freshwater spring. The word Trevi is a corruption of her name.

The fountain contains about 3 million litres (666,000 gallons) of water. Once reputed to be the sweetest water in Rome, it is now treated with chemicals. Legend has it that throwing a coin into the fountain guarantees a return to Rome.

## €3,000

of coins are thrown into the fountain every day. The money is collected and given to charity.

### LA CITTÀ DELL'ACQUA

♿ 📍 H5 📍 Vicolo del Puttarello 25 🕐 3–7pm Tue, Thu & Sat, 10am–2pm Wed, Fri & Sun 🌐 vicuscaprarius.com

In 2001 a stretch of the Acqua Vergine aqueduct (built in Augustan times and still feeding the Trevi Fountain) was revealed during restoration of an old cinema. Part of the underground archaeological area of "The City of Water" can now be visited, including the aqueduct and the ruins of an ancient Roman apartment block (insula) that was later converted into a single family home. Artifacts uncovered in the area are also on display.

## LA DOLCE VITA

Federico Fellini's 1960 film is about a paparazzo (played by Marcello Mastroianni) drifting through the decadent nightlife of Rome, and meeting a beautiful Swedish actress played by Anita Ekberg. The most famous scene – Ekberg taking a shower in the Trevi Fountain – may be largely responsible for making the Trevi the best known and most photographed fountain in the city.

## Oceanus and Chariot pulled by Tritons and Horses

The central statue standing in a triumphal arch is of Oceanus, the personification of an enormous river encircling the world from which all streams of water are derived in ancient mythology. The statue was carved by Pietro Bracci, who took over work on the fountain after the death of Nicola Salvi, his long-time friend, in 1751.

Oceanus's conch-shell chariot is powered by two horses steered by Tritons. One Triton struggles to master an unruly beast, while the other leads a far more docile animal. The horses were intended to symbolize the different moods of the sea.

↑ Trevi Fountain with *(inset)* detail of its sculpture, depicting Triton steering a horse

2 (icons)

# PALAZZO MASSIMO ALLE TERME

L4  Largo di Villa Peretti 1  H, 36, 38, 40, 64, 170 and other routes to Piazza del Cinequecento  Repubblica, Termini  2–7:45pm Tue–Fri, 10:30am–7:45pm Sat & Sun; by appt only  coopculture.it

**The main site of the Museo Nazionale Romano, the airy 19th-century Palazzo Massimo alle Terme holds an exceptional collection of antiquities dating from the 2nd century BC to the end of the 4th century AD.**

Founded in 1889, the museum contains one of the world's leading collections of Classical art, comprising frescoes, mosaics, statues and other artifacts found in Rome since 1870. The exhibits are beautifully displayed on several floors. The courtyard, with its portico of statues dappled with light and shade, is a wonderful introduction to this spectacular collection. The museum has many highlights, but the exquisite frescoes from Livia's Villa are a particular must see.

The Museo Nazionale Romano has four sites. The other branches are in the Baths of Diocletian, just around the corner from Palazzo Massimo alle Terme, the Crypta Balbi (p172) and Palazzo Altemps (p133). The same entry ticket is valid for all four sites for three consecutive days.

←

Courtyard of the 19th-century Palazzo Massimo alle Terme, lined with statues

## BATHS OF DIOCLETIAN

📍L4 🏛Terme di Diocleziano, Viale
E de Nicola 79 🕐2–7:45pm Tue–Fri,
10:30am–7:45pm Sat & Sun; by appt
only 🌐coopculture.it

Built under Emperor Diocletian between
AD 298 and 306, this bath complex was
the largest in ancient Rome. Parts were
later converted into the church of Santa
Maria degli Angeli e dei Martiri *(p193)*. The
Baths now house the Museo Nazionale
Romano's collection of funerary monuments and inscriptions. Highlights include
a display about the history of writing and
a section on amulets and magic.

↑ Fresco depicting a garden
with birds and fruit trees
from the dining room of
Livia's Villa at Prima Porta,
north of Rome

*Collection Highlights*

### Frescoes and Mosaics

Some of the most joyous displays are on the
second floor, where wall paintings and mosaics
have been brought from ancient villas excavated
in and around Rome. The most incredible are
the four exquisite floor-to-ceiling illusionistic
frescoes from the underground dining room of a
villa that belonged to Emperor Augustus's wife
Livia. They portray a garden with flowers, fruit
trees and birds, and were created to give diners
the impression they were eating al fresco.

### Objects

In the basement, objects evoke the reality of
everyday life in ancient Rome. There are ivory
dice, sewing needles,
sets of compasses
and a miniature
abacus, along with
tiny spoons used for
mixing cosmetics. Don't
miss the haunting
Grottarossa Mummy, the
mummified remains of an
eight-year-old girl, buried
with her jewellery and doll.

### Sculpture

Exhibits on the first floor evoke the luxury
enjoyed by the elite of ancient Rome, typified
by the elaborate bronze fittings - including lion
heads and a Medusa - from the opulent boats
which Emperor Caligula used for parties on the
Lake of Nemi. Other highlights include an ivory
Mask of Apollo and a striking bronze sculpture of
a Boxer whose lips and wounds
have a red hue.

# EXPERIENCE MORE

## ❸ Castor and Pollux

📍 J5 📌 Piazza del Quirinale
🚌 H, 40, 64, 70, 170 and many routes along Via del Tritone

Castor and Pollux and their prancing horses stand in the Piazza del Quirinale. Over 5.5 m (18 ft) high, these statues are huge Roman copies of 5th-century BC Greek originals. They once stood at the entrance to the nearby Baths of Constantine. Pope Sixtus V had them restored and placed here in 1588. They gave the square its familiar name of Monte Cavallo (horse hill).

The obelisk between them was brought here in 1786 from the Mausoleum of Augustus. In 1818 the composition was completed by the addition of a massive granite basin, once a cattle trough in the Forum.

## ❹  Palazzo del Quirinale

📍 J5 📌 Piazza del Quirinale
🚌 H, 40, 64, 70, 170 and many routes along Via del Tritone 🚫 Closed due to COVID-19 with no date for reopening 🌐 quirinale.it

By the 1500s, the Vatican had a reputation as an unhealthy location because of the high incidence of malaria, so Pope Gregory XIII chose this site as a papal summer residence. Work began in 1573. Piazza del Quirinale has buildings on three sides, while the fourth is open, with a splendid view of the city. Many great architects worked on the palace.

After Rome became the capital city of the new united Italy in 1870, the palace became the official residence of the king, then, in 1947, of the president of the republic.

The immaculately manicured gardens are open to the public only once a year, on Republic Day (2 June).

## ❺ Palazzo Colonna

📍 H5 📌 Via della Pilotta 17
🚌 H, 40, 64, 70, 170 and many routes to Piazza Venezia 🕐 9am–1:15pm Sat only (guided tour in English at noon) or by appt (call 06-679 4350 to book) 🌐 galleriacolonna.it

Pope Martin V Colonna (reigned 1417–31) began building the palazzo, but most of the structure dates from the 18th century. It has belonged to over twenty

↑ Annibale Carracci's *The Bean Eater*, on display in Galleria Colonna

generations of the Colonna family. The Galleria Colonna, built by Antonio del Grande between 1654 and 1665, is the only part of the palazzo open to the public. The pictures are numbered but unlabelled, so remember to pick up a guide at the start of your visit. Go up the stairs and through the antechamber leading to a series of three gleaming marble rooms with prominent yellow columns, the Colonna family emblem (*colonna* means "column").

The ceiling frescoes celebrate Marcantonio Colonna's victory over the Turks at the Battle of Lepanto (1571). On the walls are 16th- to 18th-century paintings, including Annibale Carracci's *The Bean Eater*. The room of landscape paintings, many by Poussin's brother-in-law Gaspare Dughet, reflects the 18th-century taste of Cardinal Girolamo Colonna. Beyond is a room with a ceiling fresco of *The Apotheosis of Martin V*. The throne room has a chair reserved for visiting popes and a copy of Pisanello's portrait of Martin V. The gallery offers a fine view of the private palace garden, site of the ruined Temple of Serapis.

← Statue of Castor and his horse in the Piazza del Quirinale

### 6

## Santi Apostoli

**H5** **Piazza dei Santi Apostoli 51** **06-699 571** **H, 40, 64, 70, 170 and many other routes to Piazza Venezia** **7am–noon & 4–7pm daily**

The 6th-century church that was originally on this site was rebuilt in the 15th century by popes Martin V Colonna and Sixtus IV della Rovere, whose oak-tree crest

decorates the capitals of the late 15th-century portico. Inside the portico on the left is Canova's 1807 memorial to the engraver Giovanni Volpato. The church itself contains a much larger monument by Canova, his Tomb of Clement XIV (1789).

The Baroque interior by Francesco and Carlo Fontana was completed in 1714. Note the 3D effect of Giovanni Odazzi's painted *Rebel Angels*, who really look as though they are falling from the sky. A huge 18th-century altarpiece by Domenico Muratori illustrates the martyrdom of the Apostles James and Philip, whose tombs are in the crypt.

↑ The Baroque nave and interior of the church of the Santi Apostoli

which were known as *tituli*. A later Romanesque building on the site burned down in 1519, but it was rebuilt by Jacopo Sansovino with a single nave and many richly decorated private chapels on either side. The imposing travertine façade was designed by Carlo Fontana in late Baroque style.

The third chapel on the right features fine frescoes of the Virgin Mary by Francesco Salviati. The decoration of the next chapel was interrupted by the Sack of Rome in 1527. Raphael's follower Perin del Vaga fled, leaving the ceiling frescoes to be completed by Daniele da Volterra and Pellegrino Tibaldi when peace returned to the city. In the nave stands a splendid marble Venetian-style double tomb made by Sansovino around 1520; this is a memorial to Cardinal Giovanni Michiel (who was the victim of a Borgia poisoning in 1503) and his nephew, Bishop Antonio Orso.

### 7

## San Marcello al Corso

**H5** **Piazza di San Marcello 5** **06-679 3910** **62, 63, 81, 85, 117, 119, 160, 492, 628** **7am–midnight Mon–Fri, 9:30am–midnight Sat & Sun**

This church was originally one of the first places of Christian worship in Rome,

## 8

# Santi Vincenzo e Anastasio

**H4** **Piazza di Trevi**
52, 53, 61, 62, 63, 71, 80, 116, 119 **9am-8pm daily**

Overlooking the Trevi Fountain is one of the most over-the-top Baroque façades in Rome. Its thickets of columns are crowned by the huge coat of arms of Cardinal Raimondo Mazzarino, better known as Cardinal Mazarin, chief minister of France, who commissioned Martino Longhi the Younger to build the church in 1650. The female bust above the door is of one of the cardinal's famous nieces, either Louis XIV's first love, Maria Mancini (1639–1715), or her younger sister, Ortensia. In the apse, memorial plaques record the popes whose *praecordia* (a part of the heart) are enshrined behind the wall. This gruesome tradition was started at the end of the 16th century by Pope Sixtus V and continued until Pius X stopped it in the early 20th century.

## 9

# Scuderie del Quirinale

**J5** **Via 24 Maggio 16**
H, 40, 60, 64, 70, 170 **For exhibitions only - check website** **scuderie quirinale.it**

The Scuderie started life as stables for the nearby Palazzo del Quirinale. Built in the early 1700s by Ferdinando Fuga over the remains (still partially visible) of the ancient Temple of Serapis, the stables were remodelled by Gae Aulenti in the 1990s. The Scuderie del Quirinale now host some of the best temporary art exhibitions in the country. The top floor has great views of Rome.

## 10

# Santa Maria in Trivio

**H4** **Piazza dei Crociferi 49** **06-678 9645**
52, 53, 61, 62, 63, 71, 80, 116, 119 **8am-noon & 4-8pm daily**

It has been said that Italian architecture is one of façades, and nowhere is this clearer than in the 1570s façade of Santa Maria in Trivio, delightfully stuck on to the building behind it. Note the false windows. There is illusion inside too, particularly in the ceiling frescoes, which show scenes from the New Testament by Antonio Gherardi (1644–1702).

The name of this beautiful little church probably means "St Mary-at-the-meeting-of-three-roads".

> **The Scuderie del Quirinale now host some of the best temporary art exhibitions in the country.**

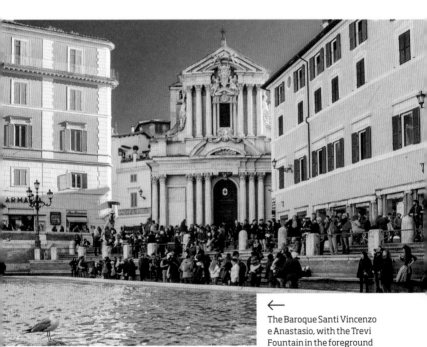

← The Baroque Santi Vincenzo e Anastasio, with the Trevi Fountain in the foreground

←

*Self-portrait* by Lavinia Fontana in the Accademia Nazionale di San Luca

the many IHS emblems (*Iesus Hominum Salvator* – Jesus Saviour of Mankind).

The site for the church was wide but shallow, so Bernini pointed the long axis of his oval plan not towards the altar, but towards the sides; he then leads the eye round to the altar end. Here Bernini ordered works of art in various media which function not in isolation, but together. The crucified St Andrew (Sant'Andrea) of the altarpiece looks up at a stucco version of himself, who in turn ascends towards the lantern and the Holy Spirit.

The rooms of St Stanislas Kostka in the adjacent convent should not be missed. The quarters of the Jesuit novice, who died in 1568 at the age of 19, reflect not his own spartan taste, but the richer style of the 17th-century Jesuits. The Polish saint has been brilliantly immortalized in marble by Pierre Legros (1666–1719).

## ⑪ Accademia Nazionale di San Luca

**⑨ H4 ⌂ Piazza dell' Accademia di San Luca 77 🚌 52, 53, 61, 62, 63, 71, 80, 116, 119 and many routes along Via del Corso and Via del Tritone ⊙ 10am–12:30pm Mon-Sat 🌐 accademiasanluca.eu**

St Luke is supposed to have been a painter, hence the name of Rome's academy of fine arts. Appropriately, the gallery contains a painting of *St Luke Painting a Portrait of the Virgin* by Raphael and his followers. The academy's heyday was in the 17th and 18th centuries, when many members gave their work to the collection. Canova donated a model for his famous marble group, *The Three Graces*.

Of particular interest are three fascinating self-portraits painted by women: the 17th-century Italian Lavinia Fontana; the 18th-century Swiss Angelica Kauffmann, whose painting is copied from a portrait of her by Joshua Reynolds; and Elisabeth Vigée-Lebrun, the French painter of the years before the 1789 Revolution.

## ⑫ Sant'Andrea al Quirinale

**⑨ J5 ⌂ Via del Quirinale 29 📞 06-487 4565 🚌 116, 117 and routes to Via del Tritone ⊙ 9am-noon & 3-6pm Tue-Sun**

Known as the "Pearl of the Baroque" because of its beautiful roseate marble interior, Sant'Andrea was designed by Bernini and executed by his assistants between 1658 and 1670. It was built for the Jesuits, hence

---

# STAY

**Villa Spalletti Trivelli**
With the feel of an elegant country-house retreat, this luxury villa has atmosphere and style in abundance. Fine antiques grace every room, a sweeping staircase leads to sumptuous guest rooms upstairs, and there's even a garden - a rarity in central Rome.

**⑨ J5 ⌂ Via Piacenza 4 🌐 villaspalletti.it**

€€€

---

↑ The interior of the small church of San Carlo alle Quattro Fontane

### 13

## San Carlo alle Quattro Fontane

📍J4 🏛 Via del Quirinale 23 ☎06-488 3261 🚌116, 117 and routes to Piazza Barberini Ⓜ Barberini 🕙10am-1pm Mon-Sat

In 1634, the Trinitarians, a Spanish order whose role was to pay the ransom of Christian hostages to the Arabs, commissioned Borromini to design a church and convent at the Quattro Fontane crossroads. The church, so small it would fit inside one of the piers of St Peter's, is also known as "San Carlino".

Although dedicated to Carlo Borromeo, the 16th-century Milanese cardinal canonized in 1620, San Carlo is as much a monument to Borromini. Both the façade and interior employ bold curves that give light and life to a small, cramped site. The oval dome and tiny lantern are particularly ingenious. Finished in 1667, the façade is one of Borromini's last works.

There are further delights in the playful inverted shapes in the cloister and the stucco work in the refectory.

In a small room off the sacristy hangs a portrait of Borromini himself wearing the Trinitarian cross. Borromini

→ The once-controversial Fontana delle Naiadi in the Piazza della Repubblica

committed suicide in 1667, and in the crypt a small curved chapel reserved for him remains empty.

### 14

## Le Quattro Fontane

📍J4 🏛Intersection of Via delle Quattro Fontane and Via del Quirinale 🚌Routes to Piazza Barberini or Via Nazionale Ⓜ Barberini

These four small fountains are attached to the corners of the buildings at the intersection of two narrow, busy streets. They date from the great redevelopment of Rome in the reign of Sixtus V (1585–90). Each fountain has a statue of a reclining deity. The river god accompanied by the she-wolf is clearly the Tiber; the other male figure may be the Arno. The female figures represent Strength and Fidelity or the goddesses Juno and Diana.

The crossroads is at the highest point of the Quirinal Hill and commands splendid views of three distant landmark obelisks: those placed by Sixtus V in front of Santa Maria Maggiore and Trinità dei Monti, and the one that stands in Piazza del Quirinale.

### 15

## Moses Fountain

📍K4 🏛Fontana dell'Acqua Felice, Piazza San Bernardo 🚌36, 60, 61, 62, 492 Ⓜ Repubblica

Officially known as the Fontana dell'Acqua Felice, this fountain owes its popular name to the statue of Moses in the central niche. The massive structure with its three elegant arches was

designed by Domenico Fontana to mark the terminal of the Acqua Felice aqueduct, so called because it was one of the many great improvements commissioned by Felice Peretti, Pope Sixtus V. Completed in 1587, the

# DRINK

### Trimani Il Wine Bar

This celebrated *enoteca* offers plenty of wines by the glass and has been selling its wares to thirsty Romans since 1821. There's also a menu of dishes far above the usual wine-bar fare. Staff can advise on the perfect choice to pair with your meal.

📍L3 🏛Via Cernaia 37B 🌐trimani.com

acqueduct brought clean piped water to this quarter of Rome for the first time since the fall of the Roman Empire.

The notorious statue of Moses striking water from the rock is larger than life and the proportions of the body are obviously wrong. Sculpted either by Prospero Bresciano or Leonardo Sormani, it is a clumsy attempt at re-creating the awesome appearance of Michelangelo's *Moses* in the church of San Pietro in Vincoli (*p207*). As soon as it was unveiled to the public, it met with ridicule; it was said to be frowning at having been brought into the world by such an inept sculptor. The side reliefs by minor sculptors also illustrate water stories from the Old Testament: Aaron leading the Israelites to water and Joshua pointing the army towards the Red Sea. The fountain's four lions are copies of Egyptian originals (now in the Vatican Museums), which Sixtus V had put there for the public's "delight".

**16**

## Santa Maria degli Angeli e dei Martiri

📍 L4  🏛 Piazza della Repubblica  📞 06-488 0812  🚌 36, 60, 61, 62, 64, 90, 116, 170, 492, 910  Ⓜ Repubblica, Termini  🕐 7am-6:30pm Mon-Sat, 7am-7:30pm Sun

Parts of the ruined Baths of Diocletian (*p187*) provided building material and setting for this church, constructed by Michelangelo in 1563. The church was so altered in the 18th century that it has lost most of its original character.

**17**

## Piazza della Repubblica

📍 K4  🚌 36, 60, 61, 62, 64, 90, 170, 492, 646, 910  Ⓜ Repubblica

Romans often refer to the piazza by its old name, Piazza Esedra, so called because it follows the shape of an exedra

(a semicircular recess) that was part of the Baths of Diocletian. The piazza was included in the great redevelopment undertaken when Rome became capital of a unified Italy. Under its sweeping 19th-century colonnades there were once elegant shops, but they have been ousted by banks, travel agencies and cafés.

In the middle of the piazza stands the Fontana delle Naiadi. Mario Rutelli's four naked bronze nymphs caused a scandal when unveiled in 1901. Each reclines on an aquatic creature symbolizing water in its various forms: a seahorse for the oceans, a water snake for rivers, a swan for lakes, and a curious frilled lizard for subterranean streams. The figure in the middle, added in 1911, is of the sea god Glaucus.

→ Santi Domenico e Sisto, with a painting of the Madonna above the altar

# EAT

### Alle Carrette

This cheerful pizzeria serves up delicious thin-crust Roman-style pizzas. The tables outside on the cobbled street are in high demand in summer.

📍J6 🏠 Via della Madonna dei Monti 95
📞 06-679 2270

€€€

---

### Hostaria al Boschetto

This family-run trattoria specializes in Roman cuisine and traditional dishes based on porcini mushrooms, including delectable grilled mushrooms.

📍J5 🏠 Via del Boschetto 30
🌐 hostariaal boschetto.it

€€€

---

### La Carbonara

The scribblings of diners that cover every inch of the walls say it all: this buzzy, relaxed restaurant has plenty of satisfied customers. The speciality is, of course, carbonara, but there are plenty of other pastas, as well as good meaty mains.

📍K5 🏠 Via Panisperna 214
🌐 lacarbonara.it

€€€

---

**18**

## Sant'Agata dei Goti

📍J5 🏠 Via Mazzarino 16 and Via Panisperna 29
📞 06-4893 0456 🚌 40, 60, 64, 70, 71, 117, 170 🕐 7am–1pm & 4-7pm daily

The Goths (*Goti*) who gave their name to this church occupied Rome in the 6th century AD. They were Aryan heretics who denied the divinity of Christ. The church was founded between AD 462 and 470, shortly before the main Gothic invasions, and the beautiful granite columns date from this period. The most delightful part of the church is the 18th-century courtyard built around a well.

---

**19** 🏛️🍴☕🛍️

## Palazzo delle Esposizioni

📍J5 🏠 Via Nazionale 194
🚌 40, 60, 64, 70, 116T, 170
🕐 10am-8pm Tue-Sun (to 10:30pm Fri & Sat), by appt only 🌐 palazzo esposizioni.it

This grandiose building, with wide steps, Corinthian columns and statues, was designed as an exhibition centre by the architect Pio Piacentini and built by the city of Rome in 1882 during the reign of Umberto I. The main entrance looks like a triumphal arch.

The restored palazzo still hosts high-profile exhibitions of modern and contemporary art that change every three to six months and include sculptures, paintings and photography. Live performances, films and lectures also take place here.

---

**20**

## Santi Domenico e Sisto

📍J6 🏠 Largo Angelicum 1
📞 06-670 2201 🚌 40, 60, 64, 70, 71, 117, 170 🕐 3-6pm Sat, booking required

The church has a tall, slender Baroque façade rising above a steep flight of steps. This divides into two curving flights that sweep up to the terrace in front of the entrance. The pediment of the façade is crowned by eight flaming candlesticks.

The interior has a vaulted ceiling with a large fresco of *The Apotheosis of St Dominic* by Domenico Canuti (1620–84). The first chapel on the right was decorated by Bernini, who may also have designed the sculpture of Mary Magdalene meeting the risen Christ in the Garden of Gethsemane. This

→ The tranquil gardens of Villa Aldobrandini, with fountains and statues fine marble group was executed by Antonio Raggi (1649). Above the altar is a 15th-century terracotta plaque of the Virgin and Child. On the left, over a side altar, is a large painting of the Madonna from the same period, attributed to Benozzo Gozzoli (1420–97), a pupil of Fra Angelico.

---

**㉑**
## Villa Aldobrandini

📍 J5 🏠 Via Panisperna
🚌 40, 60, 64, 70, 71, 117, 170 🔑 To the public Gardens: Via Mazzarino 1
🕐 Dawn-dusk daily

Built in the 16th century for the Dukes of Urbino and acquired for his family by Pope Clement VIII Aldobrandini (reigned 1592–1605), the villa is now government property and houses an international law library.

The villa, decorated with the family's six-starred coat of arms, is closed to the public, but the gardens and terraces, hidden behind a high wall that runs along Via Nazionale, can be reached through an iron gate in Via Mazzarino. Steps lead up past 2nd-century AD ruins into the gardens, highly recommended as an oasis of tranquillity in the city centre. Raised some 10 m (30 ft) above street level, the Villa Aldobrandini garden offers excellent views of the Forum and Piazza Venezia. Gravel paths lead between formal lawns and clearly marked specimen trees.

> Raised some 10 m (30 ft) above street level, the Villa Aldobrandini garden offers excellent views of the Forum and Piazza Venezia.

---

**㉒**
## Santa Maria ai Monti

📍 J6 🏠 Via Madonna dei Monti 41 📞 06-485 531
🚌 75, 117 Ⓜ Cavour 🕐 7am-10pm Mon-Thu & Sun; 7am-midnight Fri & Sat

Designed by Giacomo della Porta, this church, dating from 1580, has a splendid dome. Over the high altar is a stunning medieval painting of the Madonna dei Monti, patroness of this quarter of Rome. The altar in the left transept houses the tomb and effigy of the unworldly French saint Benoît-Joseph Labre, who died here in 1783, having spent his life as a solitary pilgrim. He slept rough in the ruins of the Colosseum, gave away any charitable gifts he received, and came regularly to worship. His faith could not sustain his body: in his mid-thirties, he collapsed and died outside the church. The foul rags he wore are preserved.

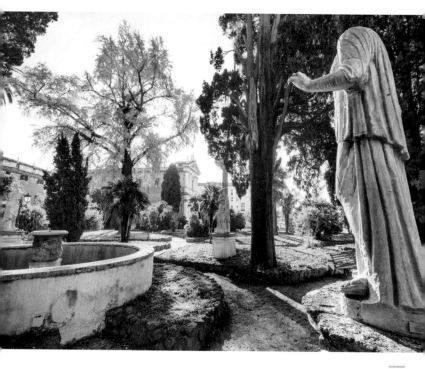

# A SHORT WALK
# THE QUIRINAL HILL

**Distance** 0.7 km (0.4 mile)  **Nearest bus** H, 40, 64, 70, 170
**Time** 15 minutes

Even though Palazzo del Quirinale is usually closed to the public, it is well worth walking up the hill to the palace to see the giant Roman statues of Castor and Pollux in the piazza and enjoy fine views of the city. Come down the hill by way of the narrow streets and stairways that lead to one of Rome's unforgettable sights, the Trevi Fountain. Many small churches lie hidden away in the back streets. Towards Piazza Venezia there are grand palazzi, including that of the Colonna, one of Rome's most ancient and powerful families.

*The Accademia Nazionale di San Luca art academy has works by famous former members (p191).*

*Santa Maria in Via is famous for its medieval well and miraculous 13th-century icon of the Madonna.*

*The attractive façade of the tiny Santa Maria in Trivio conceals a rich Baroque interior (p190).*

*The Trevi, Rome's grandest and best-known fountain, almost fills the tiny Piazza di Trevi (p184).*

*San Marcello al Corso contains a stark Crucifixion by Van Dyck in the sacristy (p189).*

*Palazzo Odescalchi has a Bernini façade from 1664, with a balustrade and richly decorated cornice. The building faces Santi Apostoli.*

VIA POLI

VIA DELLE MURATTE

VIA DELLE VERGINI

VIA DELL'UMILTÀ

VIA DEL CORSO

0 metres   75   N
0 yards    75

↑ Obelisk and statues of Castor and Pollux on Piazza del Quirinale

The grand façade of the small Baroque Santi Vincenzo e Anastasio is on a corner facing the Trevi Fountain (p190).

**Locator Map**
*For more detail see p182*

QUIRINAL AND MONTI

VIA DEL LAVATORE

DI SAN VINCENZO

VIA DELLA DATARIA

PIAZZA DELLA PILOTTA

PIAZZA DEI SANTI APOSTOLI

VIA BATTISTI

PIAZZA DEL QUIRINALE

The magnificent gardens of the presidential palace Giardini del Quirinale are open to visitors just once a year, on 2 June.

Palazzo del Quirinale, the old papal palace, is now the home of the president of Italy. Palace guards in uniform can often be seen outside (p188).

**FINISH**

The Castor and Pollux statues are grouped with an obelisk and a fountain (p188).

Piazza della Pilotta is dominated by the imposing façade of the Gregorian University.

Palazzo Colonna houses an art gallery. One of its finest old masters is Annibale Carracci's The Bean Eater (p188).

The figures of Christ and the Apostles on the balustrade of Santi Apostoli were added by Carlo Rainaldi in 1681 (p189).

**START**

# A LONG WALK
# AROUND BERNINI'S ROME

**Distance** 3.5 km (2 miles) **Walking time** 1.5 hours
**Nearest metro** Repubblica

Gian Lorenzo Bernini (1598–1680) is the artist who probably left the strongest personal mark on the appearance of the city of Rome. Favourite architect, sculptor and town planner to three successive popes, he turned Rome into a uniquely Baroque city. This walk traces his enormous influence on the development and appearance of the centre of Rome. It starts from the busy Largo di Santa Susanna just northwest of Termini station, at the church of Santa Maria della Vittoria.

The Fontana del Nettuno, sitting gracefully at Piazza Navona

The **Vicolo dei Modelli** is where male models waited to be chosen by artists.

Inspired by Bernini's work, the **Trevi Fountain** (p184) is a tribute to his lasting influence on Roman taste.

The **Via di Santa Maria** has a fine Baroque façade.

**Palazzo di Montecitorio** (p114), begun by Bernini in 1650, is now home to the Italian parliament.

TREVI

PIAZZA DI SAN SILVESTRO

Palazzo di Montecitorio

CHIGI

V. DE

LARGO

VIA

VIA DI SANTA MARIA

PIAZZA DI MONTECITORIO

PIAZZA COLONNA

Trevi Fountain

VICOLO DEI MODELLI

VICOLO SCANDERBERG

Column of Marcus Aurelius

VIA DELLE MURATTE

CORSO DEL RINASCIMENTO

San Luigi dei Francesi

DEL CORSO

VIA DELL'UMILTA

**FINISH**

PIAZZA DELLA ROTONDA

PIGNA

PIAZZA NAVONA

Palazzo Madama

Pantheon

**Piazza Navona** (p124) was remodelled by Bernini for Pope Innocent X Pamphilj.

Bernini said that although St Peter's had a hundred defects, the **Pantheon** (p106) had none.

The **Column of Marcus Aurelius** (p115) is located in Piazza Colonna.

Pass down **Vicolo Scanderberg**. Its name is a tribute to the nickname of Albanian prince Giorgio Castriota (1403–68) who once lived here.

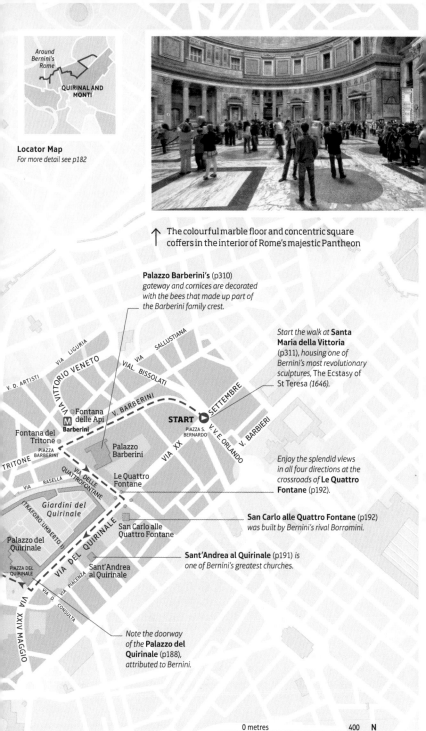

Locator Map
*For more detail see p182*

↑ The colourful marble floor and concentric square
coffers in the interior of Rome's majestic Pantheon

**Palazzo Barberini's** (p310)
*gateway and cornices are decorated
with the bees that made up part of
the Barberini family crest.*

*Start the walk at* **Santa
Maria della Vittoria**
(p311), *housing one of
Bernini's most revolutionary
sculptures, The Ecstasy of
St Teresa (1646).*

**START**

*Enjoy the splendid views
in all four directions at the
crossroads of* **Le Quattro
Fontane** *(p192).*

**San Carlo alle Quattro Fontane** (p192)
*was built by Bernini's rival Borromini.*

**Sant'Andrea al Quirinale** (p191) *is
one of Bernini's greatest churches.*

*Note the doorway
of the* **Palazzo del
Quirinale** *(p188),
attributed to Bernini.*

0 metres     400   N
0 yards     400   ↑

MARIA·VIRGO·ASSVPTA·E·AD·ETHEREV·THALAMV·INQVO·REX·REGV·STELLATO·SEDET·SOI

EXALTATA·EST·SANCTA·DEI·GENITRIX·SVPER·CHOROS·ANGELORVM·ADCELESTIA·REGNA·

# ESQUILINE

The Esquiline is the largest of Rome's seven hills.
In Imperial Rome the western slopes overlooking
the Forum housed the crowded slums of the
Suburra. On the eastern side there were a few
villas belonging to wealthy citizens such as
Maecenas, patron of the arts and adviser to
Augustus. Ancient Rome gave the Esquiline
the remains of the Baths of Titus, the Baths of
Trajan and Nero's Domus Aurea. The district's
main interest, however, lies in its churches.
Many of these were founded on the sites of
private houses where Christians met to worship
secretly in the days when their religion was
banned. Nowadays, the Esquiline is home to
Rome's Chinese community and Piazza Vittorio
is popular among Romans for hosting the yearly
Chinese New Year's celebrations. The colourful
Nuovo Mercato Esquilino market reflects the
international spirit of the neighbourhood, with
food stands catering to all the different immigrant
communities who live in this area. Bangladeshi,
Indian and Senegalese dishes are all represented.

# ESQUILINE

**Must See**

① Santa Maria Maggiore

**Experience More**

② Santa Pudenziana
③ San Martino ai Monti
④ Arch of Gallienus
⑤ San Pietro in Vincoli
⑥ Santa Prassede
⑦ Domus Aurea
⑧ Santa Bibiana
⑨ Piazza Vittorio Emanuele II
⑩ Auditorium of Maecenas
⑪ Sette Sale

**Eat**

① Trattoria Monti
② Palazzo del Freddo di Giovanni Fassi

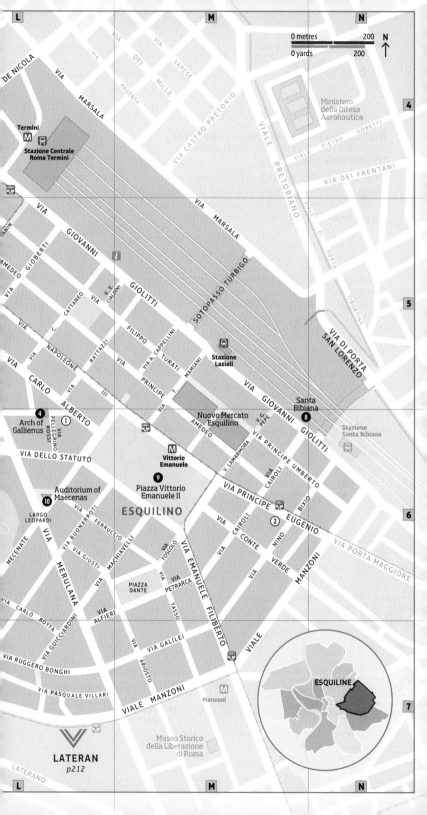

❶ 🛍️

# SANTA MARIA MAGGIORE

📍L5 🏛️Piazza di Santa Maria Maggiore ☎06-6988 6800 🚌16, 70, 71, 714 🚋14 Ⓜ️Termini, Cavour 🕐7am-6:45pm daily

Of all the great Roman basilicas, Santa Maria Maggiore has the most successful blend of different architectural styles. One of the four papal basilicas, it has a beautiful interior with sparkling mosaics.

This is the biggest of the 26 churches in Rome dedicated to the Virgin Mary. Originally built by Pope Liberius in the 4th century, Santa Maria Maggiore was renovated and improved upon by many popes over the centuries, although it still retains its early medieval structure. The colonnaded nave is part of the original 5th-century building. The Cosmatesque marble floor and delightful Romanesque bell tower, with its blue ceramic roundels, are medieval. The Renaissance saw a new coffered ceiling, and the Baroque gave the church twin domes and its imposing front and rear façades. The mosaics are Santa Maria's most famous feature and are some of the oldest in Rome. From the 5th century come the biblical scenes in the aisle and the spectacular mosaics on the triumphal arch. Medieval highlights include a 13th-century enthroned Christ in the loggia.

*Flaminio Ponzio designed this richly decorated chapel (1611) for Pope Paul V Borghese.*

↑ The 18th-century exterior of Santa Maria Maggiore on the piazza of the same name

*The gilded coffered ceiling, possibly by Giuliano da Sangallo, was a gift of Alexander VI Borgia at the end of the 15th century. The gold is said to be the first brought from America by Columbus.*

## Timeline

**420**
Probable founding date.

**432–40**
△ Sixtus III completes church.

**1288–92**
▽ Nicholas IV adds apse and transepts.

**1347**
Cola di Rienzo crowned Tribune of Rome in Santa Maria Maggiore.

**1673**
Carlo Rainaldi rebuilds apse.

**1743**
Ferdinando Fuga adds main façade on orders of Benedict XIV.

A series of wonderful apse mosaics of the Virgin by Jacopo Torriti (1295) is here.

The Baldacchino was the work of Ferdinando Fuga.

The Gothic Tomb of Cardinal Rodriguez (1299) contains Cosmatesque marblework.

This Sistine Chapel was built for Pope Sixtus V (1584–7) by Domenico Fontana and houses his tomb.

↑ Detail of the mosaic in the apse showing angels, by Jacopo Torriti

↑ Illustration showing the layout of the vast Santa Maria Maggiore basilica

### LEGEND OF THE SNOW

In 356 Pope Liberius had a dream in which the Virgin told him to build a church on the spot where he found snow. When it fell on the Esquiline, on the morning of 5 August in the middle of a baking Roman summer, he naturally obeyed. The miracle of the snow is commemorated each year by a service during which thousands of white petals float down from the ceiling of Santa Maria. Originally roses were used, but nowadays the petals are more usually taken from dahlias.

meet in the house of a man named Equitius. In the 4th century, after Constantine had legalized Christianity, Pope Sylvester I built a church, one of the very few things he did during his pontificate. In fact he was so insignificant that in the 5th century a more exciting life was fabricated for him – which included tales of him converting Constantine and curing him of leprosy.

Pope Sylvester's church was replaced in about AD 500 by St Symmachus, rebuilt in the 9th century and then transformed completely in the 1630s. The only immediate signs of its age are the ancient Corinthian columns dividing the nave and aisles. The most interesting interior features are a series of frescoed landscapes of the countryside around Rome (campagna romana) by the 17th-century French artist Gaspare Dughet, Poussin's brother-in-law, in the right aisle.

# EXPERIENCE MORE

## ❷ Santa Pudenziana

**◉ K5 ⌂ Via Urbana 160**
**✆ 06-481 4622 ▥ 16, 75, 105, 714 Ⓜ Cavour ◷ 8:30am-noon & 3-6pm daily**

Churches tend to be dedicated to existing saints, but this church, through a linguistic accident, created a brand new saint. In the 1st century AD a Roman senator called Pudens lived here, and is said to have allowed St Peter to lodge with him. In the 2nd century a bath house was built on this site and in the 4th century a church was established inside the baths, known as the *Ecclesia Pudentiana* (the church of Pudens). In time it was assumed that "Pudentiana" was a woman's name and a life was created for her – she became the sister of Prassede and was credited with caring for Christian victims of persecution. In 1969 both saints were declared invalid.

The 19th-century façade of the church retains an 11th-century frieze depicting both Prassede and Pudenziana. The apse has a remarkable 4th-century mosaic influenced by Classical pagan art.

## ❸ San Martino ai Monti

**◉ L6 ⌂ Viale del Monte Oppio 28 ✆ 06-478 4701 ▥ 16, 714 Ⓜ Cavour, Vittorio Emanuele ◷ 8:30am-noon & 4-7pm daily**

Christians have worshipped on the site of this church since the 3rd century, when they used to

## ❹ Arch of Gallienus

**◉ L6 ⌂ Via Carlo Alberto ▥ 16, 71, 714 Ⓜ Vittorio Emanuele**

Squashed between two buildings just off Via Carlo Alberto is the central arch of an originally three-arched gate erected in memory of Emperor Gallienus, who was

### Did You Know?

The horns on Michelangelo's *Moses'* head should be beams of light, but the Old Testament text was mistranslated.

assassinated by his Illyrian officers in AD 262. It was built on the site of the old Esquiline Gate in the Servian Wall, parts of which are visible nearby.

---

**5**

## San Pietro in Vincoli

📍K6 🏠Piazza di San Pietro in Vincoli 4A 📞06-9784 4950 🚌75, 117 Ⓜ️Cavour, Colosseo 🕐8am-12:30pm & 3-7pm (Oct-Mar: until 6pm) daily

According to tradition, the two chains *(vincoli)* used to shackle St Peter while he was being held in the depths of the Mamertine Prison (p99)

were subsequently taken to Constantinople. In the 5th century, Empress Eudoxia deposited one in a church there and sent the other to her daughter Eudoxia in Rome. She in turn gave hers to Pope Leo I, who had this church built to house it. Some years later the second chain was brought to Rome, where it linked miraculously with its partner.

The chains are still here, displayed below the high altar, but the church is now best known for Michelangelo's *Tomb of Pope Julius II*. When it was commissioned in 1505, Michelangelo spent eight months searching for perfect blocks of marble at Carrara in Tuscany, but Pope Julius became more interested in the building of a new St Peter's and the project was laid aside. After the pope's death in 1513, Michelangelo resumed work on the tomb, but had only finished the statues of *Moses* and *The Dying Slaves* when Pope Paul III persuaded him to start work on the Sistine Chapel's *Last Judgment*. Michelangelo had planned a vast monument with over 40 statues, but the tomb that was built – mainly by his pupils – is simply a façade with six niches for statues. *The Dying Slaves* are in Paris and Florence, but the tremendous bearded *Moses* is here, nearly 2.5 m (8 feet) in height, with his huge muscular arms and intense expression.

---

**6**

## Santa Prassede

📍L5 🏠Via Santa Prassede 9A 📞06-488 2456 🚌16, 70, 71, 75, 714 Ⓜ️Vittorio Emanuele 🕐7am-noon & 3-6:30pm daily

The church was founded by Pope Paschal I in the 9th

century, on the site of a 2nd-century oratory. Although the interior has been altered and rebuilt, the structure of the 9th-century church is visible. Its three aisles are separated by rows of granite columns. In the central nave, there is a round stone slab covering the well where, according to legend, Santa Prassede is said to have buried the remains of 2,000 martyrs.

Artists from Byzantium decorated the church with glittering, jewel-coloured mosaics. Those in the apse and choir depict stylized white-robed elders, the haloed elect looking down from the gold and blue walls of heaven, spindly legged lambs, feather-mop palm trees and bright-red poppies.

In the apse, Santa Prassede and Santa Pudenziana stand on either side of Christ, with the fatherly arms of St Paul and St Peter on their shoulders. Beautiful mosaics of saints, the Virgin and Christ, and the Apostles also cover the walls and vault of the Chapel of St Zeno, built as a mausoleum for Pope Paschal's mother, Theodora. Part of a column brought back from Jerusalem, allegedly the one to which Christ was bound and flogged, also stands here.

→

Michelangelo's *Moses* in San Pietro in Vincoli

# ⑦ ⚡ Ⓜ 🏛

## Domus Aurea

📍K6 🏛 Viale della Domus Aurea 🚌 85, 87, 117, 186, 810, 850 🚊 3 Ⓜ Colosseo 🎫 For guided tours (on weekends only) book online; virtual tours are available online also 🌐 coopculture.it

After allegedly setting fire to Rome in AD 64, Nero decided to build himself an outrageous new palace. The Domus Aurea (sometimes called Nero's Golden House) occupied part of the Palatine and most of the Celian and Esquiline hills – an area approximately 25 times the size of the Colosseum. The vestibule on the Palatine side of the complex contained a colossal gilded statue of Nero. There was an artificial lake, with gardens and woods where imported wild beasts were allowed to roam free. According to Suetonius in his *Life of Nero*, the Domus Aurea's walls were adorned with gold and mother-of-pearl, rooms had ceilings that showered guests with flowers or perfumes, the dining hall rotated and the baths were fed with both sulphurous water and sea water.

Tacitus described Nero's debauched garden parties, with banquets served on barges and lakeside brothels

serviced by aristocratic women. Since Nero killed himself in AD 68, however, he did not have long to enjoy his new home.

Nero's successors, anxious to distance themselves from the monster-emperor, did their utmost to erase all traces of the palace. Vespasian drained the lake and built the Colosseum (*p88*) in its place, Titus and Trajan each erected a complex of baths over the palace, and Hadrian placed the Temple of Venus and Rome (*p87*) over the vestibule.

Rooms from one wing of the palace have survived, buried beneath the ruins of the Baths of Trajan on the Oppian Hill. Excavations have revealed large frescoes and mosaics that are thought to be a panorama of Rome from a bird's-eye perspective.

Visitors are advised to bring a jacket as the temperature inside the building is around 10° C (50° F).

---

# ⑧

## Santa Bibiana

📍M6 🏛 Via Giovanni Giolitti 154 ☎ 06-446 5235 🚌 71 🚊 5, 14 Ⓜ Vittorio Emanuele 🕐 7:30-10am & 4:30-7:30pm Mon-Sat, 7:30am-12:30pm & 4:30-7:30pm Sun

The deceptively simple façade of Santa Bibiana was Bernini's first foray into architecture. It is a clean, economic design with superimposed pilasters and deeply shadowed archways. The church itself was built on the site of the palace belonging to Bibiana's family. This is where the saint was buried after being flogged to

← A bust of Emperor Nero at the park entrance to the Domus Aurea

> **The Domus Aurea's walls were adorned with gold and mother-of-pearl, rooms had ceilings that showered guests with flowers or perfumes.**

death with leaded cords during the brief persecution of the Christians in the reign of Julian the Apostate (361–3). Just inside the church is a small column against which Bibiana is said to have been whipped. Her remains, along with those of her mother Dafrosa and her sister Demetria, who also suffered martyrdom, are preserved in an alabaster urn below the altar.

In a niche above the altar stands a statue of Santa Bibiana by Bernini – the first fully clothed figure he ever sculpted. He depicts her standing beside a column, holding the cords with which she was whipped, apparently on the verge of a deadly swoon.

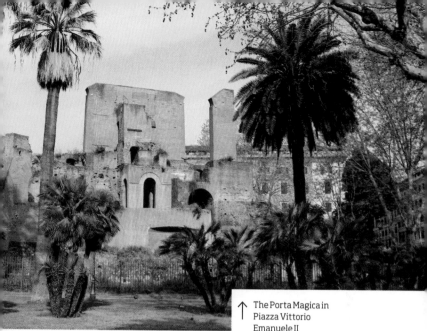

↑ The Porta Magica in Piazza Vittorio Emanuele II

## 9 Piazza Vittorio Emanuele II

📍 M6 🚌 4, 9, 71 🚊 5, 14
Ⓜ Vittorio Emanuele

Rome's largest square, Piazza Vittorio, as it is called for short, was once one of the city's main open-air food markets. The market moved around the corner to covered premises in 2001 and is now called Nuovo Mercato Esquilino (p51). The arcaded square was built as part of the urban development that was undertaken following the unification of Italy in 1861. It was named after Italy's first king, but there is nothing regal about its appearance today. The garden area in the centre of the square contains a number of mysterious ruins, including a large mound, part of a Roman fountain from the 3rd century AD and the Porta Magica, a curious 17th-century doorway inscribed with alchemical signs and formulae, which belonged to a marquis whose home was often visited by alchemists and magicians.

## 10 Auditorium of Maecenas

📍 L6 🏛 Largo Leopardi 2
📞 06-0608 🚌 16, 714
Ⓜ Vittorio Emanuele 🕐 By appt; phone in advance

Maecenas, a fop, gourmet and patron of the arts, was also an astute adviser and colleague of the Emperor Augustus. Fabulously rich, he created a fantastic villa and gardens on the Esquiline Hill, most of which have long disappeared beneath the modern city. The partially reconstructed auditorium, isolated on a traffic island, is all that remains.

Inside, a semicircle of tiered seats suggests that it may have been a place for readings and performances. If it was, then Maecenas would have been entertained here by his protégés, the lyric poet Horace and Virgil, author of the *Aeneid*, reading their latest works. However, water ducts have also been discovered and it may well have been a *nympheum* – a kind of summerhouse – with fountains. Traces of frescoes remain on the walls: you can make out garden scenes and a procession of miniature figures.

## 11 Sette Sale

📍 L6 🏛 Via delle Terme di Traiano 📞 06-0608 🚌 85, 87, 117, 186, 810, 850 🚊 3
Ⓜ Colosseo 🕐 By appt; phone in advance

Not far from Nero's Domus Aurea is the cistern of the Sette Sale, built here to supply the enormous quantities of water needed for the Baths of Trajan. These were built for Emperor Trajan in AD 104 on parts of the Domus Aurea that had been damaged by a fire.

A set of stairs leads down into the cistern, well below street level. There is not much to see here now, but you can walk through the huge, echoing cistern where light rays illuminate the watery surfaces. The nine sections, 30 m (98 ft) long and 5 m (16 ft) wide, had a capacity of eight million litres.

# A SHORT WALK
# THE ESQUILINE HILL

**Distance** 1 km (0.6 mile) **Nearest metro** Vittorio Emmanuele **Time** 20 minutes

The sight that draws most people to this rather scruffy part of Rome is the great basilica of Santa Maria Maggiore. But it is also well worth searching out some of the smaller churches on the Esquiline: Santa Pudenziana and Santa Prassede with their celebrated mosaics, and San Pietro in Vincoli, home to one of Michelangelo's most famous sculptures. To the south, in the Colle Oppio park, are the scattered remains of the Baths of Trajan.

↑ Sculpture of *Moses* by Michelangelo in San Pietro in Vincoli

*The apse of the ancient Santa Pudenziana has a magnificent 4th-century mosaic of Christ surrounded by the Apostles (p206).*

*San Pietro in Vincoli's treasures include Michelangelo's Moses and the chains that bound St Peter (p207).*

*To the Colosseum*

**START**

PIAZZA DI SAN PIETRO IN VINCOLI

*The Baths of Trajan (AD 109) were the first to be built on the massive scale later used in the Baths of Diocletian and of Caracalla.*

VIA CAVOUR

VIA DEI QUATTRO CA

VIA SFORZA

VIA GIOVANNI LANZA

PIAZZA S MARTINO MON

VIALE DEL MONTE OP

*Piazza dell'Esquilino was furnished with an obelisk in 1587 by Pope Sixtus V. This helped to guide pilgrims coming from the north to the important church of Santa Maria Maggiore.*

*Santa Maria Maggiore's imposing rear façade was added by Baroque architect Carlo Rainaldi in 1673. Santa Maria's interior is one of the most richly decorated in Rome (p204).*

**Locator Map**
*For more detail see p202*

ESQUILINE

PIAZZA DELL' ESQUILINO

VIA DELL' ESQUILINO

*The Tomb of Pius V (died 1572) by Domenico Fontana stands in this less well-known Sistine Chapel, under the northeast dome of Santa Maria Maggiore.*

VIA DELL'OLMATA

PIAZZA DI SANTA MARIA MAGGIORE

VIA MERULANA

VIA CARLO ALBERTO

**FINISH**

*Santa Prassede's 9th-century mosaics in the Chapel of San Zeno are among the finest in Rome (p207).*

*The Arch of Gallienus was built in the 3rd century AD to replace an entrance in the old Servian Wall (p206).*

*The Torre dei Capocci, a restored medieval tower, is one of the area's most distinctive landmarks.*

*The frescoes in San Martino ai Monti include 17th-century Roman landscapes and scenes from the life of Elijah by Gaspare Dughet (p206).*

| 0 metres | 100 |
| --- | --- |
| 0 yards | 100 |

N

→

Arch of Gallienus, located just off Via Carlo Alberti

# LATERAN

In the Middle Ages the Lateran Palace was the residence of the popes, and the Basilica of San Giovanni beside it rivalled St Peter's in splendour. After the return of the popes from Avignon at the end of the 14th century, the area declined in importance. Pilgrims still continued to visit San Giovanni and Santa Croce in Gerusalemme, but the area remained sparsely inhabited. Ancient convents were situated amid gardens and vineyards until Rome became capital of Italy in 1870 and a network of residential streets was laid out here to house the influx of newcomers. Archaeological interest lies chiefly in the Aurelian Wall and the ruins of the Aqueduct of Nero.

# LATERAN

### Must Sees

**1** San Giovanni in Laterano
**2** San Clemente

### Experience More

**3** Museum of Musical Instruments
**4** Santa Croce in Gerusalemme
**5** Amphiteatrum Castrense
**6** Porta Asinaria
**7** Scala Santa and Sancta Sanctorum
**8** Santo Stefano Rotondo
**9** Porta Maggiore
**10** Aqueduct of Nero and the Freedmen's Tombs
**11** Museo Storico della Liberazione di Roma
**12** Baker's Tomb
**13** Santi Quattro Coronati

### Eat

① Trattoria Luzzi

### Stay

② Palazzo Manfredi

# SAN GIOVANNI IN LATERANO

**1** (icons)

**◉** M8 **🏠** Piazza di San Giovanni in Laterano 4 **📞** 06-6988 6433 **🚌** 16, 81, 85, 87, 186, 650, 850 **🚋** 3 **Ⓜ** San Giovanni **🕐** Cathedral: 7am-6:30pm; Cloister: 9am-6pm; Museum: 10am-5:30pm; Baptistry: 9am-12:30pm & 4-6:30pm

In the 4th century, the Laterani family were disgraced and their land taken by Emperor Constantine to build Rome's first Christian basilica, San Giovanni in Laterano. This is the cathedral of Rome's bishopric.

↑ Fresco detail showing the pope proclaiming the Holy Year of 1300, attributed to Giotto

Today's church retains the original shape, but has been destroyed by fire twice and rebuilt several times. Borromini undertook the last major rebuild of the interior in 1646, and the main façade is an 18th-century addition. Before the pope's move to Avignon in 1309, the adjoining Lateran Palace was the official papal residence, and until 1870 all popes were crowned in the church. This is the city's main cathedral, and the seat of the Bishop of Rome, the pope, who celebrates Maundy Thursday Mass here. This is also where the pope attends the annual blessing of the people. The church has the world's first baptistry – its octagonal shape formed the model for all those to come.

> **This is the city's main cathedral, and the seat of the Bishop of Rome, the pope, who celebrates Maundy Thursday Mass here.**

### TRIAL OF A CORPSE

Fear of rival factions led the early popes to extraordinary lengths. At the Lateran Palace in 897 Pope Stephen VI tried the corpse of his predecessor, Formosus, for disloyalty to the Church. The corpse was found guilty, its right hand was mutilated and it was thrown into the Tiber.

↑ The elegant north façade, added by Domenico Fontana in 1586

↑ Papal altar with the Gothic baldacchino, decorated with frescoes dating from the 14th century

## ② ✍️

# SAN CLEMENTE

**📍 K7** 🏛 Via di San Giovanni in Laterano 🚌 85, 87, 117, 186, 810, 850 🚋 3 Ⓜ Colosseo 🕐 9am-12:30pm & 3-6pm Mon-Sat, noon-6pm Sun 🌐 basilicasanclemente.com

San Clemente gives visitors a chance to travel back through three layers of history, providing an insight into how buildings were modified over the years.

↑ Courtyard of the San Clemente basilica

At street level, the present-day basilica dates to the 12th century. It features medieval mosaics and Renaissance frescoes, notably those depicting St Catherine of Alexandria by the 15th-century Florentine artist Masolino da Panicale. Underneath lies a 4th-century church built to honour San Clemente, the fourth pope, who was exiled to the Crimea and martyred by being tied to an anchor and drowned. His life is illustrated in some of the frescoes. This 4th-century church was built over a temple dedicated to the cult of Mithras, which in turn was built inside a 1st-century AD aristocratic house.

The site was taken over in the 17th century by Irish Dominicans, who still continue the excavations begun by Father Mullooly in 1857.

←

A fresco by Masolino da Panicale showing a scene from the life of St Catherine of Alexandria

**Timeline**

**Late 2nd century**
△ Temple of Mithras built.

**4th century**
First church built over courtyard of earlier Roman building.

**1084**
Church destroyed during Norman invasion led by Robert Guiscard.

**1108**
New church built over 4th-century church.

**1857**
Original 4th-century church rediscovered by Father Mullooly.

**1861**
△ Church is excavated. Roman ruins discovered.

## THE CULT OF MITHRAS

In 3rd-century Rome the all-male cult of Mithras rivalled Christianity. Followers believed that Mithras had brought life to the world by spilling the blood of a bull and that faith in Mithras guaranteed salvation. Would-be cult members underwent initiation ceremonies, including trials by ice, fire, hunger and thirst. Ritual banquets were held in the triclinium, a room with stone benches on either side of an altar.

↑ The 12th-century apse mosaic of the *Triumph of the Cross* representing the crucified Christ as a Tree of Life

# EXPERIENCE MORE

↑ The cross and angels adorning Santa Croce in Gerusalemme

## Museum of Musical Instruments

**9** P7 **⌂** Piazza di Santa Croce in Gerusalemme 9A 🚌 16, 81, 649, 810 🚊 3 🕐 9am-7pm Tue-Sun; booking recommended, call 06-701 4796 **🌐** museostrumenti musicali.beniculturali.it

One of Rome's lesser-known museums, the Museum of Musical Instruments stands on the site of the Sessorianum, the great Imperial villa belonging to Empress St Helena, later included in the Aurelian Wall. It houses a collection of more than 3,000 outstanding musical instruments from all over the world, and wind, string and percussion instruments of all ages (including ancient Egyptian, Greek and Roman).

There are also sections dedicated to church and military music. The greater part of the collection comprises Baroque instruments: be sure to see the gorgeous Barberini harp (dating to 1605–20), which is remarkably well-preserved, on the first floor in Room 13. There are also fine examples of spinets, harpsichords and clavichords, and one of the first pianos ever made, dating from 1722.

## ④ 🏛 Santa Croce in Gerusalemme

**9** P7 **⌂** Piazza di Santa Croce in Gerusalemme 12 🚌 16, 81, 649, 810 🚊 3 🕐 7am-12:45pm & 3:30-7:30pm daily **🌐** santacroce roma.it

Emperor Constantine's mother St Helena founded this church in AD 320 in the grounds of her private palace. Although the church stood at the edge of the city, the relics of the Crucifixion that St Helena had brought back from Jerusalem made it a centre of pilgrimage. Most important were the pieces of Christ's Cross (*croce* means "cross") and part of Pontius Pilate's inscription in Latin, Hebrew and Greek: "Jesus of Nazareth King of the Jews".

In the crypt is a Roman statue of Juno, found at Ostia (*p316*), transformed into a statue of St Helena by replacing the head and arms.

The 15th-century apse fresco shows the medieval legends that arose around the Cross. Helena is shown holding it over a dead youth and restoring him to life. Another episode shows its recovery from the Persians by the Byzantine Emperor Heraclitus after a bloody battle. In the centre of the apse is a tomb by Jacopo Sansovino made for Cardinal Quiñones, Emperor Charles V's confessor (died 1540).

## ⑤ 🏛 Amphiteatrum Castrense

**9** P7 **⌂** Between Piazza di Santa Croce in Gerusalemme and Viale Castrense **📞** 06-3996 7702 🚌 649 🚊 3 🕐 Guided tours only on first and third Sat of month

This small 3rd-century amphitheatre was used for games and baiting animals. It owes its preservation to being part of the Aurelian Wall (*p239*), but its graceful arches framed by brick semi-columns were blocked up. The amphitheatre is best seen from outside the walls, from where there is also a good view of the bell tower of Santa Croce in Gerusalemme.

## ⑥ Porta Asinaria

**9** M8 **⌂** Between Piazza di Porta San Giovanni and Piazzale Appio 🚌 16, 81, 85, 87 🚊 3 **Ⓜ** San Giovanni

The Porta Asinaria (Gate of the Donkeys) is one of the minor gateways built between 270 and 273 in the Aurelian

18th-century piano at the Museum of Musical Instruments ↓

↑ The 28 steps of the Scala Santa, with devotees kneeling and praying

Wall (p239). Twin circular towers were added and a small enclosure was built around the entrance; the remains are still visible. From outside the walls you can see the gate's white travertine façade and two rows of small windows, giving light to two corridors built into the wall above the gateway. In AD 546 treacherous barbarian soldiers serving in the Roman army opened this gate to the hordes of the Goth Totila, who mercilessly looted the city. In 1084 the Holy Roman Emperor Henry IV entered Rome via Porta Asinaria with the antipope Guibert to oust Pope Gregory VII. The gate was badly damaged in the conflicts that followed.

The area close to the gate in the Via Sannio is the home of a large flea market held from 8am to 1pm Monday to Friday and 8am to 6pm on Saturday.

**7** 📷

## Scala Santa and Sancta Sanctorum

📍M7 🏛Piazza di San Giovanni in Laterano 14 📞06-772 6641 🚌16, 81, 85, 87, 186 and other routes to Piazza di San Giovanni in Laterano 🚊3 Ⓜ San Giovanni ⏰6am-1:30pm & 3-6:30pm daily (from 7am on Sun; to 7pm in summer).

On the east side of Piazza di San Giovanni in Laterano, a building by Domenico Fontana (1589) houses two surviving parts of the old Lateran Palace. One is the Sancta Sanctorum, the other the holy staircase, the Scala Santa. The 28 steps, said to be those that Christ ascended in Pontius Pilate's house during his trial, are said to have been brought from Jerusalem by St Helena, the mother of Constantine.

This belief, however, cannot be traced back any earlier than the the 7th century.

The steps were moved to their present site by Pope Sixtus V (reigned 1585–90) when the old Lateran Palace was destroyed. No foot may touch the holy steps, so they are covered by wooden boards. They may only be climbed by the faithful on their knees, especially on Good Friday. In the vestibule there are various 19th-century sculptures including an *Ecce Homo* by Giosuè Meli (1874).

The Scala Santa and two side stairways lead to the Chapel of St Lawrence or Sancta Sanctorum (Holy of Holies), built by Pope Nicholas III in 1278. Decorated with fine Cosmatesque marble-work, the chapel contains many important relics, the most precious being an image of Jesus – the *Acheiropoeton* or "picture painted without hands", said to be the work of St Luke, with the help of an angel. It was taken on procession in medieval times to ward off plagues.

On the walls and in the vault, restoration work has revealed 13th-century frescoes which for 500 years had been covered by later paintings.

**8**

## Santo Stefano Rotondo

🔲 K8  🏠 Via di Santo Stefano Rotondo 7  📞 06-421199  🚌 81, 117, 673  🕐 10am-1pm & 3:30-6:30pm (2-5pm winter) daily  📅 Three weeks in Aug

One of Rome's earliest Christian churches, Santo Stefano Rotondo was built between 468 and 483. It has an unusual circular plan with four chapels in the shape of a cross. It is lit by 22 high windows, a few of them restored or blocked by restorations carried out under Pope Nicholas V (reigned 1447–55), who consulted the Florentine architect Leon Battista Alberti. The archway in the centre may have been added during this period.

In the 16th century the church walls were frescoed by Niccolò Pomarancio with particularly gruesome illustrations of the martyrdom of innumerable saints. Some of the medieval decor remains: in the first chapel to the left of the entrance is a 7th-century mosaic of Christ with San Primo and San Feliciano.

**9**

## Porta Maggiore

🔲 N7  🏠 Piazza di Porta Maggiore  🚌 105  🚋 3, 5, 14, 19

Originally the arches of Porta Maggiore were not part of the city wall, but part of an aqueduct built by the Emperor Claudius in AD 52. They carried the water of the Aqua Claudia over the Via Labicana and Via Prenestina, two of ancient Rome's main south-bound roads. You can still see the original roadway beneath the gate. In the large slabs of basalt – a hard volcanic rock used in all old Roman roads – note the great ruts created by centuries of cartwheel traffic. On top of the arches separate conduits carried the water of two aqueducts: the Aqua Claudia, and its offshoot, the Aqueduct of Nero. They bear inscriptions from the time of the Emperor Claudius and also from the reigns of Vespasian and Titus. In all, six aqueducts from different water sources entered the city at Porta Maggiore.

The Aqua Claudia was 68 km (43 miles) long, with over 15 km (9 miles) above ground. Its majestic arches are a notable feature of the Roman countryside, and a popular mineral water bears its name. One stretch of the Aqua Claudia had its arches bricked up when it was incorporated into the 3rd-century Aurelian Wall (p239).

↑ The unusual circular plan of the church of Santo Stefano Rotondo

---

# STAY

**Palazzo Manfredi**

This chic bolthole boasts dead-ahead views of the Colosseum from its airy and impeccably tasteful rooms and suites. Guests can also enjoy the view from Aroma, the glass-walled Michelin-starred restaurant on the roof.

🔲 K7  🏠 Via Labicana 125  🌐 palazzo manfredi.com

€€€

## ⑩ Aqueduct of Nero and the Freedmen's Tombs

**♀ N6** **⌂ Intersection of Via Statilia and Via di Santa Croce in Gerusalemme** **🚌 105, 649** **🚋 3, 5, 14, 19** **🕐 By appt (call 06-0608)**

The aqueduct was built by Nero in the 1st century AD as an extension of the Aqua Claudia to supply Nero's Golden House (*p208*). Partly incorporated into later buildings, the arches make their way via the Lateran to the Celian Hill. Along the first section of the aqueduct, in Via Statilia, is a small tomb in the shape of a house, dating from the 1st century BC, bearing the names and likenesses of a group of enslaved people freed by the Statilii, the family of Claudius's notorious wife Messalina.

## ⑪ Museo Storico della Liberazione di Roma

**♀ M7** **⌂ Via Tasso 145** **☎ 06-700 3866** **Ⓜ Manzoni, San Giovanni** **🚋 3** **🕐 9am–6:30pm daily** **🚫 Aug**

This museum, dedicated to the resistance to the Nazi occupation of Rome during World War II, is housed in the ex-prison of the Gestapo. The makeshift cells with bloodstained walls make a strong impact (*see also Fosse Ardeatine p324*).

## ⑫ Baker's Tomb

**♀ N7** **⌂ Piazzale Labicano** **🚌 105** **🚋 3, 5, 14, 19**

In the middle of the tram junction near Porta Maggiore stands the well-preserved tomb of the rich baker Eurysaces and his wife Atistia, which was built in 30 BC. Roman custom forbade burials within city walls, and the roads leading out of cities became lined with tombs and monuments for the middle and upper classes. This tomb is shaped like a baking oven, and a low-relief frieze at the top shows Eurysaces presiding over his enslaved people through the various phases of the bread-making process. The inscription on the tomb proudly asserts his origins and also reveals him as a freed enslaved man, probably of Greek origin. Many men like Eurysaces saved money from their meagre salaries to earn their freedom and set up their own businesses, becoming the backbone of Rome's economy.

> **The implied idea of the pope as heir to the Roman Empire would affect the whole course of medieval European history.**

## ⑬ Santi Quattro Coronati

**♀ L7** **⌂ Via Santi Quattro Coronati 20** **☎ 06-7047 5427** **🚌 85, 117** **🚋 3** **Cloister and church: 🕐 10–11:45am & 4–5:45pm Mon–Sat** **🚫 Sun**

The name of this convent (Four Crowned Saints) refers to the Christian soldiers martyred for refusing to worship a pagan god. Erected in the 4th century AD, it was rebuilt after the invading Normans set fire to the neighbourhood in 1084. Hidden within is the garden of the delightful inner cloister (admission on request), one of the earliest of its kind, built c.1220.

The convent's main feature is the Chapel of St Sylvester – its remarkable frescoes (1246) recount the legend of the conversion to Christianity of the Emperor Constantine by Pope Sylvester I (reigned 314–35). Stricken by the plague, Constantine is prescribed a bath in children's blood. Unable to bring himself to obey, Constantine is visited in a dream by St Peter and St Paul. They advise him to find Sylvester, who cures him and baptizes him. The final scene shows the emperor kneeling before the pope. The implied idea of the pope as heir to the Roman Empire would affect the whole course of medieval European history.

← 

A tram running through an arch of the 1st-century AD Aqueduct of Nero

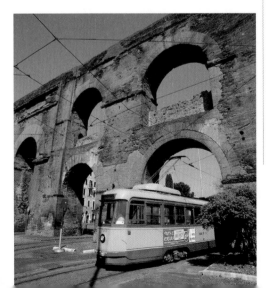

# A SHORT WALK

# PIAZZA DI SAN GIOVANNI

**Distance** 0.5 km (0.6 mile) **Nearest metro** San Giovanni
**Time** 15 minutes

Stroll along San Giovanni's modern avenues to the Basilica of San Giovanni and the Lateran Palace, which look out over a huge open area, the Piazza di San Giovanni, laid out at the end of the 16th century with an Egyptian obelisk, the oldest in Rome, in the centre. Sadly the traffic streaming in and out of the city through Porta San Giovanni tends to detract from its grandeur. Across the square is the building housing the Scala Santa (the Holy Staircase), one of the most revered relics in Rome and the goal for many pilgrims. The area is also a venue for political rallies.

*The Chapel of Santa Rufina, originally the portico of the baptistry, has a 5th-century mosaic of spiralling foliage in the apse.*

VIA DI SANTO STEFANO ROTONDO

VIA DELL´AMBA ARADAM

VIA DEI LATERANI

*The Chapel of San Venanzio is decorated with a series of 7th-century mosaics on a gold background. This detail from the apse shows one of the angels flanking the central figure of Christ. San Venanzio was an accomplished 6th-century Latin poet.*

*The Cloister of San Giovanni fortunately survived the two fires that destroyed the early basilica. A 13th-century masterpiece of mosaic work, the cloister now houses fragments from the medieval basilica.*

←

Grand 18th-century façade of San Giovanni in Laterano

Piazza di San Giovanni in Laterano boasts an ancient obelisk and parts of Nero's Aqueduct.

The Lateran Palace, residence of the popes until 1309, was rebuilt by Domenico Fontana in 1586.

Borromini's interior of San Giovanni in Laterano dates from the 17th century, but the grand façade by Alessandro Galilei, with its giant statues of Christ and the Apostles, was added in 1735 (p216).

**Locator Map**
*For more detail see p214*

**START**

PIAZZA DI SAN GIOVANNI IN LATERANO

The Scala Santa door at the top of the Holy Staircase leads to the Sancta Sanctorum (p221).

↑ Byzantine apse mosaic in San Giovanni in Laterano

VIA D. FONTANA

PIAZZA DI PORTA SAN GIOVANNI

The Triclinio Leoniano is a piece of wall and a mosaic from the dining hall of the 8th-century Pope Leo III.

**FINISH**

The Porta Asinaria, a minor gateway no longer in use, is as old as the Aurelian Wall, dating back to the 3rd century AD (p220).

| 0 metres | 100 |
| 0 yards | 100 |

N

# A LONG WALK
# ROME'S BEST MOSAICS

**Distance** 3.5 km (2 miles) **Walking time** 1.5 hours **Nearest metro** San Giovanni

In imitation of the audience chambers of Imperial palaces, Rome's early Christian churches were decorated with colourful mosaics. This walk highlights a few of Rome's churches decorated in this beautiful medium, demonstrating how fragments of glass and pieces of marble and stone have been intricately fused with gold leaf to create stunning masterpieces. The colours and subjects portrayed along this path give the faithful a glimpse of the heavenly court of the King of Kings.

The **Santa Maria Maggiore** (p204) houses a series of apse mosaics of the Virgin by Jacopo Torriti (1295) arch.

The Chapel of St Zeno at **Santa Prassede** (p207) contains the most important Byzantine mosaics in Rome.

Dating to AD 390, the **Santa Pudenziana** (p206) apse mosaic is one of the oldest in Rome.

**San Martino ai Monti** (p206) has a 6th-century mosaic portrait of Pope St Sylvester near its crypt.

The **Baths of Trajan**, built in 104 AD for Emperor Trajan , covers an area of over 100,000 sq m.

**Colle Oppio** park, with views of the Colosseum, contains the ruins of the Domus Aurea palace.

The 12th-century apse mosaic in the **Church of San Clemente** (p218) shows the cross set in a swirling pattern of acanthus leaves.

The convent of **Santi Quattro Coronati** (p223) has remarkable frescoes in the Chapel of St Sylvester.

The **San Tommaso in Formis** has a 13th-century mosaic entitled Christ between Two Freed Slaves.

The **Church of Santa Maria in Domnica**'s (p235) Chapel of Ss. Primo e Feliciano has superb mosaics commissioned by Pope Paschal I.

A chapel of the **Church of Santo Stefano Rotondo** (p222) has a Byzantine mosaic honouring two martyrs buried here.

**Locator Map**
For more detail see p214

The intricate interior of the Bapistry of San Giovanni and *(inset)* its octagonal exterior

VIA CATTANEO
V. C. NAPOLEONE III
VIA CARLO ALBERTO
V. S. VITO
V. D. STATUTO
Museo Nazionale d'Arte Orientale
LARGO LEOPARDI

0 metres 400
0 yards 400
N ↑

VIA RUGGERO BONGHI
VIA P. VILLARI
VIALE MANZONI
Ⓜ Manzoni
LABICANA
MERULANA
VIA T. TASSO
IN LATERANO
V. D. FONTANA
ROTONDO
PIAZZA SAN GIOVANNI IN LATERANO
PIAZZA DI P.TA SAN GIOVANNI
Bapistry of San Giovanni
Palazzo Laterano
⏵ START
San Giovanni in Laterano
Porta Asinaria
VIA DELL'AMBA ARADAM
VIA DEI LATERANI

The heavily restored mosaic of the **Triclinio Leoniano** shows Christ among the Apostles.

The Chapel of Santa Rufina in the **Bapistry of San Giovanni** (p216) has a beautiful apse mosaic from the 5th century.

The 13th-century apse mosaic in **San Giovanni in Laterano** (p216) depicts Christ flanked by Mary and John the Baptist.

# CARACALLA

The Celian Hill overlooks the Colosseum, and takes
its name from Caelius Vibenna, the legendary
hero of Rome's struggle against the Tarquins.
In Imperial Rome this was a fashionable place
to live, and some of its vanished splendour is
still apparent in the vast ruins of the Baths of
Caracalla. Today, thanks to the Archaeological
Zone established at the beginning of the 20th
century, it is a peaceful area, a green wedge
from the Aurelian Wall to the heart of the city.
Through it runs the cobbled Via di Porta San
Sebastiano, part of the old Via Appia. This road
leads to Porta San Sebastiano, one of the best-
preserved gates in the ancient city wall.

Colosseo

**CAMPITELLI**

Arch of
Janus

VIA CELIO VIBENNA

Tempio
di Cibele

Criptoportico

VIA DI S. TEODORO

Casa di
Livia

Domus
Flavia

PIAZZA
BOCCA D.
VERITA

Parco
del Celio

VIA DEL PARCO DEL CELIO

**FORUM AND
PALATINE**
*p76*

VIA

Casa di
Romolo

Domus
Augustana

Tempio di
Claudio

Santa Maria
in Cosmedin

V DELLA
GRECA

VLE DEL PARCO DEL CELIO

**PALATINE**

Santi Giovanni
e Paolo and
the Case Romane

**2**

DEI

CLIVO DI SCAURO

Parco di
Savello

VIA DEL CIRCO MASSIMO

*Parco del
Circo Massimo*

CERCHI

**3**

San Gregorio
Magno

VIA DI SAN GREGORIO

PIAZZALE UGO
LA MALFA

VIA DI VALLE DELLE CAMEN

**8**

**RIPA**

VIA D. TERME DECIANE

VIA DEL CIRCO MASSIMO

LARGO
ARRIGO VII

VIALE DELLE TERME L

PIAZZA
TEMPIO
DI DIANA

VIA DI S. PRISCA

Circo
Massimo Ⓜ

**FAO**

VIALE GUIDO BACCELLI

STADIO DELLE
TERME

VIA

VIA ANTONINA

VIALE AVENTINO

S. ALESSIO

*Parco di
Porta Capena*

PIAZZA DI S.
BALBINA

**9**

PIAZZA
ALBANIA

Santa
Balbina **17**

VIA DI SANTA BALBINA

VIALE GUIDO
BACCELLI

VIALE M. GELSOMINI

**AVENTINE**
*p242*

VIA AVENTINA

Baths of
Caracalla **1**

V. ERCOLE ROSA

*Parco della
Resistenza
dell'8
Settembre*

V. D. PIRAMIDE CESTIA

LARGO E.
FIORITTO

VIA LEON
BATTISTA
ALBERTI

*Parco
Egerio*

PIAZZA DI
PONTA
S. PAOLO

VIA A. PALLADIO

LARGO C.
LAZZERINI

VIA DI VILLA PEPOLI

VIALE GUIDO BACCELLI

PIAZZALE
OSTIENSE

VIALE    GIOTTO

VIALE GIOTTO

VIA GUERRIERI

VIALE DI PORTA ARDEATINA

VIA TATA

**10**

VIA C.
BELTRAMI

VIALE DI PORTA ARDEATINA

V. LUCIO FABIO CILONE

VIALE O.
BECCARI

Sangall
Bastio
**16**

**CARACALLA**

VIALE MARCO POLO

VIA LUIGI ROBECCHI BRICHETTI

VIA LUCIO FABIO CILONE

**H**

**J**

# CARACALLA

## Must See

**1** Baths of Caracalla

## Experience More

**2** Santi Giovanni e Paolo

**3** San Gregorio Magno

**4** Arch of Dolabella

**5** Santa Maria in Domnica

**6** Villa Celimontana

**7** San Sisto Vecchio

**8** Santi Nereo e Achilleo

**9** San Cesareo

**10** San Giovanni a Porta Latina

**11** San Giovanni in Oleo

**12** Columbarium of Pomponius Hylas

**13** Tomb of the Scipios

**14** Arch of Drusus

**15** Museo delle Mura

**16** Sangallo Bastion

**17** Santa Balbina

LATERAN p212

**1**

# BATHS OF CARACALLA

📍K9 🏠 Viale delle Terme di Caracalla 52 🚌160, 628 🚊3 Ⓜ Circo Massimo 🕐9am-2pm Mon, 9am-approximately 1 hour before sunset Tue-Sun 🌐coopculture.it

Completed by Emperor Caracalla in AD 217, the baths functioned for around 300 years until the acqueducts feeding them were sabotaged by invading Goths. This is one of the most enjoyable and best preserved ancient sites in the city.

Over 1,600 bathers at a time could enjoy the facilities, which included not only baths and gymnasia but gardens, shops selling food and drink, a library, art galleries, lecture rooms and, inevitably doing a roaring trade, a host of pimps, gigolos and prostitutes. In summer the Baths of Caracalla now hosts a hugely popular festival of opera and ballet in the *caldarium*.

## Inside the Baths

The *apodyterium* (changing room) was where people removed their clothes before bathing. They would then head to a hot steam room *(laconia)*, designed like Turkish baths, to induce sweat. This was followed by a hot bath in a bronze tub *(caldarium)*. The skin was then scraped to remove dead skin and dirt. Bathers then headed into the luke-warm waters of the *tepidarium*, followed by a plunge into the freezing-cold indoor pool, the *frigidarium*. The final stage was a swim in the outdoor pool *(natatio)*.

> 💬 INSIDER TIP
> ## Virtual Reality Tours
>
> The Baths of Caracalla can be brought to life with virtual reality goggles. Reconstructions of the entire site are viewable in 3D through the headsets, along with audio commentary. Ask for goggles at the ticket office.

↑ The two *apodyteria* (changing rooms), with remains of mosaic floor tiles

### PALAESTRA

Propped up against the walls of the gymnasia *(palaestra)* are fractured mosaics of athletes. Opening off the main space are smaller rooms where wrestlers were massaged with oil and wax to make the skin more supple, then sprinkled with dust to stop them being slippery, before engaging in matches. During the 1960 Olympics the *palaestra* were used for gymnastics events.

← The *caldarium*, where skin was scraped clean with a *strigil* after a hot bath

↑ Ruins of the Baths of Caracalla, surrounded by towering umbrella pines

# EXPERIENCE MORE

## ② Santi Giovanni e Paolo

📍K8 🏛Piazza Santi Giovanni e Paolo 13 ☎06-772711 🚌75, 81, 117, 673 🚊3 Ⓜ️Colosseo or Circo Massimo ⏰8:30am-noon & 3:30-6pm daily

Santi Giovanni e Paolo is dedicated to two martyred Roman officers whose house originally stood on this site. Giovanni (John) and Paolo (Paul) had served the first Christian emperor, Constantine. When they were later called to arms by the pagan emperor Julian the Apostate, they refused and were beheaded and buried in secret in their own house in AD 362.

Built towards the end of the 4th century, the church retains many elements of its original structure. The Ionic portico dates from the 12th century, and the apse and bell tower were added by Nicholas Breakspeare, the only English pope, who reigned as Adrian IV (1154–9). The base of the impressive 13th-century Romanesque bell tower was part of the Temple of Claudius that stood on this site. The interior, which was remodelled in 1718, has granite piers and columns. A tomb slab in the nave marks the burial place of the martyrs, whose relics are preserved in an urn under the high altar. In a tiny room near the altar, a magnificent 13th-century fresco depicts the figure of Christ flanked by his Apostles (to see it, ask the sacristan who will be able to unlock the door).

Excavations carried out beneath the church have revealed two 2nd- and 3rd-century Roman houses, the **Case Romane del Celio**, that were used as a Christian burial place. Well worth a visit, the Roman houses, which include 20 rooms and a labyrinth of corridors, have beautifully restored pagan and Christian frescoes. The walls are painted to resemble precious marble. The arches that are found to the left of the church were originally part of a 3rd-century street of shops.

**Case Romane del Celio**
🏛Clivo di Scauro ⏰10am-4pm daily (to 2pm on Tue & Wed) 🌐caseromane.it

> **Well worth a visit, the Roman houses, which include 20 rooms and a labyrinth of corridors, have beautifully restored pagan and Christian frescoes.**

The basilica of Santi Giovanni e Paolo on the Celian Hill

## ❸ San Gregorio Magno

📍J8 🏛Piazza di San Gregorio 1 📞06-700 8227 🚌75, 81, 117, 673 🚋3 Ⓜ Circo Massimo 🕐9am–1pm & 3:30-7pm daily

Historically, this church has links with England, for it was from here that St Augustine was sent on his mission to convert England to Christianity. The church was founded in AD 575 by San Gregorio Magno (St Gregory the Great), who turned his family home on this site into a monastery. It was rebuilt in medieval times and restored in 1629–33 by Giovanni Battista Soria. The church is reached via steps from the street.

The forecourt contains some interesting tombs. To the left is that of Sir Edward Carne, who came to Rome several times between 1529 and 1533 as King Henry VIII's envoy to gain the pope's consent to the annulment of Henry's marriage to Catherine of Aragon.

The interior, remodelled by Francesco Ferrari in the mid-18th century, is Baroque, apart from the fine mosaic floor and some ancient columns. At the end of the right aisle is the chapel of St Gregory. Leading off it, another small chapel, believed to have been the saint's own cell, houses his episcopal throne – a Roman chair of sculpted marble. The Salviati Chapel, on the left, contains a picture of the Virgin said to have spoken to St Gregory.

Outside, amid the cypresses to the left of the church, stand three small chapels, dedicated to St Andrew, St Barbara and St Sylvia (Gregory the Great's mother). The chapels contain frescoes by Domenichino and Guido Reni.

### Did You Know?

In summer Villa Celimontana hosts an excellent jazz festival.

## ❹ Arch of Dolabella

📍K8 🏛Via di San Paolo della Croce 🚌81, 117, 673 🚋3 Ⓜ Colosseo

The arch was built in AD 10 by consuls Caius Junius Silanus and Cornelius Dolabella, possibly on the site of one of the old Servian Wall's gateways. It was made of travertine blocks and later used to support Nero's extension of the Claudian aqueduct, built to supply the Imperial Palace on the Palatine Hill.

## ❺ Santa Maria in Domnica

📍K8 🏛Piazza della Navicella 12 📞06-7720 2685 🚌81,117, 673 🚋3 Ⓜ Colosseo 🕐For Mass only while construction work is undertaken on Metro C; call for latest information

The church overlooks the Piazza della Navicella (little boat) and takes its name from the 16th-century fountain. Dating from the 7th century, the church was probably built on the site of an ancient Roman firemen's barracks, which later became a meeting place for Christians. In the 16th century Pope Leo X added the portico and the coffered ceiling.

In the apse behind the modern altar is a superb 9th-century mosaic commissioned by Pope Paschal I. Wearing the square halo of the living, the pope appears at the feet of the Virgin and Child. The Virgin, surrounded by a throng of angels, holds a handkerchief like a fashionable lady at a Byzantine court.

## ❻ Villa Celimontana

📍K8 🏛Piazza della Navicella 🚌81, 117, 673 Park: 🕐7am–dusk daily

The Dukes of Mattei bought this land in 1553 and transformed the vineyards that covered the hillside into a formal garden. As well as palms and other exotic trees, the garden has its own Egyptian obelisk. Villa Mattei, built in the 1580s and now known as Villa Celimontana, houses the Italian Geographical Society.

The Mattei family used to open the park to the public on the day of the Visit of the Seven Churches, an annual event instituted by San Filippo Neri in 1552. Starting from the Chiesa Nuova (p130), Romans went on foot to the city's seven major churches and, on reaching Villa Mattei, were given bread, wine, salami, cheese, an egg and two apples. The pine-shaded park, now owned by the city of Rome, makes an ideal place for a picnic and has a playground with swings.

↑ The Egyptian obelisk in the grounds of Villa Celimontana

Detail of a 9th-century mosaic in the church of Santi Nereo e Achilleo ↑

## San Sisto Vecchio

📍K9 🏠 Piazzale Numa Pompilio 8 📞 06-7720 5174 🚌 160, 628, 671, 714 🕐 9-11am & 3-5:30pm daily

This small church is of great historical interest, as it was granted to St Dominic in 1219 by Pope Honorius III. The founder of the Dominican order soon moved his own headquarters to Santa Sabina (p249), San Sisto becoming the first home of the order of Dominican nuns, who still occupy the monastery. The church, with its 13th-century bell tower and frescoes, is also a popular place for weddings.

## ⑧ Santi Nereo e Achilleo

📍K9 🏠 Via delle Terme di Caracalla 28 📞 06-687 3124 🚌 160, 628, 671, 714 🕐 noon-12:30pm Sun (for half an hour only)

According to legend, St Peter, after escaping from prison, was fleeing the city when he lost a bandage from his wounds. The original church was founded here in the 4th century on the spot where the bandage fell, but it was later re-dedicated to the 1st-century AD martyrs St Nereus and St Achilleus.

Restored at the end of the 16th century, the church has retained many medieval features, including several fine 9th-century mosaics on the triumphal arch. A magnificent pulpit rests on an enormous porphyry pedestal which was found nearby in the Baths of Caracalla. The walls of the side aisles are decorated with grisly 16th-century frescoes by Niccolò Pomarancio, showing in clinical detail how each of the Apostles was martyred.

## ⑨ San Cesareo

📍K9 🏠 Via di Porta San Sebastiano 📞 338-491 6838 🚌 218, 628 🕐 10am-4pm Sat, 10am-noon Sun 🚫 Aug

This splendid old church was built over Roman ruins of the 2nd century AD. The lovely Renaissance façade was designed by Giacomo della Porta. The fine Cosmatesque mosaic work and carving inside rival that of any church in Rome. The episcopal throne, altar and pulpit are decorated with delightful animals. The church was restored in the 16th century by Pope Clement VIII, whose coat of arms decorates the ceiling.

> The splendid old San Cesareo church was built over Roman ruins of the 2nd century AD. The lovely Renaissance façade was designed by Giacomo della Porta.

## San Giovanni a Porta Latina

📍 L10 🏛 Via di San Giovanni a Porta Latina 📞 06-7047 5938 🚌 218, 360, 628 🕐 7:30am-12:30pm & 3-7pm daily

The church of St John at the Latin Gate, founded in the 5th century, rebuilt in 720 and restored in 1191, is one of the most picturesque of the old Roman churches. Classical columns support the medieval portico, and the 12th-century bell tower is superb. A tall cedar tree shades an ancient well standing in the forecourt. The interior has been restored, but it preserves the rare simplicity of its early origins, with ancient columns of varying styles lining the aisles. Traces of early medieval frescoes can still be seen within the church. The beautiful 12th-century frescoes created by several different artists under the direction of one master, show 46 different biblical scenes, from both the Old and New Testaments and are among the finest of their kind in Rome.

---

⑪ ♨

## San Giovanni in Oleo

📍 L10 🏛 Via di Porta Latina 📞 06-7740 0032 🚌 628 🕐 Ask at San Giovanni a Porta Latina

The name of this charming octagonal Renaissance chapel or oratory means "St John in Oil". The tiny building marks the spot where, according to legend, St John was boiled in oil – and came out unscathed, or even refreshed. An earlier chapel is said to have existed on the site; the present one was built in the early 16th century. The design has been attributed to Baldassare Peruzzi or Antonio da Sangallo the Younger. In the mid-17th century it was restored by Borromini, who altered the roof, crowning it with a cross supported by a sphere decorated with roses. Borromini also added a terracotta frieze of roses and palm leaves. The wall paintings inside the chapel include one of St John in a cauldron of boiling oil.

→

Detail of a medieval fresco in San Giovanni a Porta Latina *(right)* and Classical columns inside the church *(below)*

## 12

### Columbarium of Pomponius Hylas

📍L10 🏛Via di Porta Latina 10 📞06-0608 🚌218, 360, 628 🕐For guided tours only; phone ahead

Known as a columbarium because it resembles a dovecote (*columba* is the Latin word for "dove"), this kind of vaulted tomb was usually built by rich Romans to house the cremated remains of their freedmen. Many similar tombs have been uncovered in this part of Rome, which up until the 3rd century AD lay outside the city wall. This one dates from the 1st century AD. An inscription states that it is the tomb of Pomponius Hylas and his wife, Pomponia Vitalinis. Above her name is a "V" which indicates that she was still living when the inscription was made.

## 13

### Tomb of the Scipios

📍L10 🏛Via di Porta San Sebastiano 9 📞06-0608 🚌218, 360, 628 🕐For guided tours only; phone ahead

The Scipios were a family of conquering generals. Southern Italy, Corsica, Algeria, Spain and Asia Minor all fell to their Roman armies. The most famous of these generals was Publius Cornelius Scipio Africanus, who defeated the great Carthaginian general Hannibal at the Battle of Zama in 202 BC. Scipio Africanus was not buried here in the family tomb, but at Liternum near Naples, where he owned a favourite villa.

The Tomb of the Scipios was discovered in 1780, complete with various sarcophagi, statues and terracotta burial urns. Many of the originals have now been moved to the Vatican Museums and copies stand in their place.

The earliest sarcophagus was that of Cornelius Scipio Barbatus, consul in 298 BC, for whom the tomb was built. Members of his illustrious family continued to be buried here up to the middle of the 2nd century BC.

## 14

### Arch of Drusus

📍L10 🏛Via di Porta San Sebastiano 🚌218, 360

Once mistakenly identified as a triumphal arch, the so-called Arch of Drusus merely supported the branch aqueduct that supplied the Baths of Caracalla. It was built in the 3rd century AD, so had no connection with Drusus, a stepson of the Emperor Augustus. Its monumental appearance was due to the fact that it carried the aqueduct across the important route, Via Appia. The arch still spans the old cobbled road, just 50 m (160 ft) short of the gateway Porta San Sebastiano.

## 15

### Museo delle Mura

📍L10 🏛Via di Porta San Sebastiano 18 🚌218, 360 🕐9am-4pm Tue-Sun (last adm: 30 mins before closing) 🚫1 Jan, 1 May, 25 Dec 🌐museodelle muraroma.it

Most of the Aurelian Wall, begun by the Emperor Aurelian (AD 270–75) and completed by his successor Probus (AD 276–82), has survived. Aurelian ordered its construction as a defence against Germanic tribes, whose raids were penetrating deeper and deeper into Italy. Some 18 km (11 miles) round, with 18 gates and 381 towers, the wall took in all the seven hills of Rome. It was raised to almost twice its original height by Maxentius (AD 306–12).

The wall was Rome's main defence until 1870, when it was breached by Italian artillery just by Porta Pia, close to today's British Embassy. Many of the gates are still in use, and although the city has spread, most of its noteworthy historical and cultural sights still lie within the wall.

Porta San Sebastiano, the gate leading to the Via Appia Antica (*p321*), is the largest and best-preserved gateway in the Aurelian Wall. It was rebuilt by Emperor Honorius in the 5th century AD.

← Visitors at the Columbarium of Pomponius Hylas

The fortified Porta San Sebastiano, the best preserved gateway in the Aurelian Wall

Originally the Porta Appia, in Christian times it gradually became known as the Porta San Sebastiano, because the Via Appia led to the basilica and catacombs of San Sebastiano, which were popular places of pilgrimage.

It was at this gate that the last triumphal procession to enter the city by the Appian Way was received in state – that of Marcantonio Colonna after the victory of Lepanto over the Turkish fleet in 1571. Today the gate's towers house a free museum with prints and models showing the wall's history. From here you can take a short walk along one of the best-preserved stretches of the wall.

## 16 Sangallo Bastion

**K10** Viale di Porta Ardeatina 160

Haunted by the memory of the Sack of Rome in 1527 and fearing attack by the Turks, Pope Paul III asked Antonio da Sangallo the Younger to reinforce the Aurelian Wall. Work on the huge projecting bastion began in 1537. Its massive bulk can only be admired from outside.

## 17 Santa Balbina

**J9** Piazza di Santa Balbina 8 06-575 0969 160 3 Circo Massimo By appt only; phone ahead

Overlooking the Baths of Caracalla, this isolated church is dedicated to Santa Balbina, a 2nd-century virgin martyr. It is one of the oldest in Rome, dating back to the 5th century, and was built on the remains of a Roman villa. Consecrated by Pope Gregory the Great, in the Middle Ages Santa Balbina was a fortified monastery and over time has changed in appearance several times, regaining its Romanesque aspect in the 1920s. It contains many works of art.

From the piazza in front of the church, a staircase leads up to a three-arched portico. Inside, light streams in from a series of high windows along the length of the nave. The remains of St Balbina and her father, St Quirinus, are in an urn at the high altar, though the church's real treasure is situated in the far right-hand corner: the magnificent sculpted and inlaid tomb of Cardinal Stefanis de Surdis by Giovanni di Cosma (1303).

Other features worth noting are a 13th-century episcopal throne and various fragments of medieval frescoes. These include a lovely *Madonna and Child*, an example of the school of Pietro Cavallini, in the second chapel on the left. Fragments of 1st-century Roman mosaics were also discovered in the 1930s. Depicting birds and signs of the zodiac, these are now set into the church floor.

---

**PICTURE PERFECT**
### Aurelian Wall

A highlight of a visit to the Porta San Sebastiano ramparts of the restored Aurelian Wall is the matchless views of the Appian Way and the green hills beyond, which make for a superb photo opportunity.

# A SHORT WALK
# THE CELIAN HILL

**Distance** 1 km (0.6 mile) **Nearest metro** Circo Massimo
**Time** 20 minutes

In the course of a morning exploring the green slopes of the Celian Hill, you will see a fascinating assortment of archaeological remains and beautiful churches. A good starting point is the church of San Gregorio Magno, from where the Clivo di Scauro leads up to the top of the hill. The steep narrow street passes the ancient porticoed church of Santi Giovanni e Paolo with its beautiful Romanesque bell tower soaring above the surrounding medieval monastery buildings. Of the parks on the hill, the best kept and most peaceful is the Villa Celimontana with its formal walks and avenues. There are few bars or restaurants in the area but the green spaces are great for a picnic.

*Clivo di Scauro, the Roman Clivus Scauri, leads up to Santi Giovanni e Paolo, passing under the flying buttresses that support the church.*

*VIA DI SAN GREGORIO*

*CLIVO DI SCAUR*

▶ START

*La Vignola is a delightful Renaissance pavilion, reconstructed here in 1911 after it had been demolished during the creation of the Archaeological Zone around the Baths of Caracalla.*

*To Circo Massimo Metro*

*San Gregorio Magno monastery and chapel were founded here by Pope Gregory the Great at the end of the 6th century (p235).*

↑ Villa Celimontana, located in a pine-shaded public park

*The beautiful Villa Celimontana, built for the Mattei family in the 16th century, is now the centre of a public park (p235).*

Trams passing over the Celian Hill from the Colosseum rumble up a picturesque narrow track through the Parco del Celio.

Locator Map
For more detail see p230

CARACALLA

Ruins of the Temple of Claudius are visible over a large area of the Celian Hill. Look out for the travertine blocks that were incorporated in the base of the bell tower of Santi Giovanni e Paolo.

The nave of Santi Giovanni e Paolo, lit by a blaze of chandeliers, has been restored many times, assuming its present appearance in the 18th century (p234).

VIALE DEL PARCO DEL CELIO

VIA DI SAN PAOLO DELLA CROCE

VIA CLAUDIA

FINISH

The gateway of San Tommaso in Formis is decorated with a wonderful 13th-century mosaic showing Christ with two freed enslaved men, one white, one black.

The Arch of Dolabella was built in the 1st century AD, probably as an entrance to the city. It was later incorporated in Nero's aqueduct to the Palatine (p235).

Santa Maria in Domnica is famed for its 9th-century mosaics, notably the apostles on the triumphal arch above the apse flanking a medallion containing the figure of Christ (p235).

↑ The interior of the much-renovated ancient church of Santi Giovanni e Paolo

0 metres    100
0 yards     100

N

# AVENTINE

This is one of the most peaceful, leafy areas within the walls of the city. Although it is largely residential, with romantic villas, there are some unique historic sights. From the top of the Aventine Hill, crowned by the magnificent basilica of Santa Sabina, there are fine views across the river to Trastevere and St Peter's. At the foot of the hill, ancient Rome is preserved in the two tiny temples of the Forum Boarium and the Circus Maximus. The liveliest streets are in Testaccio, which has shops, restaurants and clubs, while to the south, beside Rome's solitary pyramid, the Protestant Cemetery is another oasis of calm.

# AVENTINE

CAPITOL
*p62*

**H** ⑤ Santa Maria
della Consolazione

**J**

⑥ Area
Archeologica di
Sant'Omobono

② San Teodoro

Casa dei
Crescenzi
⑨

⑧
San
Giovanni
Decollato

San Giorgio
in Velabro ①

Orti
Farnesiani

AVENTINE

**7**

Ponte
Rotto

Ponte
Palatino

④ Arch of
Janus

PIAZZA
BOCCA D.
VERITA

③ Santa Maria
in Cosmedin

Tempio
di Cibele

Casa di
Romolo

Temples of
the Forum
Boarium
⑦

V DELLA
GRECA

**FORUM AND PALATINE**
*p76*

Parco del
Circo Massimo

Parco di
Savello

PIAZZALE UGO
LA MALFA

⑱
Circus
Maximus

San Gregorio
Magno

**8**

Santa
Sabina
⑩

RIPA

LARGO
ARRIGO
VII

PIAZZA
TEMPIO
DI DIANA

Circo Massimo Ⓜ

PIAZZA DI
PORTA
CAPENA

FAO

STADIO
DELLE
TERME

Santi
Bonifacio
e Alessio
⑪

⑫
Piazza dei
Cavalieri di
Malta

⑤

PIAZZA
ALBANIA

**CARACALLA**
*p228*

**9**

PIAZZA DEI
SERVILI

PIAZZA
REMURIA

LARGO E.
FIORITTO

CARGO M.
GELSOMINI

④

Parco della
Resistenza
dell'8
Settembre

⑰
San Saba

PIAZZA G. L.
BERNINI

**TESTACCIO**

PIAZZA DI
PONTA
SAN PAOLO

Pyramid of
Caius Cestius
⑯

PIAZZA
OSTIENSE
Piramide Ⓜ

VIALE   GIOTTO

VIALE DI PORTA ARDEATINA

VIA TATA

**10**

⑬
Protestant
Cemetery

Stazione
Porta San Paolo

0 metres          200

0 yards           200

N
↑

**H**                    **J**

# ①

## San Giorgio in Velabro

**⦿H7 ⌂Via del Velabro 19
☎06-6979 7536 🚌23, 44,
81, 160, 170, 280, 628, 715,
716, 780 🕐10am-12:30pm
& 4-6:15pm Tue, Fri & Sat**

In the hollow of the street
named after the Velabrum,
the swamp where Romulus
and Remus are said to have
been found by the she-wolf,
is a small church dedicated
to St George, whose bones
lie under the altar.

The 7th-century basilica
has suffered over time from
floods. Careful restoration
has, however, returned it to its
original appearance. A double
row of granite and marble
columns (taken from ancient
Roman temples) divides the
triple nave. The austerity of
the grey interior is relieved by
golden frescoes in the apse
(attributed to Pietro Cavallini,
1295). The façade and the bell
tower date from the 1100s.

# ②

## San Teodoro

**⦿H7 ⌂Via di San Teodoro
7 ☎06-678 6624 🚌23,
44, 81, 160, 170, 280,
628, 715, 716 🕐9:30am-
12:30pm Sun-Fri**

This small, round 6th-century
church at the foot of the
Palatine has breathtaking 6th-
century mosaics in the apse,

↑ The ancient Bocca della
Verità, a lie detector
according to legend

and a Florentine cupola dating
from 1454. The fetching outer
courtyard was designed by
Carlo Fontana in 1705.

# ③

## Santa Maria in Cosmedin

**⦿H7 ⌂Piazza della Bocca
della Verità 18 🚌23, 44,
81, 160, 170, 280, 628, 715,
716 🕐9am-7pm Sat & Sun;
gates shut 10 mins before
closing 🌐cosmedin.org**

This beautiful unadorned
church was built in the 6th
century on the site of the
ancient city's food market.
The elegant Romanesque
bell tower and portico were
added during the 12th
century. In the 19th century a
Baroque façade was removed
and the church restored to its
original simplicity. It contains
many fine examples of
Cosmati work, in particular
the mosaic pavement, the
raised choir, the bishop's
throne and the canopy
over the main altar.

Set into the wall of the
portico is the Bocca della
Verità (Mouth of Truth). This
may have been a drain cover,
dating back to before the 4th
century BC. Medieval tradition
had it that the formidable
jaws would snap shut over the
hand of those who told lies –
a useful trick for testing the
faithfulness of spouses.

# ④

## Arch of Janus

**⦿H7 ⌂Via del Velabro
🚌23, 44, 63, 81, 160, 170,
280, 628, 715, 716, 780**

Probably dating from the
reign of Constantine, this
imposing four-faced marble
arch stood at the crossroads

→

The Renaissance exterior
of the church of Santa Maria
della Consolazione

---

**COSMATI MOSAICS**

Glass mosaics and fragments of coloured marble were
salvaged from ancient Roman buildings to adorn the
pavements, cloisters, fonts and tombs of medieval
churches in Rome with complex geometric patterns.
Discs of porphyry and serpentine were often sliced from
ancient columns to make the patchwork designs. The
most famous practitioners were the Cosmati family,
who worked in Rome in the 12th and 13th centuries.

on the edge of the Forum Boarium, near the ancient docks. Merchants did business in its shade. On the keystones above the four arches you can see small figures of the goddesses Roma, Juno, Ceres and Minerva. In medieval times the arch formed the base of a tower fortress. It was finally restored to its original shape in 1827.

## ⑤ Santa Maria della Consolazione

**⑨ H7 ⚐ Piazza della Consolazione 94 📞 06-678 4654 🚌 23, 44, 63, 81, 160, 170, 280, 628, 715, 716, 780 🕐 6:30am-6:30pm Mon-Sat, 10am-6:30pm Sun**

The church stands near the foot of the Tarpeian Rock, the site of public execution of traitors in ancient Rome.

In 1385, Giordanello degli Alberini, a condemned nobleman, paid two gold florins for an image of the Virgin Mary to be placed here, to provide consolation to prisoners in their final moments before execution. Hence the name

of the church that was constructed here in 1470. It was reconstructed between 1583 and 1600 by Martino Longhi, who provided the early Baroque façade at the same time.

The church's 11 side-chapels are owned by noble families and local crafts guild members. Taddeo Zuccari was responsible for the 1556 frescoes depicting scenes from the Passion (first chapel on the right), while the Mannerist artist Niccolò Circignani painted the scenes from the life of Mary and Jesus housed in the fifth chapel. In the presbytery is the image of Mary, attributed to Antoniazzo Romano.

## ⑥ Area Archeologica di Sant'Omobono

**⑨ H7 ⚐ Vico Jugario 4 📞 06-0608 🚌 23, 44, 63, 81, 160, 170, 280, 628, 715, 716, 780 🕐 By appt only; call in advance**

Unearthed in 1937, this important archaeological area contains the remains of a temple dedicated to Mater Matuta, goddess protectress of navigation, which date from the 6th century BC and are attributed to the time of King Tullius. The excavations have also revealed traces of a pre-Roman cult.

# EAT & DRINK

### Flavio Al Velavevodetto

This stellar trattoria, famed for its pasta dishes, backs onto Monte Testaccio; you can see the ancient amphorae through glass panels in the wall.

**⑨ G10 ⚐ Via di Monte Testaccio 97 🌐 ristorante velavevodetto.it**

€€€

---

### Mercato di Testaccio

Explore the food stands here, offering everything from assorted tasty morsels to freshly squeezed juices.

**⑨ G8 ⚐ Via Lorenzo Ghiberti 🌐 mercato ditestaccio.it**

€€€

---

### Oasi della Birra - Enoteca Palombi

The shelves of this *enoteca* are stacked with beers and wines. Fill up on the generous free buffet at *aperitivo* time on the terrace.

**⑨ G9 ⚐ Piazza Testaccio 38 📞 06-574 6122**

€€€

---

### Tram Depot

Buzzing at *aperitivo* time in summer, this little café-bar (once part of a 1903 vintage tram) has quirky seating on the pavement.

**⑨ G9 ⚐ Via Marmorata 13 📞 06-575 4406**

€€€

## ⑦ Ⓜ
### Temples of the Forum Boarium

📍H7 🏛Piazza della Bocca della Verità ☎06-3996 7700 🚌23, 44, 81, 160, 170, 280, 628, 715, 716 🕐Guided tours only, third Sun of month 🌐coopculture.it

These very well-preserved Republican temples date from the 2nd century BC and were reconsecrated as Christian churches in the Middle Ages. They offer rare examples of combined elements from Greek and Roman architecture.

The rectangular temple (formerly known as the Temple of Fortuna Virilis) was dedicated to Portunus, god of rivers and ports. Set on a podium, it has four Ionic travertine columns and 12 half-columns, embedded in the tufa wall of the *cella* – the room that housed the image of the god.

Nearby is the small circular **Temple of Hercules**, its slender Corinthian columns surrounding the central *cella*. Built around 120 BC, it is thought to be the earliest Roman marble edifice still surviving. It is often called the Temple of Vesta owing to its similarity to the one in the Forum.

### Temple of Hercules
🕐For guided tours, first and third Sun of month by appt; call 06-3996 7700

## ⑧
### San Giovanni Decollato

📍H7 🏛Via di San Giovanni Decollato 22 ☎06-679 1890 🚌23, 44, 63, 81, 160, 170, 280, 628, 715, 716, 780 🕐Only for the feast of St John, 24 Jun: 9:30am–12:30pm

Giorgio Vasari's *The Beheading of St John* (1553), from which the church takes its name, dominates the main altar. In 1490 Pope Innocent VIII gave this site to build a church for a Florentine confraternity. Clad in black robes and hoods, the Florentine monks would encourage prisoners to repent of their sins and give them a decent burial after they had been hanged. In the cloisters there are seven manholes that were used to receive the bodies. The confraternity still exists, with church funds going towards assisting prisoners' families.

The oratory features a cycle of frescoes by Florentine Mannerists Francesco Salviati

↑ The tower of 11th-century Casa dei Crescenzi

and Jacopino del Conte depicting events in the life of St John the Baptist.

## ⑨
### Casa dei Crescenzi

📍H7 🏛Via Luigi Petroselli 🚌23, 44, 63, 81, 160, 170, 280, 628, 715, 716, 780

Studded with archaeological fragments, this house is what remains of an 11th-century tower fortress. The Crescenzi family built it to keep an eye on the docks and bridge where they collected a toll. It is only viewable from outside.

Temple of Hercules and fountain in the Forum Boarium

## ⑩
## Santa Sabina

📍 G8 🏛 Piazza Pietro
d'Illiria 1 📞 06-579 401
🚌 23, 280, 716 Ⓜ Circo
Massimo ⏰ 7:15am–8pm
daily

High on the Aventine stands
an early Christian basilica,
founded by Peter of Illyria in
AD 425 and restored to its
original simplicity in the early
20th century. Light filters
through 9th-century windows
upon a wide nave framed by
white Corinthian columns
supporting an arcade
decorated with a marble
frieze. Over the main door is
a 5th-century blue and gold
mosaic dedicatory inscription.
The pulpit, carved choir and
bishop's throne date from
the 9th century.

The church was given to
the Dominicans in the 13th
century and in the nave is
the magnificent mosaic
tombstone of one of the first
leaders of the order, Muñoz
de Zamora (died 1300).

The side portico has 5th-
century panelled doors
carved from cypress wood,
representing scenes from
the Bible, including one
of the earliest Crucifixions
in existence.

↑ The 13th-century
Romanesque bell tower of
Santi Bonifacio e Alessio

---

# STAY

### San Anselmo
A quiet and peaceful
choice in a leafy
neighbourhood, this
villa offers luxurious
guest rooms, marble
bathrooms, attentive
staff and good
breakfasts.

📍 G9 🏛 Piazza di
Sant'Anselmo 2
🌐 aventinohotels.com/
sananselmo

 €€€

---

## ⑪
## Santi Bonifacio
## e Alessio

📍 G8 🏛 Piazza di
Sant'Alessio 23 📞 06-574
3446 🚌 23, 280, 716
Ⓜ Circo Massimo ⏰ For
special events only

The church is dedicated to
two early Christian martyrs,
whose remains lie under the
main altar. Legend has it that
Alessio, son of a rich senator
living on the site, fled east to
avoid an impending marriage
and became a pilgrim. Return-
ing home after many years,
he died as a servant,
unrecognized, under the
stairs of the family entrance
hall, clutching the manuscript
of his story for posterity.

The original 5th-century
church has undergone many
changes over time. Note-
worthy are the 18th-century
façade with its five arches,
the restored Cosmati doorway
and pavement, and the
magnificent Romanesque
five-storey bell tower (1217).

An 18th-century Baroque
chapel by Andrea Bergondi
houses part of the staircase.

---

## ⑫
## Piazza dei
## Cavalieri di Malta

📍 G8 🚌 23, 280, 716
Ⓜ Circo Massimo

Surrounded by cypress trees,
this ornate walled piazza
decorated with obelisks and
military trophies was designed
by Piranesi in 1765. It is named
after the Order of the Knights
of Malta (Cavalieri di Malta),
whose priory (at No. 3) is
famous for the bronze keyhole
through which there is a
miniature view of St Peter's,
framed by a tree-lined avenue.
The priory church, Santa Maria
del Priorato, was restored in
Neo-Classical style by Piranesi
in the 18th century. To visit the
church, ask permission in
person at the Order's building
at Via Condotti 48. At the
southwest corner of the square
is Sant'Anselmo, the international Benedictine church,
where Gregorian chant may be
heard on Sundays.

### 13
## Protestant Cemetery

🅖G10 🅐Cimitero Acattolico, Via Caio Cestio 6 ☎06-574 1900 🚌23, 280, 716 🚋3 Ⓜ Piramide 🕓9am-5pm Mon-Sat, 9am-1pm Sun (last adm: 30 mins before closing); donation expected

The peace of this well-tended cemetery, which is situated beneath the Aurelian Wall, is profoundly moving. As implied by its name, non-Catholics, mainly English and German, have been buried here since 1738. In the oldest part are the graves of the poet John Keats (died 1821), whose epitaph reads "Here lies One Whose Name was writ in Water", and his friend Joseph Severn (died 1879);

not far away are the ashes of Percy Bysshe Shelley (died 1822). Goethe's son Julius is also buried here.

### 14
## Monte Testaccio

🅖G10 🅐Via Galvani ☎06-0608 Ⓜ Piramide 🚌23, 83, 719 🚋3 🕓By appt only

Between about 140 BC and AD 250 the Monte Testaccio was created through the dumping of millions of *testae* (hence Testaccio) – pieces of the amphorae that were used to carry goods to nearby warehouses. The full archaeological significance of this 36 m- (118 ft-) high artificial hill was not realized until the late 18th century.

↑ The graves of English Romantic poets in the Protestant Cemetery

### 15 🖉
## Il Mattatoio

🅕F10 🅐Piazza Orazio Giustiniani 4 🕓4-10pm Tue-Sun (only during exhibitions) 🖥 matta-toioroma.it

For much of the 20th century the Testaccio neighbourhood was a gutsy working-class quarter, dominated by its vast 19th-century slaughterhouse, the Mattatoio, which is considered to be one of the industrial architectural landmarks of the city. Testaccio has now become one of Rome's trendiest areas. The large halls of the Mattatoio have been transformed into a cutting-edge gallery hosting temporary modern and contemporary art exhibitions by established and emerging artists, and art-related events.

Other parts of the complex are home to the Città dell'Altra Economia, which is committed to fair trade economies. It has an organic café and restaurant, a children's play area, a bookshop, crafts shops and

---

**TESTACCIO'S FOOD TRADITIONS**

Traditional Roman cuisine originated in the Testaccio area, near the old slaughterhouse, where the butchers were paid partly in cash and partly in meat - or more specifically, in offal. They received the "fifth quarter" (*quinto quarto*), which included head, trotters, tail, intestines and brain. When carefully cooked and richly flavoured with herbs and spices, these offcuts are a culinary delight, and such robust dishes still feature on the menus of many of Rome's restaurants.

alternative energy and recycling projects. There is also a fair trade market in Città dell'Altra Economia.

## 16
## Pyramid of Caius Cestius

**9** H10 **A** Piazzale Ostiense **C** 06-574 3193; 06-3996 7700 **🚌** 23, 280, 716 **🚋** 3 **M** Piramide **O** By appt 11am 3rd & 4th Sat & Sun of month; all other Sat & Sun

Caius Cestius, a wealthy *praetor* (senior Roman magistrate), died in 12 BC. His main claim to fame is his tomb, an imposing pyramid faced in white marble, set in the Aurelian Wall near Porta San Paolo.

It stands 36 m (118 ft) high and, according to an inscription carved upon it, took 330 days to build. Unmistakable as a landmark, it must have looked almost as incongruous when it was built as it does today.

## 17
## San Saba

**9** H9 **A** Via di San Saba **C** 06-6458 0140 **🚌** 75, 673 **🚋** 3 **O** 8am-noon & 4-7:10pm Mon-Sat, 9:30am-1pm & 4-7:30pm Sun

Tucked away in a residential street on the Little Aventine Hill, San Saba began life as an oratory for Palestinian monks fleeing from Arab invasions in the 7th century. The existing church dates from the 10th century and has undergone much restoration. The portico houses a fascinating collection of archaeological remains and a fresco depicting St Sabas.

The church has three naves in the Greek style and a short fourth 11th-century nave to the left with vestiges of 13th-century frescoes of the life of St Nicholas of Bari. Particularly intriguing is a scene of three naked young ladies lying in bed, who are saved from penury by the gift of a bag of gold from St Nicholas, the future Santa Claus. The beautiful marble inlay in the

main door, the floor an remains of the choir are 13th-century Cosmati w

## 18
## Circus Maximus

**9** J8 **A** Via del Circo Massimo **🚌** 81, 160, 628, 715 **🚋** 3 **M** Circo Massimo

What was once ancient Rome's largest stadium is today little more than a long grassy esplanade. Set in the valley between the Palatine and Aventine hills, the Circus Maximus was continually embellished and expanded from the 4th century BC until AD 549 when the last races were held. The grandstands held some 300,000 spectators, cheering wildly at the horse and chariot races, athletic contests and animal fights.

The Circus had a central dividing barrier *(spina)* with seven large egg-shaped objects on it for counting the laps of a race. These were joined in 33 BC by seven bronze dolphins for a similar purpose. In 10 BC Augustus built the Imperial box under the Palatine and decorated the *spina* with the obelisk that is now in the centre of Piazza del Popolo *(p152)*. A second obelisk, added in the 4th century by Constantine II, is now in Piazza di San Giovanni in Laterano *(p216)*.

←
The ancient Pyramid of Caius Cestius, a striking and unusual landmark

# A SHORT WALK
# PIAZZA DELLA BOCCA DELLA VERITÀ

**Distance** 0.8 km (0.5 mile) **Nearest bus** 23, 44, 81, 160, 170, 280, 628, 715, 716, 780 **Time** 20 minutes

A quiet corner of the city, this area beside the Tiber is great for escaping the crowds. The site was ancient Rome's first port and its busy cattle market; substantial Classical remains include two small temples from the Republican age and the Arch of Janus from the later Empire. In the 6th century the area became home to a Greek community from Byzantium, who founded the churches of San Giorgio in Velabro and Santa Maria in Cosmedin. Follow tradition and place your hand inside the Bocca della Verità (the Mouth of Truth), a mythological stone sculpture in the portico of Santa Maria in Cosmedin.

Sant'Omobono, dating to the 16th century, stands in isolation in the middle of an important archaeological site where the remains of sacrificial altars and two temples from the 6th century BC have been discovered.

**START**

The 11th-century Casa dei Crescenzi has columns and capitals from ancient Roman temples (p248).

The temples of the Forum Boarium (the tiny round Temple of Hercules and its neighbour, the Temple of Portunus) are the best preserved of Rome's Republican temples (p248).

Ponte Rotto, as this forlorn ruined arch in the Tiber is called, means simply "broken bridge". Built in the 2nd century BC, its original name was Pons Aemilius.

LUNGOTEVERE DEI PIERLEONI

TEVERE

PONTE PALATINO

↑ The well-preserved Temple of Hercules in the Forum Boarium

The Fontana dei Tritoni by Carlo Bizzaccheri was built here in 1715. The style shows the powerful influence of Bernini.

The 16th-century church of Santa Maria della Consolazione used to serve a hospital nearby (p247).

Medieval interior of Santa Maria in Cosmedin ↑

Locator Map
For more detail see p244

AVENTINE

The 15th-century portal of the ancient round San Teodoro church is decorated with the insignia of Pope Nicholas V (p246).

FINISH

The plain Renaissance façade of San Giovanni Decollato was completed in about 1504 (p248).

San Giorgio in Velabro's simple 12th-century portico of Ionic columns was destroyed by a bomb in 1993 but has been restored (p246).

VIA DEI FIENILI

VIA DI SAN TEODORO

GIOVANNI DECOLLATO

The Arco degli Argentari, dedicated to Emperor Septimius Severus in AD 204, is decorated with scenes of religion and war.

The square Arch of Janus with arches on each side dates from the 4th century AD (p246).

PIAZZA DELLA BOCCA DELLA VERITA

VIA DEI CERCHI

VIA DELLA GRECA

The medieval church of Santa Maria in Cosmedin has a fine marble mosaic floor and a Gothic baldacchino (p246).

0 metres 100
0 yards 100

N ↑

# A LONG WALK
# THE AVENTINE

**Distance** 3.5 km (2 miles) **Walking time** 1.5 hours
**Nearest metro** Repubblica

Rising just across the Circus Maximus from the Palatine, the residential Aventine Hill has served as a leafy haven of villas and mansions since Imperial times. This southernmost of Rome's legendary seven hills is still an oasis where traffic noise all but disappears. Yet few visitors walk here – despite the lure of fine old churches, lovely city panoramas, and rarely visited ancient ruins. You will also explore Testaccio, a fine area for authentic local cuisine, and see a Roman pyramid.

**Parco di Savello** *is a garden of orange trees with a panoramic river view.*

*The basilica of* **Santa Sabina** *has one of the earliest depictions of the Crucifixion.*

*View the fine Cosmati work in the church of* **Santi Bonifacio e Alessio** (p249).

*The* **Piazza dei Cavalieri di Malta** *offers a tiny view of St Peter's dome through the keyhole at No 3.*

*The church of* **Sant'Anselmo** *houses a mosaic of Orpheus.*

**Monte Testaccio** (p250) *is an ancient rubbish tip made up entirely of potsherds.*

**Ex-Mattatoio** (p250) *is a defunct abattoir whose workers were paid, in part, with the day's offal.*

*The striking* **Pyramid of Caius Cestius** (p251) *stands here.*

*The* **Protestant Cemetery** (p250) *is where such luminaries as Keats and Shelley lie in peace.*

*The* **Porta di San Paolo** *is one of the oldest city gates, dating to AD 402.*

**Centrale Montemartini** (p325) *is an early Industrial Age power plant now stuffed with ancient sculptures.*

Santa Sabina

Santi Bonifacio e Alessio

Parco di Savello

Sant' Anselmo

PIAZZA DEI CAVALIERI DI MALTA

PIAZZA DEI SERVILI

VIA DI PORTA LAVERNALE

PIAZZA TEMPIO DI DIANA

VIA S. MELANIA

VIA S. ALESSIO

VIA S. ALBERTO MAGNO

VIALE M. GELSOMINI

VIA MARMORATA

VIA GALVANI

LARGO M. GELSOMINI

**TESTACCIO**

Monte Testaccio

Ex-Mattatoio

VIALE DEL CAMPO BOARIO

Pyramid of Caius Cestius

Protestant Cemetery

Porta di San Paolo

PIAZZALE OSTIENSE

**Piramid** M

**Stazione Porta San Paolo**

VIA OSTIENSE

**FINISH**

Centrale Montemartini

0 metres 500

0 yards 500

N ↑

Built in the 3rd century, the **Church of Santa Prisca** includes a Passignano altarpiece.

Ascend the stairs of **San Gregorio Magno** (p235) for great views of the Palatine.

**Locator Map**
For more detail see p244

AVENTINE

The Aventine

Circus Maximus

San Gregorio Magno

Santa Maria in Domnica

Villa Celimontana

CELIO

VIA DEL CIRCO MASSIMO

VIA DELLA NAVICELLA

VIA DI VALLE DELLE CAMENE

PA

Church of Santa Prisca

VIALE AVENTINO

VIA D. FONTE DI FAUNO

**M** Circo Massimo

FAO

VIALE DELLE TERME DI CARACALLA

Parco di Porta Capena

VIALE G. BACCELLI

STADIO DELLE TERME

PIAZZA DI S. BALBINA

VIA ANTONINA

San Sisto Vecchio

PIAZZA ALBANIA

Santi Nereo e Achilleo

PIAZZALE NUMA POMPILIO

The **FAO** has housed the UN's Food and Agriculture Organization since 1952.

Baths of Caracalla **START**

Parco Egerio

VIA ANTONINIANA

**San Sisto Vecchio** (p236) was the first home of the Dominican nuns.

The church of **Santi Nereo e Achilleo** (p236) has stunning 9th-century mosaics.

The **Baths of Caracalla** (p232) is where plebeian and patrician alike once bathed (and, much later, where the poet Shelley found inspiration for Prometheus Unbound).

↑ Relaxing and enjoying a serene spot upon Rome's beautiful Aventine Hill

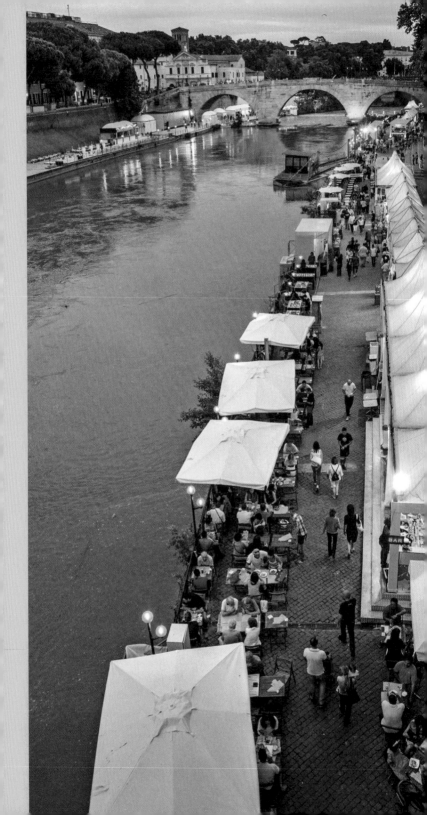

# TRASTEVERE

The proud and aggressively independent inhabitants of Trastevere, the area "across the Tiber", consider themselves the most authentic of Romans. In one of the most picturesque old quarters of the city, it is still possible to glimpse scenes of everyday life that seem to belong to bygone centuries despite the proliferation of fashionable boutiques, cafés and restaurants that characterize the area today. Some of Rome's most fascinating medieval churches lie hidden away in the patchwork of narrow, cobbled back-streets, the only clue to their location an occasional glimpse of a Romanesque bell tower. Of these, Santa Cecilia was built on the site of the martyrdom of the patron saint of music, San Francesco a Ripa commemorates St Francis of Assisi's visit to Rome, and Santa Maria in Trastevere is the traditional centre of the spiritual and social life of the area.

**D**

Gianicolo

Monumento a
G. Garibaldi

PASSEGGIATA GIANICOLO

PASSEGGIATA GIANICOLO

PIAZZALE
AURELIO

**7**

**E**

Palazzo Corsini &
Galleria Nazionale
d'Arte Antica

**JANICULUM**
p270

Casa della
Fornarina
**2**

Ponte
Sisto
**3**

VIA DI S. DOROTEA

PIAZZA
TRILUSSA

①

VIA DEL (

Santa Maria
della Scala
**4**

VICOLO BOLOGNA

VIA DELLA SCALA

VIC. DEL CINQUE

VIA GARIBALDI

VICOLO DEL
LEOPARDO

V. D. MATTONATO

V. DELLA PELLICCIA

V. DEI PANIERI

Sant'Egidio and
Museo di Roma
in Trastevere
**5**

PIAZZA D
SANT'APOLLONI
③

PIAZZA DI
SANTA MARIA

VIA DELLA PAGLIA

VIA GOFFREDO

Santa Maria
in Trastevere
**1**

VIA GIACOMO VENEZIAN

VIA GARIBALDI

VIA LUCIANO MANARA

VIA AGOSINO
BERTANI

PIAZZA
SAN COSIMATO

VIA A.
TITTONI

VIA A. MAMELI

VIA L. SANTINI

V. NATALE
DEL GRAND

VIA ANGELO MASINA

Accademia
d'America

VIA GIACOMO MEDICI

VIA PIETRO ROSELLI

FABRIZI

VIA GAETANO SACCHI

VIA ROMA
LIBERA

VIA EMILIO MOROSIN

VIA GARIBALDI

VIALE TRENTA APRILE

VIALE TRENTA APRILE

NICOLA

SCALEA DEL
TAMBURINO

VIALE

VIA DANDOLO

Ministero
della
Pubblica
Istruzione

GIANICOLENSI

VIA SENI

VIALE

VIA CALANDRELLI

Villa Sciarra
**8**

VIALE A. LEDUCQ

VIA FILIPPO CASINI

VIALE

VIA DANDOLO

GLORIOSO

VIALE
DELLE MURA

VIALE

VIALE

A.

LEDUCQ

VIA

AURELIO

SAFFI

PIAZZA
BERNARDINO
DA FELTRE

CARINI

**8**

GIACINTO

VIA

VIA GABRIELE ROSSETTI

VIA UGO
BASSI

VIALE A. SAFFI

VIALE A. SCALA RIGHETTO VIALE

VIALE ASAFFI

VIA UGO BASSI

VIALE DI TRASTEVERE

VIA B. MUSOLINO

PIAZZA
IPPOLITO
NIEVO

V. D. ORTI DI TRA STEVERE

PORTUENS

VIA

**9**

**TRASTEVERE**

VIA FRANCESCO DALL'ONGARO

**D**

**E**

# TRASTEVERE

**Must See**

❶ Santa Maria in Trastevere

**Experience More**

❷ Casa della Fornarina
❸ Ponte Sisto
❹ Santa Maria della Scala
❺ Sant'Egidio and Museo di Roma in Trastevere
❻ San Crisogono
❼ Santa Cecilia in Trastevere
❽ Villa Sciarra
❾ San Michele a Ripa Grande
❿ San Francesco a Ripa
⓫ Caserma dei Vigili della VII Coorte

**Drink**

① Enoteca Ferrara
② Big Mama
③ Ombre Rosse

**Shop**

④ Marta Ray
⑤ Pasticceria Valzani

① 🏛

# SANTA MARIA IN TRASTEVERE

**📍F7 🏛Piazza Santa Maria in Trastevere 📞06-581 4802 🚌H & 780 to Piazza San Sonnino, 23 & 280 along Lungotevere Sanzio 🚋8 from Piazza Venezia 🕐7:30am-9pm daily (8am-noon & 4-9pm Aug)**

Probably the first official Christian place of worship to be built in Rome, this basilica became the focus of devotion to the Virgin Mary. Today it is famous for its splendid mosaics.

According to legend, the church was founded by Pope Callixtus I in the 3rd century, when Christianity was still a minority cult, on the site where a fountain of oil had miraculously sprung up on the day that Christ was born. Today's church is largely a 12th-century building, remarkable for its mosaics, in particular the apse mosaic of the Coronation of the Virgin and the six mosaics by Pietro Cavallini below it of the life of the Virgin, depicted with a touching realism. The 22 granite columns in the nave were taken from the ruins of ancient Roman buildings. Despite some 18th-century Baroque additions, Santa Maria has retained its medieval character.

↑ Santa Maria in Trastevere façade, with an octagonal fountain built in the late 17th century by Carlo Fontana in front

↑ Mosaic floor, relaid in the 1870s to re-create the 13th-century Cosmatesque floor mosaics

*1291*

▽ Pietro Cavallini adds mosaics of scenes from the life of the Virgin for his patron, Bertoldo Stefaneschi.

**Timeline**

*38 BC*
Jet of mineral oil spouts from the ground on this site, later interpreted as a portent of the coming of Christ.

*AD 217–22*
Church founded by Pope Callixtus I.

*c1138*
Pope Innocent II starts rebuilding the church.

*1617*
△ Domenichino designs coffered ceiling with octagonal panel depicting the Assumption of the Virgin.

*1866–77*
Church restored by Virginio Vespignani.

**Did You Know?**

The glittering mosaics on the church's façade are illuminated at night.

The 12th-century apse mosaic and Cavallini mosaics below it ↑

# EXPERIENCE MORE

### ② Casa della Fornarina

**◎ E6 ⌂ Via di Santa Dorotea 20 ▥ 23, 280**

Not much is known about the life of Raphael's model and lover, La Fornarina, yet over the centuries she has acquired a name, Margherita Luti, and even a biography. Her father was a Sienese baker (*la fornarina* means "the baker's girl") and his shop was here in Trastevere near Raphael's frescoes in the Villa Farnesina (*p274*).

Margherita earned a reputation as a "fallen woman" and Raphael, wishing to be absolved before dying, turned her away from his deathbed. After his death she took refuge in the convent of Santa Apollonia in Trastevere.

She is assumed to have been the model for Raphael's famous portrait *La Donna Velata* housed in the Palazzo Pitti in Florence.

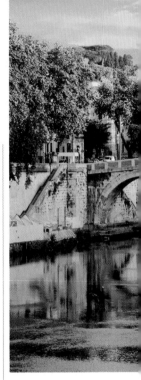

→ Ponte Sisto, with the dome of St Peter's in the background

### ③ Ponte Sisto

**◎ F6 ▥ 23, 280**

Named after Pope Sixtus IV della Rovere (reigned 1471–84), who commissioned it, this bridge was built by Baccio Pontelli in 1475 to replace an ancient Roman bridge. The enterprising pope also commissioned the Sistine Chapel (*p294*), the Hospital of Santo Spirito (*p300*) and had many churches and monuments restored. This put him in great financial difficulties and he had to sell personal collections in order to finance his projects.

### ④ Santa Maria della Scala

**◎ E7 ⌂ Piazza della Scala 23 ☎ 06-580 6233 ▥ 23, 280 ◷ 10am–1pm & 4–5:30pm daily**

This church belongs to a time of great building activity that lasted about 30 years from the end of the 16th to the early 17th century. Its simple façade contrasts with a rich interior decorated with multicoloured marbles and a number of spirited Baroque altars and reliefs, as well as a few paintings, including Carlo Saraceni's *Death of the Virgin*. In 1849, the church was used as a hospital to treat the soldiers of Garibaldi's army.

← *Death of the Virgin* (17th century) by Carlo Saraceni in Santa Maria della Scala

**5**

### Sant'Egidio and Museo di Roma in Trastevere

📍 F7 🚌 H, 23, 280 🚊 8

Built in 1630, **Sant'Egidio** is the church of the adjoining Carmelite convent. The convent is now the **Museo di Roma**, containing material relating to the festivals, pastimes and customs of the Romans when they lived under papal rule. There are old paintings and prints of the city and tableaux showing scenes of everyday life in 18th- and 19th-century Rome, including reconstructions of shops and a tavern. The museum also has manuscripts by the poets Belli and Trilussa, in local dialect.

### Sant'Egidio

🏠 Piazza Sant'Egidio 3a
🌐 santegidio.org

### Museo di Roma

♿🏠 Piazza Sant'Egidio 1
🕐 10am–8pm Tue–Sun (last adm 7pm) 🌐 museo-diromaintrastevere.it

---

**6**

### San Crisogono

📍 F7 🏠 Piazza Sonnino 44
📞 06-5810 0076 🚌 H, 23, 280, 780 🚊 8 🕐 7–11:30am & 4–7:30pm Mon–Sat, 8am–1pm & 4–7:30pm Sun

This church was built on the site of one of the city's oldest *tituli* (private houses used for Christian worship). An 8th-century church with 11th-century frescoes can still be seen beneath the present church. It is possible to see the excavations. The ground-level church dates from the early 12th century. Most of the church's columns were taken from previous buildings, including the great porphyry columns of a triumphal arch. The mosaic floor is made of recycled precious marble from various Roman ruins. Pietro Cavallini designed the apse mosaic. The Baroque ceiling painting is by Guercino.

---

**FESTA DE' NOANTRI**

Every year Trastevere hosts its very own carnival, the Festa de' Noantri, in late July. Street processions, concerts, poetry readings, theatre performances, a market and fireworks are all held in the area.

Piazza di Santa Maria in Trastevere

The ornate interior of Santa Cecilia in Trastevere and *(inset)* a detail of a fresco

## 7
## Santa Cecilia in Trastevere

📍 G7 🏛 Piazza di Santa Cecilia 📞 06-589 9289
🚌 H, 23, 44, 280 🚊 8
🕐 10am-1pm & 4-7pm daily

St Cecilia, aristocrat and patron saint of music, was martyred here in AD 230. After an attempt at scalding her to death, she was beheaded. A church was founded, perhaps in the 4th century, on the site of her house.

The **excavations and crypt** beneath the church are well worth a visit. Her body turned up in the Catacombs of San Callisto *(p323)* and was buried here in the 9th century by Pope Paschal I, who rebuilt the church. A fine apse mosaic survives from this period.

The **fresco** of *The Last Judgment* by Pietro Cavallini, reached through the convent, dates from the 1200s. In front of the altar is a statue of St Cecilia by Stefano Maderno, who used her preserved remains as a model when she was briefly disinterred in 1599.

### Excavations and Crypt
⬧ 🕐 10am-1pm and 4-7pm daily; **Cavallini fresco** 🕐 10am-12:30pm Mon-Fri (from 11:30am public hols)

---

## 8
## Villa Sciarra

📍 E8 🏛 Via Calandrelli 35
🚌 44, 75 Park: 🕐 9am-sunset daily

In Roman times the site of this small, attractive public park was a nymph's sanctuary. Shaded by trees, Villa Sciarra is a tranquil place to get away from the hustle and bustle of the surrounding streets. It is especially picturesque in spring when its wisterias are in full bloom. The paths through the park are decorated with Romantic follies, fountains and statues, and there are splendid views over the bastions of the Janiculum. It also contains the headquarters of the Italian Institute for Germanic Studies.

→

Bernini's *Ecstasy of Beata Ludovica Albertoni* in San Francesco a Ripa

## ⑨ San Michele a Ripa Grande

📍 G8 🏠 Via di San Michele 25 📞 06-6723 1440 🚌 23, 44, 75, 280 🎫 For special exhibitions only

This huge, imposing complex, now housing the Ministry of Culture, stretches 300 m (985 ft) along the River Tiber. It was built on the initiative of Pope Innocent XII and contained a home for the abandoned elderly, a boys' reform school, a woollen mill and various chapels. Today, contemporary art exhibitions are occasionally held here.

## ⑩ San Francesco a Ripa

📍 F8 🏠 Piazza San Francesco d'Assisi 88 📞 06-581 9020 🚌 H, 23, 44, 75, 280 🚋 8 🕐 7am–1pm & 4-7pm daily

St Francis of Assisi lived here in a hospice when he visited Rome in 1219, and his stone

> **Entirely rebuilt in the 1680s by Cardinal Pallavicini, the San Francesco a Ripa church is rich in sculptures.**

pillow and crucifix are preserved in his cell. The church was rebuilt by his follower, the nobleman Rodolfo Anguillara, who is portrayed on his tombstone wearing the Franciscan habit.

Entirely rebuilt in the 1680s by Cardinal Pallavicini, the church is rich in sculptures. Particularly flamboyant are the 18th-century Rospigliosi and Pallavicini monuments in the transept chapel.

The Paluzzi-Albertoni Chapel (fourth on the left, along the nave) contains Bernini's breathtaking *Ecstasy of Beata Ludovica Albertoni*, completed in 1674.

## ⑪ Caserma dei Vigili della VII Coorte

📍 G7 🏠 Via della VII Coorte 9 📞 06-0608 🚌 H, 23, 280, 780 🚋 8 🎫 For restoration; call for details

Not all Roman ruins are Imperial villas or grand temples; one that illustrates the daily life of a busy city is the barracks of the guards of the VII Coorte (7th Cohort), the Roman fire brigade. It was built in Augustus's reign, in the 1st century AD, and the excavated courtyard is where the men would rest while waiting for a call out.

# DRINK

### Enoteca Ferrara

This cosy *enoteca* has a vast wine list and there's a smart restaurant attached, although the wine bar's generous *aperitivo* buffet might leave you too full for dinner.

📍 F7 🏠 Piazza Trilussa 41 🌐 enotecaferrara.it

### Big Mama

A basement jazz club hosting international musicians several nights a week (from 10.30pm), this is an intimate place for a nightcap. There is a €10 admission charge.

📍 F8 🏠 Vicolo di San Francesco a Ripa 18 🌐 bigmama.it

### Ombre Rosse

The terrace of this bar is a great spot for a pre-dinner Prosecco. There's live music several nights a week.

📍 F7 🏠 Piazza di Sant'Egidio 12 🌐 ombrerosse intrastevere.it

# A SHORT WALK
# TRASTEVERE

**Distance** 2 km (1.2 miles)  **Nearest bus** 23, 280
**Time** 30 minutes

It is best to appreciate the antique charm of Trastevere's narrow streets in the more tranquil atmosphere of the early morning. All year round Trastevere is a major attraction both for its restaurants, clubs and cinemas, and for its picturesque maze of narrow cobbled alleyways. On summer evenings the streets are packed with jostling groups of pleasure-seekers. Café and restaurant tables spill out over pavements, especially around Piazza di Santa Maria in Trastevere and outside the pizzerias along Viale di Trastevere. Kiosks sell slices of watermelon and *grattachecca*, a mixture of syrup and grated ice.

Raphael's mistress is said to have lived at the Casa della Fornarina. There is now a flourishing restaurant in the back garden (p262).

The Santa Maria della Scala's unassuming façade conceals a rich Baroque interior (p262).

The church of Santa Maria dei Sette Dolori (1643) is a minor work by Borromini.

Sant'Egidio and Museo di Roma in Trastevere has a 17th-century fresco of Sant'Egidio by Pomarancio in the left-hand chapel. The convent next door is a museum of Roman life and customs (p263).

Vicolo del Piede is one of the picturesque narrow streets lined with restaurant tables leading off Piazza di Santa Maria in Trastevere.

Santa Maria in Trastevere is famous for its 13th-century mosaics by Pietro Cavallini but it also has earlier works to the left of the apse (p260).

The fountain of Piazza di Santa Maria in Trastevere by Carlo Fontana (1692) is a popular meeting place. At night it is floodlit and dozens of young people sit on the steps around its octagonal base.

↑ People relaxing at the fountain on Piazza di Santa Maria in Trastevere

**Locator Map**
*For more detail see p256*

TRASTEVERE

*Ponte Sisto was built on the orders of Sixtus IV in 1474 to link Trastevere to central Rome (p262).*

PIAZZA TRILUSSA

PONTE SISTO

↑ The pedestrianized 15th-century Ponte Sisto spanning the Tiber river

LLICCIA

TEVERE

LUNGOTEVERE SANZIO

VIA DELLA RENELLA

VIA DELLA LUNGARETTA

PIAZZA

BELLI

PONTE GARIBALDI

*Piazza Belli is named after Giuseppe Gioacchino Belli (1791–1863), who wrote satirical sonnets in Roman dialect rather than academic Italian. At the centre of the piazza stands a statue of the poet (1913).*

*The Torre degli Anguillara (13th century) is the only survivor of the many medieval towers that once dominated the Trastevere skyline.*

PIAZZA SONNINO

VIA DI SAN GALICANO

VIALE DI TRASTEVERE

*San Crisogono's Romanesque bell tower dates from the early 12th century. The plain portico is a later addition (1626), but is in keeping with the spirit of this ancient church (p263).*

*The courtyard of the Caserma dei Vigili della VII Coorte, Rome's ancient fire station, still stands (p267).*

# JANICULUM

Overlooking the Tiber on the Trastevere side of the river, the Janiculum Hill has often played its part in the defence of the city. The last occasion was in 1849 when Garibaldi held off the attacking French troops – the park at the top of the hill is filled with monuments to Garibaldi and his men. A popular place for walks, the park provides a welcome escape from the densely packed streets of Trastevere, and you will often come across puppet shows and other children's amusements. In medieval times most of the hill was occupied by monasteries and convents. Bramante built his miniature masterpiece, the Tempietto, in the convent of San Pietro in Montorio. The Renaissance also saw the development of the riverside area along Via della Lungara, where the rich and powerful built beautiful houses such as the Villa Farnesina.

VATICAN
*p282*

## JANICULUM

### Must See
❶ Villa Farnesina

### Experience More
❷ Giuseppe and Anita Garibaldi Monuments
❸ Galleria Corsini
❹ Porta Settimiana
❺ Botanical Gardens
❻ Sant'Onofrio
❼ San Pietro in Montorio
❽ Tempietto
❾ Fontana dell'Acqua Paola

### Eat
① Antico Arco

0 metres 200
0 yards 200
N

JANICULUM

SASSIA

Ponte Principe
Amedeo Savoia
Aosta

Palazzo
Salviati

VIA GIULIA

LUNGOTEVERE DEI SANGALLO

Fiume

Tevere

CORSO VITTORIO EMANUELE II

PARIONE

Palazzo della
Cancelleria

VIA DEL PELLEGRINO

VIA DELLA LUNGARA

VIA DEGLI ORTI D'ALIBERT

VIA DELLE MANTELLATE

Carcere di
Regina Coeli

FRANCESCO DI SALES

V.S. FRANCESCO DI SALES

V. S. FRANCESCO DI SALES

Gianicolo

VIA DELLA PENITENZA

VIA DELLA LUNGARA

VIA DEI RIARI

LUNGOTEVERE DELLA FARNESINA

Ponte
Giuseppe
Mazzini

LUNGOTEVERE DEI TEBALDI

**CAMPO
DE' FIORI**
*p160*

CAMPO
DE' FIORI

PIAZZA
FARNESE

Palazzo
Farnese

**① Villa
Farnesina**

**③ Galleria
Corsini**

Casa della
Fornarina

Palazzo
Spada

LUNGOT. D. VALLATI

**6**

Ponte
Sisto

**⑤ Botanical Gardens**

**④ Porta
Settimiana**

LUNGOTEVERE R. SANZIO

VIA D. SCALA

VIA GARIBALDI

VIC. DEL CEDRO

PIAZZA S.
APOLLONIA

Santa
Maria in
Trastevere

**7**

PASSEGGIATA GIANICOLO

VIA DI PORTA SAN PANCRAZIO

**Tempietto ⑧**

**⑨ Fontana
dell'Acqua Paola**

VIA GARIBALDI

**San Pietro in ⑦
Montorio**

VIA GOFFREDO MAMELI

VIA LUCIANO MANARA

VIA S. FRANCESCO

VIA ANGELO MASINA

Accademia
d'America

VIA GIACOMO MEDICI

**TRASTEVERE**
*p256*

VIA GARIBALDI

❶ ⊘ ⊗ ⊡

# VILLA FARNESINA

**⊙ E6 ⌂ Via della Lungara 230 ▦ 23, 280 to Lungotevere ⊙ 9am–2pm Mon–Sat & 2nd Sun of every month ⊠ Aug ⊛ villafarnesina.it**

A perfect example of Renaissance architecture, Villa Farnesina was built in the early 16th century for the fabulously wealthy Sienese banker Agostino Chigi, and served as a sophsticated retreat where he could entertain and hold magnificent banquets.

Having established the headquarters of his far-flung financial empire in Rome, Agostino Chigi commissioned the villa in 1508 from his compatriot, painter and architect Baldassare Peruzzi. The simple, harmonious design, with a central block and projecting wings, made this one of the earliest true Renaissance villas. The decoration was carried out between 1510 and 1519 and has been restored. Peruzzi frescoed some of the interiors himself. Later, Sebastiano del Piombo, Raphael and his pupils added more elaborate works. The frescoes illustrate Classical myths, and the vault of the main hall, the Sala di Galatea, is adorned with astrological scenes showing the position of the stars at the time of Chigi's birth. Artists, poets, cardinals, princes and the pope himself were entertained here in magnificent style by their wealthy and influential host. In 1577 the villa was bought by Cardinal Alessandro Farnese. Since then, it has been known as the Villa Farnesina.

> **Artists, poets, cardinals, princes and the pope himself were entertained here in magnificent style by their wealthy and influential host.**

Triumph of Galatea by Raphael

Frescoes in the Room of Galatea

← 

The elegant, classical exterior of the Renaissance Villa Farnesina, designed by Peruzzi

Lunette in the Room of Galatea

Salone delle
Prospettive

← Drawing showing
the layout of the
Villa Farnesina

### AGOSTINO CHIGI

A super-wealthy banking tycoon and Renaissance playboy, Agostino Chigi was fond of throwing extravagant parties. At a dinner party, held in a riverside pavilion in the grounds of Villa Farnesina, the food was served on gold and silver platters which were flung into the Tiber at the end of each course. The demonstration of wealth was not quite as reckless as it first seemed – Chigi had taken the precaution of having nets laid on the river bed so that his dinner service could be retrieved after the guests had gone home.

Loggia of Cupid
and Psyche

① Loggia of Cupid and Psyche

② *The Three Graces* by Raphael in the Loggia of Cupid and Psyche

③ *Perseus Beheading Medusa* fresco by Peruzzi in the Room of Galatea

# EXPERIENCE MORE

**2**

## Giuseppe and Anita Garibaldi Monuments

📍D6 🏛Piazzale Giuseppe Garibaldi 🚌870

Dominating a huge open piazza on the summit of the Janiculum Hill is an equestrian statue of Giuseppe Garibaldi, hero of the Italian Unification. The statue and piazza commemorate the weeks in 1849 when Garibaldi and his men, based on the hill, fended off attacks from highly superior French forces, before finally being overwhelmed and escaping. In 2011, to mark the 150th anniversary of the Italian Republic, a low wall was erected, inscribed with the country's constitution.

A short distance away is a dramatic monument to Garibaldi's wife Anita, who fought alongside him. She is depicted on a leaping horse, a pistol in her right hand and her baby under her left arm.

← 
Dramatic equestrian statue of Anita Garibaldi riding into battle

**3**

## Galleria Corsini

📍E6 🏛Via della Lungara 10 🚌23, 280 🕐For renovations; check website for details 🌐barberinicorsini.org

The history of Palazzo Corsini is intimately entwined with that of Rome. Built for Cardinal Domenico Riario in 1510–12, it has boasted among its many distinguished guests Bramante, the young Michelangelo, Erasmus and Queen Christina of Sweden, who died here in 1689. The old palazzo was completely rebuilt for Cardinal Neri Corsini by Ferdinando Fuga in 1736. As Via della Lungara is too narrow for a good frontal view, Fuga designed the façade so it could be seen from an angle.

Palazzo Corsini houses the Galleria Nazionale d'Arte Antica, also known as Galleria Corsini. This outstanding collection includes paintings by Rubens, Van Dyck, Murillo, Caravaggio and Guido Reni, together with 17th- and 18th-century Italian regional art. The palazzo is also home to the Accademia dei Lincei, a learned society founded in 1603 that once included Galileo among its members.

In 1797 French General Duphot (the fiancé of Napoleon's sister Pauline) was killed here during a skirmish between papal troops and Republicans. The consequent French occupation of the city and the deportation of Pope Pius VI led to the proclamation of a short-lived Roman Republic (1798–9).

**4**

## Porta Settimiana

📍E6 🏛Between Via della Scala and Via della Lungara 🚌23, 280

This gate was built in 1498 by Pope Alexander VI Borgia to replace a minor passageway in the Aurelian Wall. The Porta Settimiana marks the start of Via della Lungara, a long road built in the early 16th century.

**5**

## Botanical Gardens

📍E6 🏛Largo Cristina di Svezia 24, off Via Corsini 📞06-4991 7108 🚌23, 280 🕐9am-6:30pm Mon-Sat (Nov-Mar: to 5:30pm) 🕐Public hols

Sequoias, palm trees and collections of orchids and bromeliads are cultivated in Rome's Botanical Gardens (Orto Botanico). These tranquil gardens contain more than 7,000 plant species. Indigenous and exotic species are grouped to illustrate their botanical families and their adaptation to different climates and ecosystems. The gardens were originally part of the Palazzo Corsini but now belong to the University of Rome.

**6**

## Sant'Onofrio

📍D5 🏛Piazza di Sant'Onofrio 2 📞06-686 4498 🚌870 🕐9am-1pm & 3-6pm Sun-Fri 🕐Aug

Beato Nicola da Forca Palena, whose tombstone guards the entrance, founded this church

The monumental Fontana dell'Acqua Paola, built in 1612

in 1419 in honour of the hermit St Onofrio. It retains the flavour of the 15th century in the simple shapes of the portico and the cloister. In the early 17th century the portico was decorated with frescoes by Domenichino.

The monastery next to the church has a small **museum** that is dedicated to the 16th-century Italian poet Torquato Tasso, who died there.

### Museum

🏠 Piazza di Sant'Onofrio 2
📞 06-687 7341 ⏰ By appt

---

### ❼ San Pietro in Montorio

📍 E7 🏠 Piazza San Pietro in Montorio 2 📞 06-581 3940
🚌 44, 75 ⏰ 8am-noon & 3-4pm daily (times may vary in summer)

San Pietro in Montorio – the church of St Peter on the Golden Hill – was founded in the Middle Ages near the spot where St Peter was presumed to have been crucified. It was rebuilt by order of Ferdinand and Isabella of Spain at the end of the 15th century, and decorated by outstanding artists of the Renaissance.

The single nave ends in a deep apse that once contained Raphael's *Transfiguration*, now in the Vatican. Two wide chapels, one on either side of the nave, were decorated by some of Michelangelo's most famous pupils. The left-hand chapel was designed by Daniele da Volterra, who was also responsible for the altar painting, *The Baptism of Christ*. The chapel on the right was the work of Giorgio Vasari, who included a self-portrait (in black, on the left) in his altar painting, *The Conversion of St Paul*.

The first chapel to the right of the entrance contains a powerful *Flagellation*, by the Venetian artist Sebastiano del Piombo (1518); Michelangelo is said to have provided the original drawings. Work by Bernini and his followers can be seen in the second chapel on the left and in the flanking De Raymondi tombs.

---

### ❽ Tempietto

📍 E7 🏠 Piazza San Pietro (in courtyard) 🚌 44, 75
⏰ 10am-6pm Tue-Sun

Around 1502 Bramante completed what many consider to be the first true Renaissance building in Rome – the Tempietto, a perfectly circular Doric temple. The name means simply "little temple". Its circular shape echoes early Christian *martyria*, chapels built on the site of a saint's martyrdom. This was believed to be the place where St Peter was crucified.

Bramante chose the Doric order for the 16 columns surrounding the domed chapel. Above the columns is a Classical frieze and a delicate balustrade. Though the scale of the Tempietto is tiny, Bramante's masterly use of Classical proportions creates a satisfyingly harmonious whole. The Tempietto illustrates the great Renaissance dream that the city of Rome would once again relive its ancient glory.

---

### ❾ Fontana dell'Acqua Paola

📍 E7 🏠 Via Garibaldi
🚌 44, 75

This fountain marks the reopening in 1612 of an aqueduct built in AD 109. It was renamed the "Acqua Paola" after Paul V, the Borghese pope who ordered its restoration. The original fountain had five small basins. In 1690 Carlo Fontana added the huge basin you can see today.

---

## EAT

### Antico Arco
This chic restaurant has a short menu of gourmet Italian dishes made with top-notch ingredients, such as sea bass with Roman broccoli and black truffle. It is the ideal dining choice for a special occasion.

📍 D7 🏠 Piazzale Aurelio 7
🌐 anticoarco.it

€€€

The perfectly proportioned Tempietto, within the cloister of San Pietro in Montorio

# A SHORT WALK
# A TOUR OF THE JANICULUM

**Distance** 1 km (0.6 mile) **Nearest bus** 23, 280, 870 **Time** 15 minutes

The long hike to the top of the Janiculum is rewarded by wonderful views over the city. The park's monuments include a lighthouse and statues of Garibaldi and his wife Anita. There is also a cannon which is fired at noon each day. In Via della Lungara, between the Janiculum and the Tiber, stand Palazzo Corsini, with its national art collection, and the Villa Farnesina, decorated by Raphael for his friend and patron, the fabulously wealthy banker Agostino Chigi.

*Tasso's Oak is a memorial to the poet Torquato Tasso, who liked to sit here in the days before he died in 1595. The tree was struck by lightning in 1843.*

*The Manfredi Lighthouse, built in 1911, was a gift to the city of Rome from Italians in Argentina.*

*The Monument to Anita Garibaldi by Mario Rutelli was erected in 1932. The great patriot's Brazilian wife lies buried beneath the statue (p276).*

*The view from Villa Lante, a beautiful Renaissance summer residence, gives a magnificent panorama of the whole city.*

*The inscription on the base of the equestrian statue of the Garibaldi Monument says "Rome or Death".*

**START**

VIALE ALDO FABRIZI

PIAZZALE GIUSEPPE GARIBALDI

← Late-Renaissance Villa Lante, with panoramic views over Rome

**Locator Map**
*For more detail see p272*

↑ The Renaissance Porta
Settimiana, part of the
Aurelian Wall

*The suburban Villa Farnesina,
which belonged to the banker
Agostino Chigi, is celebrated
for its frescoes by Raphael,
Baldassarre Peruzzi and other
Renaissance masters.*

VICOLO DELLA PENITENZA

VIA DELLA PENITENZA

VIA DELLA LUNGARA

VIA DEI RIARI

VIA CORSINI

*Looking through the
Renaissance gateway
of the Porta
Settimiana from Via
della Lungara, you
catch a glimpse of
Trastevere's warren of
narrow streets (p276).*

*The Botanical Gardens
were established in 1883
when part of the grounds
of Palazzo Corsini was
given to the University
of Rome (p276).*

*The 15th-century Palazzo Corsini
triptych by Fra Angelico hangs in
the Galleria Corsini (p276).*

0 metres     100   N

0 yards     100   ↖

**○ FINISH**

# VATICAN

As the site where St Peter was martyred and buried, the Vatican became the residence of the popes who succeeded him. Decisions taken here have shaped the destiny of Europe, and the great basilica of St Peter's draws pilgrims from all over the Christian world. The papal palaces beside St Peter's house the Vatican Museums. With the awe-inspiring attractions of Michelangelo's Sistine Chapel and the Raphael Rooms, their wonderful collections of Classical sculpture make them the finest museums in Rome. The Vatican's position as a state within a state was guaranteed by the Lateran Treaty of 1929, marked by the building of a new road, the Via della Conciliazione. This leads from St Peter's to Castel Sant'Angelo, a monument to a far grimmer past. Built originally as the Emperor Hadrian's mausoleum, this papal fortress and prison has witnessed many fierce battles for control of the city.

# VATICAN

**Must Sees**
1 St Peter's
2 Vatican Museums
3 Castel Sant'Angelo

**Experience More**
4 Porta Santo Spirito
5 Santo Spirito in Sassia
6 Hospital of Santo Spirito
7 Palazzo del Commendatore
8 Palazzo dei Convertendi
9 Palazzo dei Penitenzieri
10 Santa Maria in Traspontina
11 The Borgo
12 Palazzo Torlonia
13 Palazzo di Giustizia

**Eat and Drink**
1 Dal Toscano
2 Franchi
3 Il Simposio

**Shop**
4 Via Cola di Rienzo

VIA
SABOTINO
VIA G. GIUSEPPE ANDREOLI
VIA A. CA DALLA CHIESA
S. PELLICO
S. ANTONIO BALBAMONTI

PIAZZA
GIUSEPPE
MAZZINI
VIA LUIGI SETTEMBRINI
VIA G. FERRARI
VIALE DELLE MILIZIE
VIA LEPANTO

0 metres    200
0 yards     200
N

Ponte
G. Matteotti

1

**PIAZZA DI SPAGNA
AND
VILLA BORGHESE**
*p136*

Ponte
P. Nenni

2

Ponte
Regina
Margherita

Lepanto M
GIULIO CESARE
VIALE
VIA DEGLI SCIPIONI
VIA M. COLONNA
VIA A. FARNESE
VIA POMPEO MAGNO
VIA V. ORSINI
GRACCHI
LUNGOTEVERE MICHELANGELO

PIAZZA
DELLA LIBERTÀ

VIA DUILIO
VIA PAOLO EMILO
VIA EZIO
DEI
PIAZZA DEI
QUIRITI
PIAZZA COLA
DI RIENZO
LUNGOTEVERE DEI MELLINI

A DEGLI
PRATI
SCIPIONI
VIA MASSIMO
VIA COLA
DI RIENZO
VALADIER
VIA LUCREZIO CARO
CESI
Q. VISCONTI

3

ERMANICO
DEI GRACCHI
VIA MARIO
PIAZZA
DELL'UNITÀ
(2)
(4)
VIA A. REGOLO
VIA PLINIO
VIA VIRGILIO
VIA ORAZIO
VIA TACITO
VIA CICERONE
VIA ENNIO
VIA GIOACCHINO
VIA FEDERICO
BELLI
VIA P. PALESTRINA
COSSA
CLEMENTI

VIA V. VARRONE
VIA PROPERZIO
VIA P. LETO
VIA F. CANCELLIERI
VIA TIBULLO
VIA BOEZIO
VIA OVIDIO
VIA CASSIODORO
VIA
VIA M. DIONIGI
VIA P. CAVALLINI

VIA
CRESCENZIO
VIA ALBERICO II
PIAZZA
ADRIANA
PIAZZA CAVOUR
VIA V. COLONNA

PIAZZA
AMERIGO
CAPPONI
VIA GIOVANNI
VITELLESCHI
VIA P. D. VALLE
PIAZZA CAVOUR
Ponte
Cavour

V. PLAUTO
V. D. OMBRELLARI
VITTORIO
The Borgo (11)
BORGO
Il Passetto
Castel
Sant'Angelo
(3)
VIA TRIBONIANO
Palazzo di
Giustizia
(13)
VIA ULPIANO
LUNGOT. PRATI

4

Ponte
Umberto

**PIAZZA
NAVONA**
*p120*

Palazzo dei
nvertendi (8)
Palazzo
Torlonia (12)
Santa Maria
in Traspontina (10)
A DELLA CONCILIAZIONE
LUNGOT. VATICANO
i
LUNGOTEVERE CASTELLO
Ponte
S. Angelo
Fiume Tevere

Palazzo dei
Penitenzieri (9)

Santo (5)
Spirito in
Sassia
Palazzo del
Commendatore (7)
Ponte Vittorio
Eman. II
LT. DEGLI
ALTOVITI
LUNGOT. TOR DI NONA

Porta (4)
Santo Spirito
Hospital of
Santo Spirito (6)

VATICAN

5

RINCIPE
AOSTA
Ponte Principe
Amedeo
Savoia Aosta

**JANICULUM**
*p270*

IL GIANICOLENSE

**CAMPO
DE' FIORI**
*p160*

CORSO VITTORIO EMANUELE II
LUNGOTEVERE
DEI SANGALLO

PARIONE

① ⓂⓐⒶ

# ST PETER'S

📍 C4  🏛 Piazza San Pietro  📞 06-6988 3712 (Sacristy); 06-988 1662 (tourist info)
🚌 23, 49, 70, 180, 492  Ⓜ Ottaviano San Pietro  🕐 Basilica: 7am-6pm daily Apr-Sep
(to 6:30pm mid-Oct-Mar); Treasury: 8am-6pm daily Apr-Sep (to 5:30pm Oct-Mar);
Grottoes: 8am-6pm daily Apr-Sep (to 5pm Oct-Mar); Dome: 8am-6pm daily Apr-Sep
(to 5pm Oct-Mar)

**The centre of the Roman Catholic faith, St Peter's draws pilgrims from all over the world. The magnificent basilica holds many precious works of art.**

A shrine was erected in the 2nd century on the site where, according to Catholic tradition, St Peter was martyred and buried in AD 61. The first great basilica, ordered by Emperor Constantine, was constructed here in AD 349. By the 15th century it was falling down, so in

1506 Pope Julius II commissioned Bramante to replace the old church with a brand-new basilica. It took more than a hundred years to build and all the great architects and artists of the Roman Renaissance and Baroque had a hand in its design – not only Bramante, but

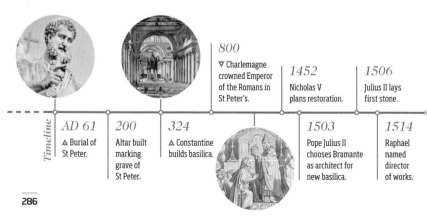

Timeline

**800**
▽ Charlemagne crowned Emperor of the Romans in St Peter's.

**1452**
Nicholas V plans restoration.

**1506**
Julius II lays first stone.

**AD 61**
△ Burial of St Peter.

**200**
Altar built marking grave of St Peter.

**324**
△ Constantine builds basilica.

**1503**
Pope Julius II chooses Bramante as architect for new basilica.

**1514**
Raphael named director of works.

↑ Piazza San Pietro
with the basilica and
Bernini's colonnade

Raphael, Bernini and Michelangelo. The
basilica was finally completed in 1626 and
is the world's second-largest church after
Yamoussoukro in Côte d'Ivoire. Few are
disappointed when they first enter the
sumptuously decorated basilica beneath the
vast dome designed by Michelangelo, the tallest
dome in the world. For a fee you can go up
into the dome. A broad ramp followed by a
spiral staircase around the inside of the dome
leads from the roof to the cupola, from where
there are stunning views over the city and of
Bernini's colonnade. Designed by Carlo Maderno,
the travertine façade features Corinthian
columns and a balustrade with 13 statues.

## MASS AND AUDIENCE WITH THE POPE

The pope presides over Mass and
addresses the crowds in St Peter's
Square on Easter Day, Christmas Day
and other major Christian festivals.
General Audiences are usually held on
Wednesdays (10–10:30am) in St Peter's
Square (or in the Paul VI Audience Hall
in bad weather). Get there very early if
you want a chance of meeting or being
blessed by the pope. Tickets to Papal
Masses and General Audiences are free.
To apply for a ticket visit www.vatican.
va/various/prefettura/index_en.html,
and download the form. There is no
email address and all applications must
be faxed. See www.papalaudience.
org/information for further details.

**1538** Da Sangallo the Younger made director of works.

**1547** △ Michelangelo named chief architect of St Peter's.

**1564** Death of Michelangelo.

**1593** Dome completed.

**1606** Carlo Maderno extends basilica.

**1614** △ Maderno finishes the façade.

**1626** ▽ New basilica of St Peter's consecrated.

## Inside St Peter's

The vast basilica's 187 m- (615 ft-) long, marble-encrusted interior contains 11 chapels, 45 altars, and a wealth of works of art. Some were salvaged from the original basilica and others commissioned from late Renaissance and Baroque artists, but much of the elaborate decoration is owed to Bernini's mid-17th-century work. The building's central focus is the Papal Altar beneath Bernini's great baldacchino, filling the space between the four piers which support the dome. From the basilica you can visit the Grottoes – where the late Pope John Paul II is buried, the Treasury and St Peter's Sacristy, or the terrace for panoramic views.

*The 136.5 m- (448 ft-) high dome, designed by Michelangelo, was not completed in his lifetime.*

*Bernini's splendid bronze baldacchino stands above St Peter's tomb.*

*The Papal Altar is above the crypt where St Peter is reputedly buried.*

*The foot of St Peter, cast in the 13th century, has worn thin from the touch of pilgrims over the centuries.*

*Michelangelo's famous marble sculpture, the Pietà*

HIDDEN GEM
**Parco Adriano**

Escape for some quiet to the green space nearest St Peter's in the small Parco Adriano, behind Castel Sant' Angelo. There is also an ice rink here in winter.

↑ Interior of St Peters, showing the papal altar, with Bernini's magnificent baldacchino (sculpted canopy)

*Michelangelo created the Pietà in 1499 when he was only 25.*

*From this balcony the pope blesses the faithful gathered in the piazza below.*

*The bronze doors from the old basilica were decorated with biblical reliefs by Filarete in 1439–45.*

→

The monumental spiral staircase designed by Giuseppe Momo in 1932

**2** 🗡️ 🚭 🍴 🛍️ 🎁

# VATICAN MUSEUMS

📍 C3 🏛️ Città del Vaticano (entrance in Viale Vaticano) 🚌 49 to entrance, 23, 81, 492, 990 Ⓜ️ Ottaviano San Pietro, Cipro 🕐 9am–6pm Mon–Sat (last admission 4pm), 9am–2pm last Sun of month (last admission 12:30pm; free entry); low-cut or sleeveless clothing, shorts, mini-skirts and hats are not allowed 🚫 Religious and public hols 🌐 museivaticani.va

Home to the Sistine Chapel and Raphael Rooms as well as to one of the world's most important art collections, the Vatican Museums are housed in palaces originally built for Renaissance popes Julius II, Innocent VIII and Sixtus IV. Most of the later additions were made in the 18th century, when priceless works of art accumulated by earlier popes were first put on show. Strung along 7 km (over 4 miles) of corridors, these incredible collections form one of the world's largest museums.

Among the Vatican's greatest treasures are its superlative Greek and Roman antiquities, together with the magnificent artifacts excavated from Egyptian and Etruscan tombs during the 19th century. Some of Italy's leading artists, such as Raphael, Michelangelo and Leonardo da Vinci, are represented in the Pinacoteca (art gallery) and parts of the former palaces, where they were employed by popes to decorate sumptuous apartments and galleries. The absolute highlights of this complex of museums are the Sistine Chapel and the Raphael Rooms, which should not be missed.

↑ The Cortile della Pigna, with a spherical bronze sculpture by Arnaldo Pomodoro

**Skipping the Queue**

Booking tickets in advance online is strongly recommended, preferably for an afternoon in the middle of the week. Saturday and Monday are the busiest days. Head straight to the Sistine Chapel, then make your way slowly backwards.

Gregorian Profane Museum

Spiral Staircase designed by Giuseppe Momo

Entrance

Belvedere Palace

Cortile della Pigna

Pio Clementino Museum

Pinacoteca

Gallery of the Candelabra

Gallery of the Tapestries

Gallery of the Maps

Borgia Apartment

Sistine Chapel

Bramante Staircase

Octagonal Courtyard

Egyptian Museum

↑ Highlights of the Vatican Museums complex

Raphael Rooms

**Timeline**

**1473**
△ Pope Sixtus IV builds Sistine Chapel.

*1503-13*
Pope Julius II starts Classical sculpture collection.

*1508*
▽ Raphael begins work on Rooms; Michelangelo begins painting the Sistine Chapel ceiling.

**1541**
Michelangelo's *Last Judgment* is unveiled.

**1655**
△ Bernini designs Royal Staircase.

**1758**
Founding of Gregorian Profane Museum.

**1771**
△ Founding of Pio Clementino Museum.

# HIGHLIGHTS OF THE VATICAN COLLECTION

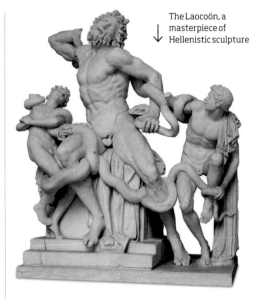

The Laocoön, a masterpiece of Hellenistic sculpture

## Pio Clementino Museum

The Vatican's prize pieces of Greek and Roman sculpture form the nucleus of this museum. Most of the works are Roman copies of lost ancient Greek originals, notably The Laocoön, a violently contorted Hellenistic work showing the Trojan priest Laocoön and his two sons struggling to escape from the writhing coils of a sea serpent. Also here is the Apollo Belvedere, considered a paragon of physical perfection by Renaissance artists, and the muscular, contorted Belvedere Torso, whose influence can be seen on Michelangelo's *ignudi* (male nudes) in the Sistine Chapel. A menagerie of animal-themed sculptures and mosaics are gathered together in the Room of the Animals.

On either side of the museum are two staircases. The original spiral stairway designed by Bramante in 1505 is open only to special tours. The modern double helix stairway, commonly called the Snail or Momo Staircase, was designed by Giuseppe Momo in 1932. It was inspired by Bramante's original.

## Did You Know?

Bramante designed the spiral staircase so that it could be ridden up on horseback.

## Gregorian Profane Museum

In a space infused with natural light, the Gregorian Profane museum spans Classical antiquity and includes large marble fragments from the Athens Parthenon, Roman copies of Greek sculptures and a striking mosaic from the Baths of Caracalla portraying full-length figures of athletes.

## Egyptian Museum

Ancient Egyptian cults and culture became extremely fashionable in Imperial Rome, and the collection here consists chiefly of Egyptian antiquities brought to the city to adorn buildings such as the Temple of Isis (which once stood near the Pantheon), Villa Adriana at Tivoli, and the Gardens of Sallust to the southeast of the Villa Borghese park. Also on display are painted mummy cases and tomb finds.

## Galleries of Maps, Tapestries and Candelabra

A long corridor is divided into three contiguous galleries. The Gallery of the Maps displays 16th-century maps of Italy's regions and papal territories painted as if Rome were literally at the centre of the world, with areas south

←

Classical sculptures gallery in the Pio Clementino Museum

The Gallery of the Maps; *(inset)* detail of a map by Egnazio Danti (1580)

→

**The Gallery of the Tapestries has early 16th- century silk, gold and wool tapestries woven in Brussels to designs inspired by Raphael.**

of Rome, such as Sicily and Calabria, appearing "upside down". The Gallery of the Tapestries has early 16th-century silk, gold and wool tapestries woven in Brussels to designs inspired by Raphael, while the Gallery of the Candelabra has immense marble candle holders.

## Pinacoteca

There are some splendid Renaissance works from all over Italy in the 18 rooms of the art gallery. Don't miss the fragments of frescoes of apostles and angel musicians in Room IV by Melozzo da Forlì or the exquisitely romantic Madonna paintings by Filippo

Lippi and Fra Angelico in Room III. Room VI is devoted to the fabulous world of the Crivelli brothers, 16th-century Venetian artists who depicted fragile doll-like Madonnas enclosed within elaborate painted frames of fruit and flowers. Raphael has an entire room (VIII) devoted to his work, notably *The Transfiguration*, which includes a woman with red-gold hair, who is thought to have been his lover, La Fornarina. Next door in Room IX is a single, rare work by Leonardo da Vinci depicting St Jerome in the desert. There are also notable paintings by Titian, Crespi, Veronese and Caravaggio.

### GALLERY GUIDE

The museum complex is absolutely vast: the Sistine Chapel and Raphael Rooms are 20 to 30 minutes' walk from the entrance, without allowing for any viewing time of other collections along the way. It is best, therefore, to be selective. Visitors have to follow a strict one-way system.

Michelangelo's breathtaking ceiling frescoes ↑

# SISTINE CHAPEL: THE CEILING

Although Michelangelo had studied fresco-painting under Ghirlandaio, until 1508 he had mainly gained fame through his work as a sculptor. Nonetheless, Pope Julius II commissioned him to paint the ceiling of the Sistine Chapel, which would result in one of the greatest masterpieces of Western art.

At the time, the ceiling was painted simply blue, with golden stars. Michelangelo frescoed over the old ceiling painting between 1508 and 1512, working on specially designed scaffolding. He persuaded the pope to give him a free hand, and spent four years painting 366 figures from the Old and New Testaments, illustrating the bibilical stories of the Creation of the World, the Fall of Man and the Coming of Christ. *Ignudi* (male nudes) are depicted around these frescoes. In the spandrels surrounding the vault are sibyls, prophetesses from pagan mythology, which, in the Renaissance, were adopted by Christian artists as figures who could foresee the Coming of Christ. The central painting, *The Creation of Adam*, portraying God reaching down from a cloudy heaven to create Adam, is one of the most reproduced religious paintings of all time.

### RESTORATION OF THE CEILING

From 1979 until 1994 a huge restoration programme was carried out. Five hundred years of soot, candle smoke and glue – along with breadcrumbs and retsina used by earlier restorers, and brush hairs and fingerprints left behind by Michelangelo – were removed. The faded, eggshell-cracked figures were discovered to have rose-petal skin, lustrous hair and to be wearing luscious strawberry-pink, lime-green, lemon and orange shot-silk robes. Critics were surprised that Michelangelo's palette was so bright.

←
*The Last Judgment* by Michelangelo, showing souls meeting the wrath of Christ

## Hall of Constantine

The frescoes here, started in 1517, were executed mainly by Raphael's pupils and show the triumph of Christianity over paganism, focusing on key moments in the life of Emperor Constantine.

## Room of Heliodorus

The theme here is divine intervention and includes *The Expulsion of Heliodorus from the Temple* and the dazzling *Liberation of St Peter*, in which an angel frees St Peter (a portrait of Julius II) from prison.

## Room of the Segnatura

The frescoes here celebrate the Renaissance ideal – the ability of the intellect to discover the truth. The key work is *The School of Athens* in which Raphael painted leading Greek philosophers in a vaulted hall.

## Room of the Fire in the Borgo

This celebrates a miracle in 847, when Pope Leo IV is said to have extinguished a fire in the quarter around the Vatican by making the sign of the cross.

# SISTINE CHAPEL: THE WALLS

## Wall Frescoes

The massive walls of the Sistine Chapel were frescoed by some of the finest artists of the 15th and 16th centuries. The twelve paintings by artists, including Perugino, Ghirlandaio, Botticelli and Signorelli, show parallel episodes from the lives of Moses and Christ. The altar wall was repainted by Michelangelo between 1534 and 1541.

## The Last Judgment

Twenty-four years after he had finished the Sistine ceiling, Michelangelo was commissioned by Pope Paul III Farnese to cover the altar wall of the chapel with a fresco of *The Last Judgment*. Michelangelo drew on Dante's *Inferno*. The painting is a bleak, harrowing work, showing the damned hurtling towards a putrid hell, the blessed being dragged up to heaven, and saints demanding vengeance for their martyrdoms, a theme chosen by the pope

### Did You Know?

Michelangelo's self-portrait is seen on the flayed skin held by St Bartholomew in *The Last Judgement*.

to warn Catholics to adhere to their faith in the turmoil of the Reformation.

# RAPHAEL ROOMS

In 1508, Pope Julius II asked Bramante to recommend an artist to redecorate his private suite of four rooms. Bramante suggested a young artist named Raphael. The resulting frescoes swiftly established Raphael as one of the leading artists in Rome, putting him on a par with Michelangelo. Raphael and his pupils took over 16 years to fresco the rooms.

→
Detail of *The School of Athens*, with Plato and Aristotle in the centre

←

Hall of Constantine, a celebration of the triumph of Christianity over paganism

**3** ⊘ Ⓜ ⊡ ⑪

# CASTEL SANT'ANGELO

📍 E4  🏠 Lungotevere Castello 50  🚌 23, 40, 62 to Lungotevere Vaticano or 34, 49, 87, 280, 492, 926, 990 to Piazza Cavour  🕑 9am-7:30pm daily  🌐 castelsantangelo. beniculturali.it

A massive brick cylinder rising from the banks of the Tiber, Castel Sant'Angelo began life in AD 139 as Emperor Hadrian's mausoleum. Since then it has served as a medieval citadel, a prison and as the residence of popes in times of political unrest.

The fortress takes its name from the vision that Pope Gregory the Great had of the Archangel Michael on this site. From the dank cells in the lower levels to the fine apartments of the Renaissance popes above, Castel Sant-Angelo is now a 58-room museum covering all aspects of the castle's history. Highlights include the Sala Paolina, decorated with illusionistic frescoes (1546–8) by Pellegrino Tibaldi and Perin del Vaga, and the armoury, which displays a wide range of weaponry of the times. The castle's terrace, scene of the last act of Puccini's opera *Tosca*, offers great views in every direction.

> **Castel Sant-Angelo is now a 58-room museum covering all aspects of the castle's history.**

*Timeline*

**271**
Tomb is incorporated into Aurelian Wall and fortified.

**1527**
Castle withstands siege during Sack of Rome.

**1870**
▽ Castle used as barracks and military prison.

**AD 130**
Hadrian begins family mausoleum.

**590**
△ Legendary date of appearance of Archangel Michael above the castle.

**1542–9**
Sala Paolina and apartments built for Pope Paul III.

↑ Courtyard of Honour with stone cannon-balls, once the castle's ammunition store

↑ Sala Paolina, decorated with frescoes for Pope Paul III Farnese

### PROTECTING THE POPE

The Vatican Corridor is an elevated 800-m (2,600-ft) passage that leads from the Vatican Palace to Castel Sant' Angelo. It was built in 1277 to provide an escape route when the pope was in danger. The pentagonal ramparts built around the castle during the 17th century improved its defences in times of siege.

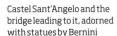

←
Castel Sant'Angelo and the bridge leading to it, adorned with statues by Bernini

# EXPERIENCE MORE

**4**

## Porta Santo Spirito

📍 D5 🏛 Via dei Penitenzieri
🚌 23, 34, 46, 62, 64, 98, 870,
881, 982

This gate is situated at what
was once the southern limit of
the "Leonine City", the area
enclosed within walls by Pope
Leo IV as a defence against
the Saracens, who had sacked
Rome in AD 845. The walls
measure 3 km (2 miles) in
circumference. Work on the
walls started in AD 846. Pope
Leo supervised the huge army
of labourers personally, and
the job was completed in four
years. He then consecrated his
massive feat of construction.

Since the time of Pope Leo
the walls have needed much
reinforcement and repair. The
gateway visible today at Porta
Santo Spirito was built by the
architect Antonio da Sangallo
the Younger in 1543–4. It is
framed by two huge bastions
that were added in 1564 by
Pope Pius IV Medici. Sadly,
Sangallo's design for a monumental entrance to the
Vatican was never completed;
the principal columns come to
an end somewhat abruptly in
a modern covering of cement.

**5**

## Santo Spirito in Sassia

📍 D4 🏛 Via dei Penitenzieri
12 📞 06-687 9310 🚌 23, 34,
46, 62, 64, 98, 870, 881, 982
🕐 7:30am–noon & 3–6:30pm
Mon-Sat, 9:30am–1pm &
3–6:30pm Sun

Built on the site of a church
erected by King Ine of Wessex,
who died in Rome in the 8th
century, this church is the
work of Antonio da Sangallo
the Younger. It was rebuilt
(1538–44) after the Sack of
Rome left it in ruins in 1527.
The façade was added under
Pope Sixtus V (1585–90). The
pretty bell tower is earlier,
dating from the reign of
Sixtus IV (1471–84).

---

**6**

## Hospital of
## Santo Spirito

📍 D5 🏛 Borgo Santo Spirito
2 📞 06-6835 2433 🚌 23, 34,
46, 62, 64 🕐 Complex and
chapel: for events only

The oldest hospital in Rome,
this is reputed to have been
founded as a result of a
nightmare experienced by

↑ Interior of Santo Spirito in
Sassia and *(inset)* detail
of *Coronation of the
Virgin Mary* by Nebbia

Pope Innocent III (1198–1216).
In the dream, an angel
showed him the bodies of
Rome's unwanted babies
dredged up from the River
Tiber in fishing nets. As a
result, the pope hastened
to build a hospice for sick
paupers. In 1475 the hospital
was reorganized by Pope
Sixtus IV to care for the poor
pilgrims expected for the
Holy Year. Sixtus's hospital
was a radical building.
Cloisters divided the different
types of patients; one area
is still reserved for orphans
and their nurses.

In order to guarantee
anonymity, unwanted infants
were passed through a revolv-
ing barrel-like contraption
called the *rota*, still visible to
the left of the central entrance
in Borgo Santo Spirito.
Martin Luther, who visited
in 1511, was shocked by the

number of abandoned children he saw, believing them to be "the sons of the pope himself".

In the centre, under the hospital's conspicuous drum, is an octagonal chapel, where Mass was said for patients. This room can be visited by prior arrangment, while the rest of the building still functions as a hospital.

---

## ❼ Palazzo del Commendatore

📍 D4 🏠 Borgo Santo Spirito 3 📞 06-6835 2353 🚌 23, 34, 46, 62, 64 🔓 Courtyard open to public

As director of the Hospital of Santo Spirito, the Commendatore not only oversaw the running of the hospital, he was also responsible for its estates and revenues. This important post was originally given to members of the pope's family.

The palazzo, built next door to the hospital, has a spacious 16th-century frescoed loggia appropriate to the dignity and sobriety of its owners. The frescoes represent the story of the founding of the Hospital of Santo Spirito. To the left of the entrance is the Spezieria, or Pharmacy. This still has the wheel used for grinding the bark of the cinchona tree to produce the drug quinine, first introduced here in 1632 by Jesuits from Peru as a cure for malaria.

Above the courtyard is a splendid clock (1827). The dial is divided into six; it was not until 1846 that the familiar division of the day into two periods of 12 hours was introduced in Rome by Pope Pius IX.

## ❽ Palazzo dei Convertendi

📍 D4 🏠 Via della Conciliazione 43 🚌 23, 34, 62, 64 🔒 To the public

With the building of Via della Conciliazione in the 1930s, Palazzo dei Convertendi was taken down and later moved to this new site nearby. The house, partly attributed to the architect Bramante, is where the artist Raphael died in 1520.

---

## ❾ Palazzo dei Penitenzieri

📍 D4 🏠 Via della Conciliazione 33 📞 06-6989 2930 🚌 23, 34, 62, 64 🕑 2:30–5pm Mon–Fri by appt only (fax) for groups

The palazzo owes its name to the fact that the place was once home to the confessors (penitenzieri) of St Peter's. Now partly housing the Hotel Columbus, it was originally built by Cardinal Domenico della Rovere between 1480 and 1490. The palazzo still bears the family's coat of arms, the oak tree (rovere means "oak"), on its graceful

courtyard well-head. On the cardinal's death, the palazzo was acquired by Cardinal Francesco Alidosi, Pope Julius II della Rovere's favourite. Suspected of treason, the cardinal was murdered in 1511 by the pope's nephew, the Duke of Urbino, who took over the palazzo. A few of the rooms of the palazzo still contain beautiful frescoes by Pinturicchio and his workshop. The most notable is Il Soffitto dei Semidei – a magnificent ceiling fresco depicting mythological and allegorical figures and animals.

→ Detail of a ceiling fresco by Pinturicchio in the Palazzo dei Penitenzieri

## ⑩ Santa Maria in Traspontina

📍 D4  🏛 Via della Conciliazione 14  📞 06-6880 6451  🚌 23, 34, 62, 64  🕐 6:30am-noon & 4-7:15pm Mon-Sat, 7:30am-1pm Sun

The church occupies the site of an ancient Roman pyramid, believed in the Middle Ages to have been the Tomb of Romulus. The pyramid was destroyed by Pope Alexander VI Borgia, but representations of it survive in the bronze doors at the entrance to St Peter's and in a Giotto triptych housed in the Vatican Pinacoteca (p293).

The present church was begun in 1566 to replace an earlier one which had been in the line of fire of the cannons defending Castel Sant'Angelo during the Sack of Rome in 1527. The papal artillery officers therefore insisted that the dome of the new church should be as low as possible, so it was built without a supporting drum. The first chapel to the right is dedicated to the gunners' patron saint, Santa Barbara, and is decorated with warlike motifs. In the third chapel on the left are two columns, popularly thought to be the ones which SS Peter and Paul were bound to before going to their martyrdom nearby.

## ⑪ The Borgo

📍 D4  🚌 23, 34, 40, 62

The Borgo's name derives from the German burg, meaning "town". Rome's Borgo is where the first pilgrims to St Peter's were housed in hostels and hospices, often for quite lengthy periods. The first of these foreign colonies, called "schools", was founded in AD 725 by a Saxon, King Ine of Wessex, who wished to live a life of penance and to be buried near the Tomb of St Peter. These days hotels and hostels have made the Borgo a colony of inter-national pilgrims once again. Much of the area's character was lost after redevelopment

The Palazzo di Giustizia, with the Ponte Umberto crossing the Tiber in the foreground

### Did You Know?

Raphael and Michelangelo count among the Borgo area's most famous past residents.

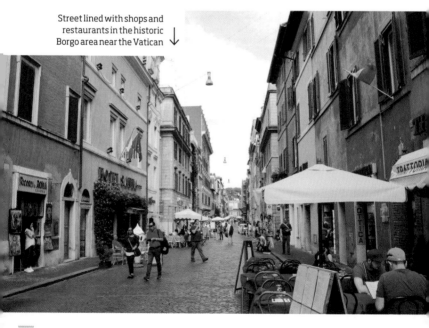

Street lined with shops and restaurants in the historic Borgo area near the Vatican ↓

in the 1930s, but it is still enjoyable to stroll the old narrow streets on either side of Via della Conciliazione.

---

**12**

## Palazzo Torlonia

📍D4 🏛 Via della Conciliazione 30 🚌23, 34, 40, 62, 64 🚫To the public

The pretty palazzo was built in the late 15th century by the wealthy Cardinal Adriano Castellesi, in a style closely resembling Palazzo della Cancelleria *(p170)*. The cardinal was a much-travelled rogue, who collected vast revenues from the bishopric of Bath and Wells which he was given by his friend King Henry VII of England. In return, he gave Henry his palazzo for use as the seat of the English ambassador to the Holy See. Castellesi was finally stripped of his cardinalate by Pope Leo X Medici and disappeared from history.

Since then the palazzo has had many owners and tenants. In the 17th century it was rented for a time by Queen Christina of Sweden. The Torlonia family, who acquired the building in 1820, owed its fortune to the financial genius of shopkeeper-turned-banker Giovanni Torlonia. He lent money to the impoverished Roman nobility and bought up their property during the Napoleonic Wars.

---

**13**

## Palazzo di Giustizia

📍F4 🏛 Piazza Cavour 🚌34, 49, 70, 87, 186, 280, 492, 913, 926, 990 🚫To the public

The monumental Palazzo di Giustizia (Palace of Justice) was built between 1889 and 1910 to house the national law courts. Its riverside façade is crowned with a bronze chariot and fronted by giant statues of the great men of Italian law.

The building was supposed to embody the new order replacing the injustices of papal rule, but it has never endeared itself to the Romans. It was soon dubbed the Palazzaccio (roughly, "the ugly old palazzo") both for its appearance and for the nature of its business. By the 1970s the building was collapsing under its own weight, but it has since been restored.

---

# EAT & DRINK

Home to modern eateries, small bistros and old pilgrim taverns, the Vatican area is filled with places to enjoy a well-earned plate of food and a restorative glass of wine after visiting the museums.

### Dal Toscano
📍C3 🏛 Via Germanico 58 🌐ristorantedal toscano.it

€€€

---

### Franchi
📍D3 🏛 Via Cola di Rienzo 200 📞06-686 5564

€€€

---

### Il Simposio
📍E3 🏛 Piazza Cavour 16 🌐ilsimposioroma.it

€€€

# A SHORT WALK

# A TOUR OF THE VATICAN

**Distance** 1 km (0.6 mile) **Nearest metro**
Cipro, Ottaviano San Pietro **Time** 15 minutes

The Vatican, a centre of power for Catholics all over the world and a sovereign state since February 1929, is ruled by the pope. About 1,000 people live here, staffing the Vatican's facilities. These include a post office and shops; Vatican radio, broadcasting to the world in over 20 languages; a daily newspaper (*L'Osservatore Romano*); Vatican offices and a publishing house.

*The Grotto of Lourdes is a replica of the grotto in the southwest of France, where in 1858 the Virgin appeared to St Bernadette.*

*Papal heliport*

*Radio Vatican is broadcast from this tower, part of the Leonine Wall built in 847.*

*The Madonna of Guadalupe shows the miraculous image of the Madonna which appeared on the cloak of an indigenous Mexican in 1531.*

*The Vatican Railway Station, opened in 1930, connects with the line from Rome to Viterbo, but is now used only for freight.*

*The Chapel of St Peter is in the Grottoes under St Peter's basilica. The rich marble decoration was added by Clement VIII at the end of the 16th century (p288).*

**Did You Know?**

If you visit every museum in the Vatican Museum complex you will have walked over 7 km (4 miles).

*The Papal Audience Chamber, by Pier Luigi Nervi, was opened in 1971. It seats up to 12,000.*

*The information office gives details of tours of the Vatican Gardens.*

PIAZZA DEL SANT'UFFIZIO

*Piazza San Pietro was laid out by Bernini between 1656 and 1667. The narrow space in front of the church opens out into an enormous ellipse flanked by colonnades.*

→

The elaborate
Eagle Fountain
in the Vatican
Gardens

**Locator Map**
*For more detail see p284*

*The Eagle
Fountain was
built to celebrate
the arrival of
water from the
Acqua Paola
aqueduct
at the Vatican.
The eagle is the
Borghese crest.*

*The Casina of Pius IV
is a delightful
summerhouse in the
Vatican Gardens built
by Pirro Ligorio in the
mid-16th century.*

*The Cortile della Pigna
is mostly the work of
Bramante. The niche for
the pine cone, once a
Roman fountain, was
added by Pirro Ligorio
in 1562.*

| 0 metres | | 150 |
| 0 yards | | 150 |

↗ N

*Entrance to
Vatican Museums*

**FINISH**

*Raphael's Madonna of Foligno
(1513) is just one of the many
Renaissance masterpieces in
the Vatican Museums (p290).*

*The Galleon Fountain is a
perfect scale model of a
17th-century ship in lead,
brass and copper. It was
made by a Flemish artist for
Pope Paul V.*

VIA DI PORTA ANGELICA

PIAZZA
SAN PIETRO

PIAZZA
PIO XII

**START**

*The obelisk was erected here
in 1586 with the help of 150
horses and 47 winches.*

→

Piazza San Pietro
and obelisk in front
of St Peter's basilica

# VIA VENETO

In Imperial Rome, this was a suburb where rich families owned luxurious villas and gardens. Ruins from this era can be seen in the excavations in Piazza Sallustio, named after the most extensive gardens in the area, the Horti Sallustiani. After the Sack of Rome in the 5th century, the area reverted to open countryside. Not until the 17th century did it recover its lost splendour, with the building of Palazzo Barberini and the now-vanished Villa Ludovisi. When Rome became capital of Italy in 1870, the Ludovisi sold their land for development. They kept a plot for a new house, but tax on the profits from the sale was so high, they had to sell that too. By 1900, Via Veneto had become a street of smart grand hotels and cafés. It featured prominently in Fellini's 1960 film *La Dolce Vita*, a scathing satire on the lives of film stars and the idle rich, but since then has lost its position as the meeting place of the famous.

# VIA VENETO

**Experience**
1. Via Veneto
2. Palazzo Barberini
3. Santa Maria della Concezione and Capuchin Crypt
4. Fontana delle Api
5. Fontana del Tritone
6. Santa Susanna
7. Santa Maria della Vittoria

**Drink**
1. Il Giardino Hotel Eden
2. Doney Café

Villa Borghese

PIAZZA DI SPAGNA AND VILLA BORGHESE
*p136*

PORTA PINCIANA

LARGO FEDERICO FELLINI

Veneto/Sardegna

Villa Medici

CAMPO MARZIO

Casino dell'Aurora

Palazzo Margherita

M Spagna

Scalinata della Trinità dei Monti

PIAZZA DI SPAGNA

Museo Keats-Shelley

PIAZZA MIGNANELLI

Via Veneto

Santa Maria della Concezione and Capuchin Capuchin Crypt

Fontana delle Api

Barberini M

PIAZZA BARBERINI

Fontana del Tritone

Palazzo Barberini

TREVI

Accademia di San Luca

LARGO CHIGI

Giardini del Quirinale

Fontana di Trevi

Palazzo del Quirinale

# EXPERIENCE

## ❶
## Via Veneto

📍 J3 🚌 52, 53, 63, 80, 116, 119, 160 and many routes to Piazza Barberini
Ⓜ Barberini

Via Veneto descends in a lazy curve from the Porta Pinciana to Piazza Barberini, lined in its upper reaches with exuberant late 19th-century hotels and canopied pavement cafés. It was laid out in 1879 over a large estate sold by the Ludovisi family in the great building boom of Rome's first years as capital of Italy. Palazzo Margherita, intended to be the new Ludovisi family palazzo, was completed in 1890. It now houses the American embassy.

In the 1960s this was the most glamorous street in Rome, its cafés patronized by film stars and plagued by paparazzi. Most of the people drinking in the cafés today are tourists, as film stars now seem to prefer the bohemian atmosphere of Trastevere or the luxury of the Parioli neighbourhood.

↑ Detail of Pietro da Cortona's ceiling fresco in Palazzo Barberini

## ❷
## Palazzo Barberini

📍 J4 🏛 Via delle Quattro Fontane 13 🚌 52, 53, 61, 62, 63, 80, 116, 492, 590
Ⓜ Barberini 🕐 10am–6pm Thu–Sun (booking recommended) 🚫 1 Jan, 25 Dec
🌐 barberinicorsini.org

When Maffeo Barberini became Pope Urban VIII in 1623 he planned a grand palace for his family on the fringes of the city. Architect Carlo Maderno designed it as a rural villa, with wings into the surrounding gardens. Maderno died in 1629 and Bernini took over, assisted by Borromini.

The pediments on some of the top-floor windows, and the oval staircase inside, are almost certainly by Borromini.

The most striking of the sumptuous rooms is the Gran Salone, with an illusionistic ceiling fresco by Pietro da Cortona. The palazzo also houses paintings from the 13th to the 16th centuries, with notable works by Filippo Lippi, El Greco and Caravaggio, as well as Guido Reni's *Beatrice Cenci*, the young woman executed for planning her father's murder (p175), and *La Fornarina*, traditionally thought to be a portrait of Raphael's mistress (p262), although not necessarily painted by him.

---

# DRINK

### Il Giardino Hotel Eden
A historic bar, revamped in 2017, the Eden's rooftop area has vast windows that offer stunning views of the city - to be enjoyed with an expertly mixed Negroni in hand. Service is top-notch.

📍 J3 🏛 Via Ludovisi 49
🌐 dorchester collection.com

---

### Doney Café
In the heart of Via Veneto, Doney re-creates *Dolce Vita* glamour with vast chandeliers and retro furnishings. Come at *aperitivo* time for a cocktail and a spot of people-watching. There's a pricey restaurant, too.

📍 J3 🏛 Via Veneto 125
🌐 restaurantdoney.com

← Elegant Via Veneto, lined with numerous chic hotels, cafés and shops

### ❸
### Santa Maria della Concezione and Capuchin Crypt

📍 J3 🏛 Via Veneto 27 🚌 52, 53, 61, 62, 63, 80, 116, 119 Ⓜ Barberini Church: 🕐 7am–1pm & 3–6pm

Pope Urban VIII's brother, Antonio Barberini was a cardinal and a Capuchin friar. In 1626 he founded this plain church at what is now the foot of the Via Veneto. When he died he was buried not, like most cardinals, in a grand marble sarcophagus, but below a simple flagstone near the altar, with the bleak epitaph in Latin: "Here lies dust, ashes, nothing".

The grim reality of death is illustrated even more graphically in the **Museum and Capuchin Crypt** beneath the church, where generations of Capuchin friars decorated the walls of the five vaulted chapels with the bones and skulls of their departed brethren. In all, some 4,000 skeletons were used over about 100 years to create this macabre *memento mori* started in the late 17th century. There are also some complete skeletons, including one of a Barberini princess who died as a child. At the exit, a Latin inscription reads: "What you are, we used to be. What we are, you will be."

**Museum and Capuchin Crypt**
🕐 9am–7pm daily

### ❹
### Fontana delle Api

📍 J4 🏛 Piazza Barberini 🚌 52, 53, 61, 62, 63, 80, 116, 119 Ⓜ Barberini

The fountain of the bees (*api*, symbol of the Barberini family) is one of Bernini's more modest works. Tucked away in a corner of Piazza Barberini, it is quite easy to miss. Dating from 1644, it pays homage to Pope Urban VIII Barberini, and features rather crab-like bees which appear to be sipping the water as it dribbles down into the basin.

### ❺
### Fontana del Tritone

📍 J4 🏛 Piazza Barberini 🚌 52, 53, 61, 62, 63, 80, 116, 119 Ⓜ Barberini

In the centre of busy Piazza Barberini is one of Bernini's liveliest creations, the Triton Fountain. It was created for Pope Urban VIII Barberini in 1642, shortly after the completion of his palace on the ridge above. Acrobatic dolphins stand on their heads, twisting their tails together to support a huge scallop shell on which the sea god Triton kneels, blowing a spindly column of water up into the air through a conch shell.

### ❻
### Santa Susanna

📍 K4 🏛 Via XX Settembre 14 🚌 60, 61, 62, 492, 910 Ⓜ Repubblica 🕐 For restoration

Santa Susanna's most striking feature is its vigorous Baroque façade by Carlo Maderno, finished in 1603. Christians have worshipped on the site since at least the 4th century. In the nave, there are four huge frescoes by Baldassarre Croce (1558–1628), painted to resemble tapestries. These depict scenes from the life of Susanna, an obscure Roman saint martyred here, and the rather better-known life of the Old Testament Susanna, who was spotted bathing in her husband's garden by two lecherous judges.

Santa Susanna is usually the Catholic church for Americans in Rome. It is closed for restoration, so the American church now meets at St Patrick's.

↑ Bernini's playful Fontana del Tritone in Piazza Barberini

### ❼
### Santa Maria della Vittoria

📍 K3 🏛 Via Settembre 17 📞 06-4274 0571 🚌 60, 61, 62, 492, 910 Ⓜ Repubblica 🕐 8:30am–noon & 3:30–6pm daily

This intimate Baroque church has a lavishly decorated candlelit interior. It contains one of Bernini's most ambitious sculptural works, *Ecstasy of St Teresa* (1646), the centrepiece of the Cornaro Chapel, built to resemble a miniature theatre. It even has an audience: sculptures of the chapel's benefactor, Cardinal Federico Cornaro, and his ancestors sit in boxes, as if watching the scene in front of them.

Visitors may be shocked or thrilled by the apparently physical nature of St Teresa's ecstasy. She lies on a cloud, her mouth half open and her eyelids closed, with rippling drapery covering her body. Looking over her with a smile, which from different angles can appear either tender or cruel, is a curly-haired angel holding an arrow with which he is about to pierce the saint's body for a second time. The marble figures are framed and illuminated by rays of divine light materialized in bronze.

# A SHORT WALK
# VIA VENETO

**Distance** 2 km (1.2 miles) **Nearest metro** Barberini
**Time** 30 minutes

The streets around Via Veneto, though within the walls of ancient Rome, contain little dating from before the unification of Italy in 1861. With its hotels, restaurants, bars and travel agencies, the area is the centre of 21st-century tourism in the way that Piazza di Spagna was the hub of the tourist trade in the Rome of the 18th-century Grand Tour. However, glimpses of the old city can be seen among the modern streets. These include Santa Maria della Concezione, the church of the Capuchin friars, whose convent once stood in its own gardens. In the 17th century Palazzo Barberini was built here for the powerful papal family. Bernini's Fontana del Tritone and Fontana delle Api have stood in Piazza Barberini since it was the meeting place of carts entering the city from surrounding vineyards.

*Santa Maria della Concezione and Capuchin Crypt is best known for the macabre collection of bones in its crypt (p311).*

*Fontana delle Api – Bernini's drinking fountain – is decorated with bees, an emblem of his Barberini patrons (p311).*

FINISH

PIAZZA BARBERINI

START

VIA VENETO

VIA DI SAN BASILIO

*Bernini's muscular sea god at the centre of the Fontana del Tritone has been spouting water skywards for over 350 years (p311).*

VIA DI SAN NICOLA DA TOLENTINO

*Barberini station*

VIA BARBERINI

## Did You Know?

Via Veneto derives its name from the Italian victory over Austro-Hungarian troops in World War I.

VIA XX SETTEMBRE

*Pietro da Cortona worked on his spectacular ceiling fresco The Triumph of Divine Providence in the Palazzo Barberini between 1633 and 1639 (p310).*

A pavilion is all that remains of the Casino dell'Aurora Ludovisi estate that once occupied most of this quarter of Rome.

**Locator Map**
For more detail see p308

The Porta Pinciana was built in AD 403. Only the central arch of white travertine is original.

VIA VENETO

Via Veneto, built during the redevelopment of Rome at the end of the 19th century and lined with smart hotels and spacious pavement cafés, enjoyed its heyday during the 1950s and 1960s.

0 metres    75    N
0 yards     75

VIA BISSOLATI

Santa Susanna is dedicated to a martyr executed during Diocletian's persecution of Christians in the 3rd century AD (p311).

The highlight of the Baroque Santa Maria della Vittoria is the Cornaro Chapel, designed to resemble a theatre. At its centre is Bernini's thrilling sculpture of The Ecstasy of St Teresa (p311).

LARGO DI SANTA SUSANNA

→

Fontana del Tritone, designed by Bernini, in Piazza Barberini

# BEYOND
# THE CENTRE

The more inquisitive visitor to Rome may wish to try a few excursions to the large parks and the catacombs on the Via Appia Antica on the outskirts of the city. With a day to spare, you can explore the villas of Tivoli and the ruins of the ancient Roman port of Ostia. More modern sights include the EUR suburb, built in the Fascist era, and the Resistance memorial at the Fosse Ardeatine.

**Must See**

1 Ostia Antica

**Experience More**

2 MAXXI (National Museum of 21st-Century Art)
3 Audiorium Parco della Musica
4 Villa Ada
5 Catacombs of Priscilla
6 Quartiere Coppedè
7 MACRO (Museo d'Arte Contemporanea di Roma)
8 Santa Costanza
9 Sant'Agnese fuori le Mura
10 Via Appia Antica
11 Catacombs of San Callisto
12 Catacombs of San Sebastiano
13 Catacombs of Domitilla
14 Fosse Ardeatine
15 Tomb of Cecilia Metella
16 EUR
17 Cinecittà Si Mostra
18 Foro Italico
19 Centrale Montemartini
20 San Paolo fuori le Mura
21 Villa Doria Pamphilj
22 Tivoli
23 Villa d'Este
24 Hadrian's Villa
25 Villa Gregoriana

MAXXI, the national museum of contemporary art

❶ ⬦ ⬚ ⬚

# OSTIA ANTICA

🏠 Viale dei Romagnoli 717. Site is 25 km (16 miles) southwest of Rome
Ⓜ Piramide, then train from Porta San Paolo station ⏰ 8:30am–1 hour
before sunset Tue–Sun Ⓦ ostiaantica.beniculturali.it

With its ivy- and creeper-covered walls rising from long grass,
scattered in spring with wild flowers, the remains of the ancient
Roman port of Ostia are among the most extensive in Italy.

Ostia was originally built on the coast, but over
the centuries silt from the Tiber has shifted the
coastline further west, and the site is now
several kilometres from the sea. In Republican
times Ostia was Rome's main commercial port
and a military base protecting the mouth of
the Tiber. It continued to flourish through
Imperial times until the 4th century, when the
harbour began to silt up, covering the old city
with sand and mud. The ruins are remarkably
well preserved and give a good picture of life
under the Roman Empire. People of all social
classes and from all over the Mediterranean
lived and worked here.

The main road through the town, the
Decumanus Maximus, would have been filled
with hurrying citizens, avoiding the jostling
carriages and cars, while tradesmen pursued
their business under the porticoes. The public
buildings included bathhouses, such as the
Baths of the Cisarrii (wagoners), the theatre,
the Forum and temples.

Mosaic of an elephant outside a shop of a North African merchant on Piazzale delle Corporazioni. The square was surrounded by businesses, each with a mosaic outside depicting a trade.

INSIDER TIP
**Picnic**

Still wild in parts, Ostia Antica is a lovely, relaxing site for a picnic accompanied by some ancient history. For picnic ingredients, shop at a great deli, Volpetti (Via Marmorata 47A; Tel 06-574 2352), near the Porta San Paolo station.

A carved stone mask displayed outside the theatre. Beneath the brick arches supporting the tiers of seats were taverns and shops

Ruins of shops, houses and apartment blocks at Ostia Antica

### THERMOPOLIUM OF VIA DIANA

The Thermopolium was a bar that served wine and hot snacks. The ruins retain an L-shaped counter and a beautiful fresco showing carrots, onions and chickpeas.

# EXPERIENCE MORE

## ② MAXXI (National Museum of 21st Century Art)

🏠 Via Guido Reni 4A 🚌 53, 217, 225, 910 🚊 2 🕒 11am–8pm Tue–Sun (to 7pm on Wed, Thu & Sun) 🚫 1 May, 25 Dec 🌐 maxxi.art

Along with the nearby Parco della Musica, MAXXI, the National Museum of 21st Century Art, has put Rome on the contemporary arts map. Completed in 2009, it is located in a stunning building designed by the late architect Zaha Hadid. The museum showcases emerging Italian and international artists. An impressive amount of space is also given over to architecture. Some of the biggest names represented include Renzo Piano, Gilbert and George, and Paolo Portoghesi.

## ③ Auditorium Parco della Musica

🏠 Viale Pietro de Coubertin 30 🚊 2 🕒 11:30am–6pm (to 8pm in summer) 🌐 auditorium.com

Designed by Renzo Piano and opened in 2002, the Auditorium Parco della Musica is not merely a beautiful concert venue but a multi-functional space with an outdoor amphitheatre, shops, restaurants and play area – and an ice rink in winter, a popular leisure space with Romans. Renzo Piano studied acoustics with contemporary composers Luciano Berio and Luigi Nono; guided tours of the auditoriums reveal how he applied the technology of musical instruments to architecture with the use of complex geometries and fine wood.

## ④ Villa Ada

🏠 Via Salaria 265 🚌 14 🚊 3, 19

Rome's second-largest park (after Villa Doria Pamphilj, *p327*), Villa Ada cuts a green swathe through the north of Rome and features land-scaped gardens, ornamental lakes and umbrella-pine-shaded lawns that lead the way to wilder wooded hills.

A royal hunting ground and residence belonging to the House of Savoy, the properties were sold in 1878 to a Swiss count who named them after his wife. The villa is now the Egyptian embassy. From late June to August,

↑ A showcase for 21st-century art, the cutting-edge MAXXI and *(inset)* its interior

Villa Ada hosts the free world-music festival Roma Incontra il Mondo, with concerts staged on the lakeside.

## Catacombs of Priscilla

⌂ Via Salaria 🚌 63, 92, 310 ☎ 06-4542 8493 ⏱ 9am-noon & 2- 5pm Tue-Sun, by appt only 🌐 catacombe priscilla.com

Tunnelling for 15 km (9 miles) on three different levels below the extensive estate of an aristocratic 1st-century AD Roman woman known only as Priscilla, these catacombs – rarely visited by tourists – are run by a small community of Benedictine sisters. They hold the tombs of more than 40,000 Christians. The sisters give personal guided tours, during which they point out tiny, telling details. The tours take in both the humble burial places of the poor and the more elaborate frescoed tombs of the wealthy. The catacombs also contain the oldest-known image of the Madonna and Child, dating back to the late 1st or early 2nd century AD.

### ⑥

## Quartiere Coppedè

⌂ Between Via Salaria and Via Tagliamento 🚌 3, 52, 53, 217, 360, 910, 926 🚋 3, 19

The Coppedè neighbourhood was created by Art Nouveau Florentine architect Gino Coppedè between 1913 and 1927 as a prestigious residential enclave for wealthy Ligurian bankers. Coppedè's imagination was given free rein, and the result is an architectural fantasia, a fairytale world that features Tuscan turrets, Venetian pinnacles, Moorish arches, Gothic gargoyles, medieval frescoes and gingerbread-house aesthetics. Start your visit on Via Tagliamento, entering via a mighty arch-way hung with an elaborate wrought-iron lamp. This emerges onto a piazza dominated by the Fontana delle Rane, which is adorned with a dozen stone frogs. In all, there are around 40 villas and apartment buildings around the square, the highlight of which is the Villini delle Fate, a complex of three villas, embellished with everything from the signs of the zodiac and a lion of St Mark to falconers and Franciscan monks.

---

🔍 HIDDEN GEM
**Whimsical Architecture**

Truly unique and unlike any other architectural style, the quirky Quartiere Coppedè provides quite a contrast to the classic Renaissance and Baroque styles in most of the rest of the city.

**7**

## Museo d'Arte Contemporanea di Roma (MACRO)

⌖ Via Nizza 138  🚌 36, 60, 90
🕐 11am–8pm Tue–Thu & Sun, 11am–10pm Fri & Sat
🌐 museomacro.it

The historic Peroni beer factory is home to the MACRO gallery of contemporary art. It has cutting-edge architecture featuring coloured lights, glass and exposed steel. As well as a permanent collection of late 20th-century art, with works by artists such as Carla Accardi and Mario Schifano, there are often interesting temporary exhibitions showcasing the latest on the local and national scene. Free screenings of oddball, experimental and arthouse short films are held in a niche just off the atrium.

> **MACRO has cutting-edge architecture featuring coloured lights, glass and exposed steel.**

**8** 

## Santa Costanza

⌖ Via Nomentana 349
📞 06-8620 5456  🚌 36, 60, 84, 90  Ⓜ S Agnese Annibaliano  🕐 9am–noon & 3–6pm Mon–Sat, 3–6pm Sun

The round church of Santa Costanza was first built as a mausoleum for Emperor Constantine's daughters, Constantia and Helena, in the early 4th century. The dome and its drum are supported by a circular arcade resting on 12 magnificent pairs of granite columns. The ambulatory that runs around the outside of the central arcade has a barrel-vaulted ceiling decorated with wonderful 4th-century mosaics of flora and fauna and charming scenes of a Roman grape harvest. In a niche on the far side of the church from the entrance is a replica of Constantia's ornately carved porphyry sarcophagus. The original was moved to the Vatican Museums in 1790.

Constantia was described by the historian Marcellinus as fury incarnate and guilty of goading her equally unpleasant husband Hannibalianus to violence. Her canonization was probably the result of some confusion with a saintly nun of the same name.

---

**9**

## Sant'Agnese fuori le Mura

⌖ Via Nomentana 349  📞 06-8620 5456  🚌 36, 60, 84, 90  Ⓜ S Agnese Annibaliano  🕐 8am–7pm Mon–Sat, between services Sun & public hols

The church of Sant'Agnese stands among a group of early Christian buildings which includes the ruins of a covered cemetery, some extensive **catacombs** and the crypt where the 13-year-old martyr St Agnes was buried in AD 304. Agnes was exposed naked by order of Emperor Diocletian, furious that she should have rejected the advances of a young man at his court, but her hair miraculously grew to protect her modesty.

The interior of Rome's contemporary art museum, MACRO, on Via Nizza ↑

Though considerably altered over the centuries, the form and much of the structure of the 4th-century basilica remain intact. In the 7th-century apse mosaic St Agnes appears as a bejewelled Byzantine empress. According to tradition she appeared like this eight days after her death, holding a white lamb. Every year on 21 January two lambs are blessed on the church altar and a vestment called the *pallium* is woven from their wool. Every newly appointed archbishop is sent a *pallium* by the pope.

**Catacombs**

⊛ ⊛ ⬤ By appt only ✖ Nov

---

**10**

# Via Appia Antica

🚌 118, 218 🌐 parcoappia antica.it

The first part of the Via Appia was built in 312 BC by the Censor Appius Claudius Caecus. When it was extended to the ports of Benevento, Taranto and Brindisi in 190 BC, the road became Rome's link with its empire in the East. It was the route taken by the funeral processions of the dictator Sulla (78 BC) and Emperor Augustus (AD 14) and it was along this road that St Paul was led as a prisoner to Rome in AD 56. Abandoned in the Middle Ages, the road was restored by Pope Pius IV in the mid-16th century. It is lined with ruined family tombs and collective burial places. Beneath the fields on each side is a vast maze of catacombs. You can still walk along the Via Appia Antica in the footsteps of many ancient Romans (*p328*). Today the road starts at Porta San Sebastiano (*p238*). Major Christian sights include the church of Domine Quo Vadis, built where St Peter is said to have met Christ while fleeing from Rome, and the Catacombs of San Callisto and San Sebastiano. The tombs lining the road include those

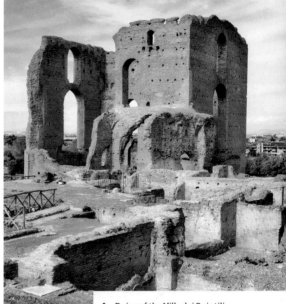

↑ Ruins of the Villa dei Quintili, a luxurious private residence in the 2nd century

of Cecilia Metella (*p323*) and Romulus (son of Emperor Maxentius) who died in 309. The remains of an ancient sumptuous private residence and baths, **Villa dei Quintili**, are 4 km (2.5 miles) away. It has some impressive mosaic floors, and the guided tour of the archaeological site includes entry to a small museum.

**Villa dei Quintili**

⊛ ⊛ ⬤ Via Appia Nuova 1092 ☎ 06-3996 7700 & 06-712 9121 ⬤ 9am-approx 1 hour before sunset Tue-Sun

---

**11** ⊛ ⊛ 🖥 🏛

# Catacombs of San Callisto

⬤ Via Appia Antica 126 🚌 118, 218 ⬤ 9am-noon & 2-5pm Thu-Tue, by appt only ✖ 1 Jan, late Jan-late Feb, Easter Sun & 25 Dec 🌐 catacombe.roma.it

In burying their dead in underground cemeteries outside the city walls, the

early Christians were simply obeying the laws of the time rather than doing so because of persecution. So many saints were buried in the various catacombs that they went on to become shrines and places of pilgrimage.

The vast Catacombs of San Callisto are laid out over four different levels, and only certain parts may be explored by visitors. The rooms and connecting passageways are hewn out of volcanic tufa. The dead were placed in niches known as *loculi*, which were able to hold two or three bodies. The most important rooms were decorated with stucco and frescoes.

The area that can be visited includes the Crypt of the Popes, where many of the early popes were buried (16 pontiffs in all), and the Crypt of Santa Cecilia, where the saint's body was discovered in 820 before being moved to her church in Trastevere (*p266*). Dozens of martyrs were also buried in these catacombs.

Ancient frescoes in the Catacombs of Domitilla, the largest catacombs in Rome

### 12 Catacombs of San Sebastiano

🏛 Via Appia Antica 136
📞 06-785 0350 🚌 118, 218
🕐 10am-4:30pm Mon-Sat
📅 1 Jan, mid-Nov-mid-Dec, 25 Dec 🌐 catacombe.org

The 17th-century church of San Sebastiano, situated above the catacombs, occupies the site of a basilica. Preserved at the entrance to the catacombs is the *triclia*, a building that once stood above ground and was used by mourners for taking funeral refreshments. Its walls are covered with graffiti that invokes St Peter and St Paul, whose remains may have been moved here during one of the periods of persecution.

### 13 Catacombs of Domitilla

🏛 Via delle Sette Chiese 282 🚌 218, 716 🕐 9am-noon & 2-5pm Wed-Mon (summer: 5:30pm) 📅 Mid-Dec-mid-Jan, Easter Sun 🌐 domitilla.info

This network of catacombs is the largest in Rome. Many of the tombs from the 1st

and 2nd centuries AD have no Christian connection. In the burial chambers there are frescoes depicting both Classical and Christian scenes, including one of the earliest depictions of Christ as the *Good Shepherd*. Above the catacombs stands the basilica of Santi Nereo e Achilleo. After centuries of rebuilding and restoration, little remains of the original 4th-century church.

### 14 Fosse Ardeatine

🏛 Via Ardeatina 174
🚌 218, 716 🕐 8:15am-3:30pm Mon-Fri, 8:15am-4:30pm Sat & Sun (museum closes 15 minutes earlier) 📅 Public hols 🌐 mausoleo fosseardeatine.it

On the evening of 24 March 1944, Nazi forces took 335 prisoners to this abandoned quarry south of Rome and shot them at point blank range. The execution was in reprisal for a bomb attack that had killed 32 German soldiers. The victims included various political prisoners, 73 Jews and ten other civilians, among them a priest and a 14-year-old boy. The Germans blew up the tunnels where the massacre had taken place, but

a local peasant had witnessed the scene and later helped find the corpses. The site is now a memorial to the values of the Resistance against the Nazi occupation, which gave birth to the modern Italian Republic (*p58*). A forbidding bunker-like monument houses the rows of identical tombs containing the victims.

Beside it is a museum of the Resistance with interesting works of modern sculpture including *The Martyrs*, by Francesco Coccia, and the gates shaped like a wall of thorns by Mirko Basaldella.

---

## EAT

### Eataly

This cathedral to gastronomy is a must for anyone who loves to eat or cook. As well as a huge number of niche producers of everything from handmade pasta to biodynamic wine, there are bars, restaurants, tastings and a packed calendar of events.

🏛 Piazzale 12 Ottobre 1492 🌐 eataly.net

€ € €

## 15 Tomb of Cecilia Metella

Via Appia Antica, km 3
06-3996 7700 118, 660 9am-approx 1 hr before sunset Tue-Sun

One of the most famous landmarks on the Via Appia Antica is the huge tomb built for the noblewoman Cecilia Metella. Her father and husband were rich patricians and successful generals of late Republican Rome, but hardly anything is known about the woman herself.

In 1302 Pope Boniface VIII donated the tomb to his family, the Caetani. They incorporated it in a fortified castle that blocked the Via Appia, allowing them to control the traffic on the road and exact tolls.

Across the road are the remains of the early 14th-century church of San Nicola.

## 16 EUR

170, 671, 714 and other routes M EUR Fermi, EUR Palasport

The Esposizione Universale di Roma (EUR), a suburb south of the city, was built for an international exhibition, a kind of "Work Olympics", that was planned by Mussolini for 1942 to celebrate Fascist Italy but never took place because of World War II. The architecture was intended to glorify Fascism and the style of the buildings is very over-blown and rhetorical. The eerie Palazzo della Civiltà del Lavoro (The Palace of the Civilization of Work) is an unmistakable landmark.

The scheme was completed in the 1950s. In terms of town planning, EUR has been quite successful and people are still keen to live here owing to its modern amenities. Many businesses have offices in the area. The great marble halls and large austere buildings inspired by ancient Imperial Roman architecture house government offices and a number of museums.

The library of the SIAE building houses the **Burcardo Theatre Museum**, featuring theatre literature, Chinese masks and puppets from all over Italy. The fascinating **Museo delle Civiltà** museum complex brings together the collections of several different museums: the Museum of Prehistory and Ethnography "Luigi Pigorini" features exhibits from different cultures and some important prehistoric remains, such as a Neanderthal cranium, prehistoric fauna and some well-preserved Neolithic boats; the Museum of Traditional and Folk Art explores Italian regional culture; while the National Museum of the Early Middle Ages presents a wealth of early medieval Italian objects and houses a spectacular reconstruction of a marble-clad room from Ostia Antica. The National Museum of Oriental Art "Giuseppe Tucci" displays objects from Italian archaeological findings in Iran, India, Pakistan, China and elsewhere in the Far East.

In the southern part of the district is a lake, a park, and the domed Palazzo dello Sport built for the 1960 Olympics.

### Burcardo Theatre Museum

Viale della Letteratura 24
06-5990 3814 9:15am-4:30pm Mon & Wed; 9:15am-1:15pm Tue, Thu, Fri

### Museo delle Civiltà

Piazza G. Marconi 14
8am-7pm Tue-Sun
W museocivilta.beni culturali.it

← The Marconi Obelisk, towering over the central square of EUR district

## 🄱 ⊗
### Cinecittà Si Mostra

🄰 Via Tuscolana 1055
Ⓜ Cinecittà 🄲 10am-
6:30pm Wed-Mon
🅆 cinecittasimostra.it

Cinecittà Si Mostra (literally translated as "Cinecittà Shows Off") offers the chance to step behind the scenes of Italy's most famous film studio. Props and costumes are exhibited, including the dress worn by Elizabeth Taylor in *Cleopatra* (1963). Tours include film sets, such as a replica Broadway created for the Martin Scorsese film *Gangs of New York* (2002) and a mock ancient Rome (which stood in for ancient Pompeii in a 2008 episode of *Doctor Who*), along with the working film studio.

**The Stadio dei Marmi is ringed by 60 colossal marble statues of idealized male athletes, each one sculpted by a young, unknown artist.**

## 🄸
### Foro Italico

🄰 Piazza Lauro de Bosis
🚌 32, 69, 186, 224, 271, 280

The Foro Italico sports complex was created by Mussolini (and originally named the Foro Mussolini) between 1928 and 1938 in the hope of securing the 1944 Olympic Games for the city; in the event, that year's Games were cancelled due to World War II. Inspired by the Fora of Imperial Rome, it still features a huge obelisk inscribed with the words "Mussolini Dux" (*dux* being the Latin for leader). The swimming pool is pure marble, with stone mosaic decorations. The Stadio dei Marmi is ringed by 60 colossal marble statues of idealized male athletes, each one sculpted by a young, unknown artist and donated by one of the 60 provinces of Italy. Overlooking it is a building that once housed the Fascist Male Academy of Physical Education, now the headquarters of the Italian Olympic Committee. Also within the complex is the Stadio Olimpico; rebuilt for the 1990 FIFA World Cup, it is the home stadium of both the Roma and Lazio football teams and is also used for international rugby and athletics and occasional big rock concerts. The Italian Open tennis tournament is staged at the complex's Campo Centrale.

→

The 17th-century Villa Doria Pamphilj with its tranquil formal gardens

**19** ⚐ Ⓜ ▱ 🏛

## Centrale Montemartini

⚐ Via Ostiense 106
🚌 23, 769 🕐 9am-7pm
Tue-Sun (last adm:
6:30pm) 🌐 centrale
montemartini.org

An enormous old industrial site was restored in 1997 to house part of the collections of the Capitoline Museums *(p66)*. Originally, the building was used as Rome's first thermo-electric power station and its two huge generators still occupy the central machine room, creating quite an intriguing contrast to the exhibits of Classical ancient Roman statuary and artifacts. Many of the statues were discovered during excavations in the late

19th and early 20th centuries and include finds from the Area Sacra di Largo Argentina *(p171)*.

---

**20** 🏛

## San Paolo fuori le Mura

⚐ Via Ostiense 186 📞 06-6988 0800 🚌 23, 128, 170, 670, 707, 761, 769 Ⓜ San Paolo 🕐 7am-6:30pm daily Cloister and museum: 🕐 8:30am-6pm daily

Today's church is a faithful reconstruction of the great 4th-century basilica destroyed by fire on 15 July 1823. Few fragments of the original church survived. The triumphal arch over the nave is decorated on one side with restored 5th-century mosaics. On the other side are mosaics by Pietro Cavallini, originally on the façade. The splendid Venetian apse mosaics (1220) depict the figures of Christ with St Peter, St Andrew, St Paul and St Luke.

←

Mosaics adorning the walls of the swimming pool at the Foro Italico, and *(inset)* detail of one of the marble figures around the Stadio dei Marmi

The fine marble canopy over the high altar is signed by the sculptor Arnolfo di Cambio (1285) "together with his partner Pietro", who may have been Pietro Cavallini. Below the altar is the *confessio*, the tomb of St Paul. To the right is an impressive Paschal candle-stick by Nicolò di Angelo and Pietro Vassalletto.

The cloister of San Paolo, with its pairs of colourful inlaid columns supporting the arcade, was spared completely by the fire. Completed around 1214, it is considered one of the most beautiful in Rome.

---

**21**

## Villa Doria Pamphilj

⚐ Via di San Pancrazio
🚌 31, 44, 75, 710, 870
Park: 🕐 dawn-dusk daily

One of Rome's largest public parks, the Villa Doria Pamphilj was laid out in the mid-17th century for Prince Camillo Pamphilj. His uncle, Pope Innocent X, paid for the magnificent summer residence, the Casino del Bel Respiro, and the fountains and summerhouses, some of which still survive.

↑ Picturesque ruins in Hadrian's Villa

## ㉒ Tivoli

🚗 31 km (20 miles) northeast of Rome
🚉 From Tiburtina
🚌 COTRAL from Ponte Mammolo (on Metro line B)

Tivoli has been a popular summer resort since the days of the Roman Republic. Among the famous men who owned villas here were the poets Catullus and Horace, Caesar's assassins Brutus and Cassius, and the emperors Trajan and Hadrian. Tivoli's main attractions were its clean air and beautiful situation on the slopes of the Tiburtini hills, its healthy sulphur springs and the waterfalls of the Aniene. The Romans' luxurious lifestyle was revived in Renaissance times by the owners of the Villa d'Este, the town's most famous sight.

In the Middle Ages Tivoli suffered frequent invasions as its position made it an ideal base for an advance on Rome.

The town's cobbled streets are still lined with medieval houses. The cathedral contains a lovely 13th-century life-size wooden group representing the *Deposition from the Cross*.

## ㉓  Villa d'Este

🏛 Piazza Trento 5, Tivoli
🚌 COTRAL from Ponte Mammolo (on Metro line B)
🕐 Villa and cloister: 8:30am–7:45pm Tue–Sun, garden closes at sunset 🚫1 Jan, 25 Dec 🌐 villadeste tivoli.info

The Villa d'Este occupies the site of an old Benedictine convent. In the 16th century the estate was developed by Cardinal Ippolito d'Este, son of Lucrezia Borgia. A palace was designed by Pirro Ligorio to make the most of its hill-top situation, but the villa's fame rests more on the terraced gardens and fountains laid out by Ligorio and Giacomo della Porta.

The grottoes and fountains still give a vivid impression of the luxury enjoyed by the princes of the church. From the loggia of the palace you descend to the Grotto of Diana and Bernini's Fontana del Bicchierone. Below to the right is the Rometta (little Rome), a model of Tiber Island with allegorical figures and the legendary she-wolf. The Fontana dell'Organo is a water-organ, in which the

force of the water pumps air through the pipes. The garden's lowest level has flower beds and fountains and splendid views.

## ㉔  Hadrian's Villa

🏛 Villa Adriana, Largo M Yourcenar 1, 6 km (4 miles) southwest of Tivoli
🚉 Tivoli, then local bus No. 4
🚌 COTRAL from Ponte Mammolo (on Metro line B)
🕐 9am–sunset daily (see website for opening hours month by month)
🌐 villaadriana.beni culturali.it

Built as a private summer retreat between AD 118 and 134, Hadrian's Villa was a vast open-air museum of the finest architecture of the Roman world. The grounds of the Imperial Palace were filled with full-scale reproductions of the emperor's favourite buildings from Greece and Egypt. Although excavations on this site began in the 16th century, many of the ruins scattered in the surrounding fields have yet to be identified with any certainty. The grounds make a very picturesque site for a picnic. The most notable buildings are signposted and several have been partially restored or reconstructed. One of the most impressive is the so-called Maritime Theatre. This is a round pool with an island in the middle, surrounded by columns. The island, reached by means of a swing bridge, was probably Hadrian's private studio, where he withdrew from the cares of the Empire to indulge in his two favourite pastimes, painting and architecture. There were also theatres, Greek and Latin libraries, two bathhouses, extensive housing for guests and the palace staff, and formal gardens with fountains, statues and pools.

Hadrian also loved Greek philosophy. One part of the gardens is thought to have been Hadrian's reproduction of the Grove of Academe, where Plato lectured to his students. He also had a replica made of the Stoà Poikile, a beautiful painted colonnade in Athens, from which the Stoic philosophers took their name. The so-called Hall of the Philosophers, close to the Poikile, was probably a library.

The most ambitious of Hadrian's replicas was the Canopus, a sanctuary of the god Serapis near Alexandria. For this a canal 119 metres (130 yards) long was dug and Egyptian statues were imported to decorate the temple and its grounds.

Below ground the emperor even built a fanciful re-creation of the underworld, Hades, reached through underground tunnels, of which there were many linking the various parts of the villa.

Plundered by barbarians, who camped here in the 6th and 8th centuries, the villa fell into disrepair and Renaissance antiquarians contributed even further to its destruction. Statues unearthed in the grounds are on display in museums around Europe. The Vatican's Egyptian Collection *(p292)* has many fine works that were found here.

---

**25**

## Villa Gregoriana

🏠 **Largo Sant'Angelo, Tivoli**
🚉 🚌 **Tivoli, then short walk**
📞 **0774-332 650** 🕐 **Mar & mid-Oct–mid-Dec: 10am–5pm Tue–Sun; Apr–mid-Oct: 10am–6:30pm Tue–Sun**

The main attractions of this steeply sloping park are the waterfalls and grottoes

← 

The Grande Cascata waterfall and Villa Gregoriana above

created by the River Aniene. The park is named after Pope Gregory XVI, who in the 1830s ordered the building of a tunnel to ward against flooding. This tunnel created a new waterfall, the Grande Cascata, plunging 160 m (525 ft) into the valley behind the town.

## ALSO WORTH SEEING

**Lake Bracciano**
🚉 **From Ostiense (c.70 min)** 🚌 **From Saxa Rubra, reached by train from Roma Nord (then bus, c.90 min)**
This volcanic lake is popular for sailing and for swimming.

**Pompeii**
🚉 **From Termini to Naples, then change to local train (c.130 min)** 🚌 **Special tours from tourist agents**
Visit the excavations of the bustling Roman city where daily life was put to a sudden end by the eruption of Vesuvius in AD 79.

**Viterbo**
🚌 **From Ostiense (c.115 min) or train from Roma Nord, Piazzale Flaminio, on Metro line A (c.150 min)** 🚌 **From Saxa Rubra, reached by train from Roma Nord (then bus, c.90 min)**
As well as a medieval quarter, this city has great thermal spas.

**Castelli Romani**
🚉 **From Termini (c.20 min)**
About 20 km (12 miles) south of Rome lie 16 hill towns known as the "Roman Castles", set amidst lush greenery. They are popular for wine-tasting tours.

# A LONG WALK
# THE VIA APPIA ANTICA

**Distance** 3 km (2 miles) **Walking time** 1 hour
**Nearest Bus** 118 from Piazzale Ostiense

Lined with cypresses and pines as it was when the ancient Romans came here by torchlight to bury their dead, the Via Appia is wonderfully atmospheric. Along the walk admire the fields strewn with ruined tombs set against the picturesque background of the Alban hills to the south. Although the marble or travertine stone facings of most tombs have been plundered along this path, a few statues and reliefs survive or have been replaced by copies.

*Start at the* **Tomb of Cecilia Metella** *(p323). In the Middle Ages this area acquired the name Capo di Bove (oxhead) from the frieze of festoons, and oxheads are still visible on the tomb.*

**START**

Tomb of Cecilia Metella

San Nicola

Torre di Capo di Bove

VIA DI SAN SEBASTIANO

VIA DI CECILIA METELLA

*The* **Gothic church of San Nicola** *was once part of the medieval fortress of the Caetani family.*

*These crossroads are home to many original Roman paving slabs made of volcanic basalt.*

*The* **Torre di Capo di Bove** *is a great mausoleum overgrown with ivy.*

↑ Walking down the ancient cobblestones of the Via Appia Antica

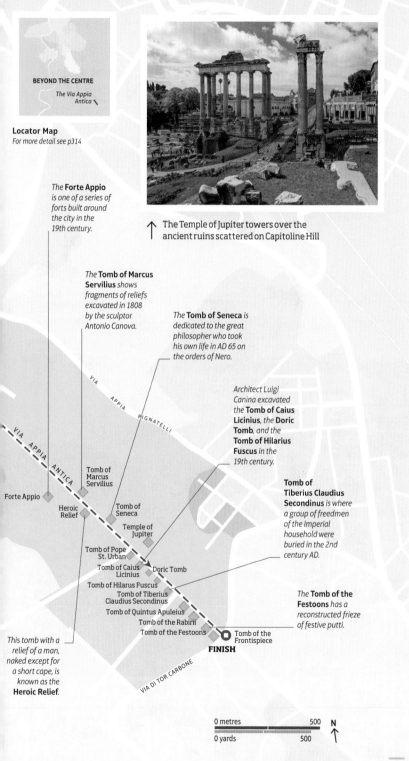

↑ The Temple of Jupiter towers over the ancient ruins scattered on Capitoline Hill

The **Forte Appio**
is one of a series of
forts built around
the city in the
19th century.

The **Tomb of Marcus
Servilius** shows
fragments of reliefs
excavated in 1808
by the sculptor
Antonio Canova.

The **Tomb of Seneca** is
dedicated to the great
philosopher who took
his own life in AD 65 on
the orders of Nero.

Architect Luigi
Canina excavated
the **Tomb of Caius
Licinius**, *the* **Doric
Tomb**, *and the*
**Tomb of Hilarius
Fuscus** in the
19th century.

**Tomb of
Tiberius Claudius
Secondinus** *is where
a group of freedmen
of the Imperial
household were
buried in the 2nd
century AD.*

Tomb of
Marcus
Servilius

Forte Appio

Heroic
Relief

Tomb of
Seneca

Temple of
Jupiter

Tomb of Pope
St. Urban

Tomb of Caius
Licinius

Doric Tomb

Tomb of Hilarus Fuscus

Tomb of Tiberius
Claudius Secondinus

Tomb of Quintus Apuleius

Tomb of the Rabirii

Tomb of the Festoons

Tomb of the
Frontispiece

**FINISH**

The **Tomb of the
Festoons** has a
reconstructed frieze
of festive putti.

*This tomb with a
relief of a man,
naked except for
a short cape, is
known as the*
**Heroic Relief**.

VIA APPIA

APPIA

PIGNATELLI

VIA APPIA ANTICA

VIA DI TOR CARBONE

| 0 metres | | 500 |
| 0 yards | | 500 |

N
↑

# NEED TO KNOW

Victor Emmanuel Monument

# BEFORE
# YOU GO

Things change, so plan ahead to make the most of your trip. Be prepared for all eventualities by considering the following points before you travel.

## AT A GLANCE

### CURRENCY
Euro (EUR)

### AVERAGE DAILY SPEND

| | | |
|---|---|---|
| SAVE **€50** | SPEND **€100** | SPLURGE **€200+** |

| BOTTLED WATER **€1.30** | COFFEE **€1.50** | BEER **€5** | DINNER FOR TWO **€60** |
|---|---|---|---|

### ESSENTIAL PHRASES

| | |
|---|---|
| Hello | Buongiorno/Ciao |
| Goodbye | Arrivederci |
| Please | Per favore |
| Thank you | Grazie |
| Do you speak English? | Parla inglese? |
| I don't understand | Non ho capito |

### ELECTRICITY SUPPLY

Power sockets are type F and L, fitting two- and three-pronged plugs. Standard voltage is 220–230v.

## Passports and Visas

For entry requirements, including visas, consult your nearest Italian embassy or check the **Polizia di Stato** website. EU nationals and citizens of the UK, US, Canada, Australia and New Zealand do not need visas for stays of up to three months.
**Polizia di Stato**
w poliziadistato.it

## Government Advice

Now more than ever, it is important to consult both your and the Italian government's advice before travelling. The **UK Foreign and Commonwealth Office**, the **US State Department**, the **Australian Department of Foreign Affairs and Trade** and the Italian **Ministero della Salute** offer the latest information on security, health and local regulations.
**Australian Department of Foreign Affairs and Trade**
w smartraveller.gov.au
**Ministero della Salute**
w salute.gov.it
**UK Foreign and Commonwealth Office**
w gov.uk/foreign-travel-advice
**US State Department**
w travel.state.gov

## Customs Information

You can find information on the laws relating to goods and currency taken in or out of Italy on the ENIT (Italy's national tourist board) website (p338).

## Insurance

We recommend that you take out a comprehensive insurance policy covering theft, loss of belongings, medical care, cancellations and delays, and read the small print carefully.
EU citizens are eligible for free emergency medical care in Italy provided they have a valid **EHIC** (European Health Insurance Card).
**EHIC**
w ec.europa.eu

## Vaccinations

No inoculations are needed for Italy.

## Booking Accommodation

Rome offers a huge variety of accommodation and the ENIT website *(p338)* provides an extensive list of options. To avoid disappointment, and inflated prices, book well in advance.

All accommodation is subject to the city tourist tax. This varies between €3 and €7 per night for a maximum of ten nights. Always check if this is included in the rate quoted to you.

Under Italian law, hotels are required to register guests at police headquarters and issue a receipt of payment *(ricevuta fiscale)*, which you must keep until you leave Italy.

## Money

Most establishments accept major credit, debit and prepaid currency cards. Contactless payments are becoming increasingly common in Rome, but it's always a good idea to carry some cash for smaller items such as coffee, gelato, pizza-by-the-slice, and when visiting markets or more remote areas. Cash is also needed for ticket machines at stations. Wait staff should be tipped €1–2 and hotel porters and housekeeping will expect €1 per bag or day.

## Travellers with Specific Requirements

Rome's historic sites and cobbled streets are ill-equipped for disabled access. Many buildings do not have wheelchair access or lifts. Always call ahead to ensure that your needs will be met.

Assistance at airports can be arranged by notifying your airline company or travel agent of your particular needs in advance of your trip. **ADR Assistance** can coordinate assistance at Rome's Ciampino or Fiumicino or airports. Train travellers with Trenitalia *(p334)* can arrange special reservations and assistance at stations.

Some museums, including the Vatican Museums, offer tours in Italian Sign Language (LIS) and American Sign Language (ASL), as well as multi-sensory tactile tours.

**ADR Assistance**

W adr.it

## Language

Italian is the official language spoken in Rome. The level of English spoken in the city varies. Many of those working in the major tourist areas speak good English. However, a little knowledge of the local language goes a long way, and locals appreciate visitors' efforts to speak Italian, even if you can only manage a few words.

## Opening Hours

> **COVID-19** The pandemic continues to affect Rome. Some museums, tourist attractions and hospitality venues are operating on reduced or temporary opening hours, and require visitors to make advance bookings for a specific date and time. Always check ahead before visiting.

**Lunchtime** Most shops, churches and some small businesses shut for a few hours in the afternoon.

**Monday** Many museums and restaurants close.

**Sunday** Restaurants usually close for lunch. Churches and cathedrals forbid tourists from visiting during Mass, and public transport runs a reduced service.

**Public holidays** Shops, churches and museums either close early or for the day.

| PUBLIC HOLIDAYS | |
| --- | --- |
| 1 Jan | New Year's Day |
| 6 Jan | Epiphany |
| Mar/Apr | Easter Sunday |
| MarApr | Easter Monday |
| 25 Apr | Liberation Day |
| 1 May | Labour Day |
| 2 Jun | Republic Day |
| 29 Jun | St Peter & St Paul Day (Patron Saints of Rome) |
| 15 Aug | Ferragosto |
| 1 Nov | All Saints' Day |
| 8 Dec | Feast of the Immaculate Conception |
| 25 Dec | Christmas Day |
| 26 Dec | St Stephen's Day |

# GETTING AROUND

Whether exploring Rome's historic centre by foot or making use of the city's public transport, here is all you need to know to navigate the city.

**PUBLIC TRANSPORT COSTS**
Tickets are valid on all forms of public transport in Rome.

ONE-WAY

**€1.50**

100 mins
transfers included

DAY TICKET

**€7**

Unlimited travel

3-DAY TICKET

**€18**

Unlimited travel

**SPEED LIMIT**

MOTORWAY

**130**
km/h
(80 mph)

DUAL CARRIAGEWAYS

**110**
km/h
(70 mph)

SECONDARY ROAD

**90**
km/h
(50 mph)

URBAN AREAS

**50**
km/h
(30 mph)

## Arriving by Air

Rome has two airports, Fiumicino and Ciampino, both served by international flights and with excellent transport links to the city centre.

For journey times and ticket pricing for transport between the airport and the city centre, see the table opposite.

## Train Travel

### International Train Travel

Regular high-speed international trains connect Italy to the main towns and cities in Austria, Germany, France and Eastern Europe. Reservations for these services are essential and tickets are booked up quickly.

You can buy tickets and passes for multiple international journeys via **Eurail** or **Interrail**; however, you may still need to pay an additional reservation fee depending on which rail service you travel with. Always check that your pass is valid before boarding.

**Eurail**
W eurail.com
**Interrail**
W interrail.eu

### Regional and Local Train Travel

**Trenitalia** is the main operator in Italy. Tickets can be bought online but there are only a fixed number available so book ahead.

For travelling between cities, **Italo Treno** (NTV) and **Trenitalia** (FS) also offer a high-speed rail service. Reservations are essential. Rome's main stations are Termini and Tiburtina.

There is a useful city line to Ostia Antica and Ostia Lido from Stazione Porta San Paolo, next to the Piramide Metro station.

Tickets must be validated by stamping them before boarding. Machines are positioned at the entrance to platforms in railway stations for this purpose. Heavy fines are levied if you are caught with an unvalidated ticket.

**Italo Treno**
W italotreno.it
**Trenitalia**
W trenitalia.com

## GETTING TO AND FROM THE AIRPORT

| Airport | Transport | Journey time | Price |
|---------|-----------|--------------|-------|
| Ciampino | Bus (Siti/Terravision) | 40 mins | €5/€6 |
| | Taxi | 30 mins | €30 |
| Fiumicino | Train (Leonardo da Vinci Express) | 35 mins | €14 |
| | Train (regionale) | 50 mins | €8 |
| | Bus (ATRAL/COTRAL/Siti/Terravision) | 1 hr | €5/€7 |
| | Taxi | 45 mins | €48 |

## Public Transport

**ATAC** is Rome's main public transport authority. Safety and hygiene measures, timetables, ticket information, transport maps and more can be obtained from ATAC kiosks, the customer service office or the ATAC website.
**ATAC**
atac.roma.it

### Tickets

Tickets (biglietti) are available from kiosks, stations, bars, newsstands or any shop with the ATAC sticker in the window. Be aware that ticket machines only accept cash. Tickets cannot be bought on board – they must be bought in advance (there are automatic ticket machines at main bus stops and Metro stations) and must be validated on the day of travel.

Tickets are valid on all modes of public transport, including buses, trams, Metro and local train lines. Regular one-way tickets (BIT) valid for 75 minutes cost €1.50, day tickets (BIG) cost €7, three-day tickets (BTI) cost €18 and weekly passes (CIS) are €24. Children under 10 travel for free with an adult.

### Metro

Rome's Metro (Metropolitana) has three lines – A, B and C. Line A runs from west to southeast and Line B runs from northeast to south. A and B meet at Termini station, and A and C at San Giovanni. Regional rail services connect with the Metro to serve the surrounding areas and the airports. Line C runs from Pantano station to San Giovanni, where it links with Line A.

Trains run every 4–10 minutes 5:30am–11:30pm daily, and 5:30am–1:30am on Friday and Saturday nights.

On street level, Metro stations are clearly marked by red and white "M" signs. At the station, use the maps to identify which line you need and then insert your ticket through the barrier to access the platform. The machine will return your ticket to you and you should keep it on you in case of inspection. Screens on the platform show the waiting time for the next train. Once you are onboard, look out for your stop, as it may not be announced.

### Trams

Trams cover the outskirts of the city centre and are a good way to get to the main sights while avoiding the crowded centre. The most useful routes are No 2 (to MAXXI) and No 19 (connecting Vatican City with Villa Borghese).

Tram stops display the tram numbers that serve them and a list of stops on each route. Approaching trams display the route number and their destination. Useful routes include Route 2 (along Via Flaminio) and Route 8 (between Largo Argentina and Trastevere).

Trams operate 5:30am–10:30pm or midnight daily, depending on the route (Route 8 runs until 3am on Friday and Saturday nights). Tickets must be stamped on board in the yellow machines.

### Buses

Bus routes cover most of the city. When not stuck in traffic, they are a quick way to reach the main sights and attractions of Rome and you can sightsee as you travel.

The main bus terminus is on Piazza dei Cinquecento outside Termini station, but there are other major route hubs throughout the city, most usefully those at Piazza del Risorgimento and Piazza Venezia.

Bus stops display the bus numbers that serve them and a list of stops on each route. Regular services generally run every 10 to 20 minutes. After 11:30pm a night bus service operates until 5.15am. Night buses are marked with the letter "N" (for *notturno*) before the route number.

Buses must be flagged down. Enter at the front or back doors and exit via the middle door. Tickets must be stamped in  the yellow machines located at the front or back of the bus. Press the button to request a stop.

For day trips, **COTRAL** blue buses run from several Rome terminals out into the suburbs and surrounding countryside.

**COTRAL**
🔲 cotralspa.it

### Long-Distance Bus Travel

Long-distance coaches terminate at Tiburtina, which is the city's main coach station. Tickets and information for coaches to European cities are available from the **Eurolines**, **Flixbus** or **Italybus** websites.

Local buses, serving villages and towns within the Lazio region, are run by COTRAL. All bus stations used by COTRAL in Rome are linked to Metro stations. Tickets are purchased on the spot and cannot be booked in advance.

**Eurolines**
🔲 eurolines.com
**Flixbus**
🔲 flixbus.it
**Italybus**
🔲 italybus.it

## Guided Bus Tours

Bus tours are the perfect way to get a quick overview of a city, especially if they come with an audioguide. **City Sightseeing Roma** offers hop-on-hop-off tours of the city aboard double-decker buses. While travelling between stops, ticket holders can listen to audio guides, which are available in eight languages and detail the history of sites outside the windows as you pass by. Tours run every 15 to 20 minutes daily, with a first departure at 9am and a last departure at 7pm. Buses can be boarded at any of the eight stops, which include the Colosseum, Trevi Fountain, Piazza Barberini and the Vatican. You can also buy "combo" tickets that include the Colosseum and the Vatican, or night tours.

The **Roma Cristiana** bus is a similar tour, but with a Christian emphasis. It runs from Termini to Piazza San Pietro with stops close to religious sights, and also includes audio guides.

**City Sightseeing Roma**
🔲 roma.city-sightseeing. it
**Roma Cristiana**
🔲 operaromanapellegrinaggi.org

## Taxis

Taxis in Rome are some of the most expensive in Europe and not all accept credit cards. They cannot be hailed; take one at an official taxi stand at stations, main piazzas or close to key tourist sights – the most useful are at Termini, Piazza Venezia, Piazza di Spagna, Piazza del Popolo and Piazza Barberini. You can also reserve **Radiotaxi 3570** online or **Chiama Taxi** by phone. When you order a taxi by phone, the meter will run from the time of your call. Official taxis are white, have a "taxi" sign on the roof and their official taxi licence number on the doors. Uber also operates in Rome.

When travelling to and from the airport, bear in mind that extra charges are added for each piece of luggage placed in the boot, for rides between 10pm and 7am, on Sundays and public holidays, and for journeys to and from airports. Report any problems with taxi drivers by calling 06 0608.

**Chiama Taxi**
📞 060609
**Radiotaxi 3570**
🔲 3570.it

## Driving

Driving in Rome is not recommended – roads are congested and parking is extremely difficult, even for locals.

### Driving to Rome

Rome is easily reachable from other European countries via E-roads, the International European Road Network connecting major roads across national borders within Europe, or by national (N) and secondary (SS) roads from neighbouring France, Switzerland, Austria and Slovenia. The city is also easily accessible from the rest of Italy.

Tolls are payable on most motorways (*autostrade*), and payment is made at the end of the journey in cash, by credit card or pre-paid magnetic VIA cards, available from tobacconists and the **ACI** (*Automobile Club d'Italia*). If you wish to avoid toll roads, there is almost always an alternative route signposted.

If you bring your own foreign-registered car to Italy, you must carry a Green Card, the vehicle's registration documents and a valid driver's licence.

**ACI**
🔲 aci.it

### Car Rental

Many car rental companies operate from the airports. To rent a car in Italy you must be over 21 and have held a valid driver's licence with no points for at least one year.

Driving licences issued by any of the European Union member states are valid throughout the EU, including Italy.

If visiting from outside the EU, you may need to apply for an International Driving Permit (IDP). Check with your local automobile association before you travel.

## Driving in Rome

City centre streets are designated ZTL *(Zona a Traffico Limitato)* which means that only residents can drive and park there.

Those arriving by car are advised to leave it in a car park outside the city centre. The **European Car Parking Guide** and **Saba** list free car parks on Rome's periphery. There are also car parks located near Villa Borghese and Piazza Partigiani. Look for a white "P" sign on a blue background. Metered parking is permitted in parking spaces identified by a blue line from 8am until 8pm.

If your vehicle is towed, call the municipal police. You can reach them by dialling 06 0606. Tell them where you parked and they will direct you to the nearest tow lot. Once you have located your vehicle, you will have to pay a fee to retrieve it as well as pay for the parking violation.

**European Car Parking Guide**
W car-parking.eu/italy/rome/pr
**Saba**
W sabait.it

## Rules of the Road

It is important to abide by the following rules. Drive on the right, use the left lane only for passing and yield to traffic from the right. Seat belts are required for all passengers in the front and back. Heavy fines are levied for using a mobile phone while driving. The drink-drive limit is strictly enforced *(p339)*. If you are drinking alcohol, use public transport or take a taxi.

During the day dipped headlights are compulsory when driving on motorways, dual carriageways and on all out-of-town roads. A red warning triangle and fluorescent vests must be carried at all times, for use in the event of an emergency.

If you have an accident or breakdown, switch on your hazard warning lights and place a warning triangle 50 m (55 yd) behind your vehicle. In the event of a breakdown, call the ACI emergency number (803 116) or the emergency services (112 or 113). The ACI will tow any foreign-registered car to the nearest ACI-affiliated garage for free.

## Hitchhiking

Hitchhiking *(autostop)* is illegal on motorways, and is not commonplace in large cities such as Rome. In more rural areas it is a common transport method for travellers on a budget. Always consider your own safety before entering an unknown vehicle or letting someone into yours.

# Cycle and Scooter Hire

Cycling in Rome can be a challenging task due to the city's hilly nature, the heavy traffic and the lack of bike paths, but it is still a green and convenient way to get around the city. If you are not up for urban cycling, a ride in Villa Borghese park can be a healthier and more enjoyable alternative. Bikes, tandems and rickshaws can all be hired by the entrance of the Pincio Gardens.

You can rent bicycles, motorcycles and scooters hourly or by the day. You may have to leave your passport with the rental shop as a deposit, and you must have a valid licence to hire a scooter or motorcycle. **Bici & Baci** and **Barberini Scooters for Rent** offer bike and scooter rental by the hour and by the day, so you can easily ride around the city like Audrey Hepburn and Gregory Peck in *Roman Holiday*.

Be aware that motorcyclists, scooter drivers and their passengers must wear helmets by law; these can be rented from most hire shops. Unless you are an experienced moped or scooter rider, it is wise not to ride in Rome because of the exceptionally busy roads.

**Barberini Scooters for Rent**
W rentscooter.it
**Bici & Baci**
W bicibaci.com

# Walking

Everything from St Peter's and the Janiculum to Villa Borghese and beyond can be seen without having to use public transport. In fact, much of the city is made up of narrow lanes and alleys, which are impenetrable to buses, and many streets are pedestrianized. You can easily visit several of the main tourist sights in a few hours.

Wandering through Rome's historic centre is one of the most enjoyable aspects of any visit to the city. You can take in the architectural details, absorb the streetlife and peek into any church, shop or bar that catches your interest. You can easily visit several of the main tourist sights in a few hours.

To travel safely on foot, wear sensible shoes, cross streets only when the green *avanti* sign is lit and wait at the crossing when the red *alt* sign is lit. In summer, keep to the shady, narrow streets rather than main piazzas, as they can be very hot. It is also advisable to wear sunscreen and carry water at this time of year.

# PRACTICAL
# INFORMATION

A little local know-how goes a long way in Rome. Here you can find all the essential advice and information you will need during your stay.

## AT A GLANCE

### EMERGENCY NUMBERS

**GENERAL EMERGENCY**

**112**

**AMBULANCE**

**118**

**FIRE SERVICE**

**115**

**POLICE**

**113**

### TIME ZONE
CET/CEST
Central European
Summer Time (CEST)
runs 31 Mar–27 Oct
2019

### TAP WATER
Unless otherwise
stated, tap water in
Rome is safe to drink.

### WEBSITES AND APPS

**www.italia.it**
The official website of ENIT, Itay's
national tourist board

**Chiama Taxi App**
Roma Servizi's handy taxi app

**ProntoTreno**
Buy train tickets, get live updates and
check journey times

**WiFi°Italia°**
Connect quickly and easily to free Wi-Fi
hotspots throughout Rome and Italy

## Personal Security

Rome is a relatively safe city to visit, where you only really need to fear becoming a victim of pickpocketing. Bag-snatching scooter drivers are a problem, so hold bags on the inside of the pavement where possible, especially in crowded tourist areas. Pickpockets are common on public transport, so be careful on popular bus routes such as 23, 40 and 64. Keep your belongings in a safe place and with you at all times.

If you have anything stolen, report the crime within 24 hours to the nearest police station and take ID with you. Get a copy of the crime report (denuncia) to make an insurance claim.

Contact your embassy if you have your passport stolen, or in the event of a serious crime or accident.

As a rule, Romans are very accepting of all people, regardless of their race, gender or sexuality. Homosexuality was legalized in 1887 and in 1982, Italy became the third country to recognize the right to legally change your gender. If you do feel unsafe, the **Safe Space Alliance** pinpoints your nearest place of refuge.

Women may receive unwanted and unwelcome attention, especially around tourist areas. If you feel threatened, head straight for the nearest police station.

**Safe Space Alliance**
🔲 safespacealliance.com

## Health

Italy has a world-class healthcare system. Emergency medical care in Italy is free for all EU and Australian citizens. If you have an EHIC card (p333), be sure to present this as soon as possible. You may have to pay after treatment and reclaim the money later.

For other visitors, payment of medical expenses is the patient's responsibility. It is therefore important to arrange comprehensive medical insurance before travelling.

Seek medicinal supplies and advice for minor ailments from pharmacies (farmacia). You can find details of the nearest 24-hour service on all pharmacy doors.

## Smoking, Alcohol and Drugs

Smoking is banned in enclosed public places. Possession of narcotics is prohibited and could result in a prison sentence.

Italians tend to drink only with meals and are unlikely to be seen drunk – obvious drunkenness is frowned upon.

Italy has a strict limit of 0.05 per cent BAC (blood alcohol content) for drivers. This means that you cannot drink more than a small beer or a small glass of wine if you plan to drive. For drivers with less than three years' driving experience the limit is 0.

## ID

By law you must carry identification with you at all times in Italy. A photocopy of your passport photo page (and visa if applicable) should suffice. If you are stopped by the police you may be asked to present the original document within 12 hours.

## Local Customs

Italians are relatively relaxed when it comes to etiquette. Strangers usually shake hands, while friends and family greet each other with a kiss on each cheek. But there are some strict rules. You can be fined for dropping litter, sitting on monument steps or eating or drinking outside churches, historic monuments and public buildings. It is an offence to swim or bathe in public fountains. You can also be fined for buying something from illegal street traders.

## Visiting Churches and Cathedrals

Entrance to churches is free, but you may be charged a small fee to see a certain area, such as a chapel, cloister or underground ruins.

Strict dress codes apply: cover your torso and upper arms, and ensure shorts and skirts cover your knees. Shoes must be worn.

## Mobile Phones and Wi-Fi

Wi-Fi is generally widely available, and cafés, bars, restaurants and some cultural venues will usually allow you to use their Wi-Fi on the condition that you make a purchase. Visitors travelling to Italy with EU tariffs will be able to use their devices abroad without being affected by roaming charges. Users will be charged the same rates for data, voice calls and SMS services as they would pay at home.

## Post

Stamps are sold in kiosks and tobacconists. The Vatican City and San Marino have their own post systems and stamps. Only letters bearing San Marino or Vatican stamps can be posted in San Marino and Vatican postboxes.

Italian post is notorious for its unreliability. Letters and postcards can take anything between four days and two weeks to arrive.

## Taxes and Refunds

VAT (IVA) is usually 22 per cent. Under certain conditions, non-EU citizens can claim a rebate.

Either claim the rebate before you buy (show your passport to the shop assistant and complete a form), or claim it retrospectively by presenting a customs officer with your receipts as you leave. Stamped receipts will be sent back to the vendor to issue a refund.

## Discount Cards

There are a number of visitor passes and discount cards available for Rome. It is worth considering carefully how many of the offers you are likely to take advantage of before purchasing one of these.

The two-day or three-day **Roma Pass** (€32/€52) includes public transport, entry to two museums or archaeological sites and discounts for various exhibitions and events. The **Omnia Rome and Vatican Pass** (€114 for three days) offers a similar package, but also includes the Vatican Museums.

Many national and city museums offer free entry to under 18s, and discounts for students.

During the *Settimana dei Beni Culturali* (Culture and Heritage week) in the Spring, admission to all state-run sites is free.

**Roma Pass**
W romapass.it
**Omnia Rome and Vatican Pass**
W romeandvaticanpass.com

# INDEX

# PHRASE BOOK

## IN EMERGENCY

| | | |
|---|---|---|
| Help! | Aiuto! | eye-**yoo**-toh |
| Stop! | Ferma! | fair-**mah** |
| Call a doctor | Chiama un medico | kee-**ah**-mah oon **meh**-dee-koh |
| Call an ambulance | Chiama un' ambulanza | kee-**ah**-mah oon am-boo-**lan**-tsa |
| Call the police | Chiama la polizia | kee-**ah**-mah ee pol-ee-**tsee**-ah |
| Call the fire brigade | Chiama i pompieri | kee-**ah**-mah ee pom-pee-**air**-ee |
| Where is the telephone? | Dov'è il telefono? | dov-**eheel** teh-leh-foh-noh? |
| The nearest hospital? | L'ospedale più vicino? | loss-peh-**dah**-leh pee-**oovee-chee**-noh? |

## COMMUNICATION ESSENTIALS

| | | |
|---|---|---|
| Yes/No | Sì/No | **see**/noh |
| Please | Per favore | pair fah-**vor**-eh |
| Thank you | Grazie | **grah**-tsee-eh |
| Excuse me | Mi scusi | mee skoo-zee |
| Hello | Buon giorno | bwon jor-noh |
| Goodbye | Arrivederci | ah-ree-veh-**dair**-chee |
| Good evening | Buona sera | **bwon**-ah sair-eh |
| morning | la mattina | lah mah-**tee**-nah |
| afternoon | il pomeriggio | eel poh-meh-**ree**-joh |
| evening | la sera | lah sair-eh |
| yesterday | ieri | ee-**air**-ee |
| today | oggi | **oh**-jee |
| tomorrow | domani | doh-**mah**-nee |
| here | qui | **kwee** |
| there | la | **lah** |
| What? | Quale? | **kwah**-leh? |
| When? | Quando? | **kwan**-doh? |
| Why? | Perchè? | pair-**keh**? |
| Where? | Dove? | **doh**-veh |

## USEFUL PHRASES

| | | |
|---|---|---|
| How are you? | Come sta? | **koh**-meh stah? |
| Very well, thank you. | Molto bene, grazie. | **moll**-toh **beh**-neh **grah**-tsee-eh |
| Pleased to meet you. | Piacere di conoscerla. | pee-ah-**chair**-eh dee coh-**noh**-shair-lah |
| See you soon. | A più tardi. | ah pee-oo tar-dee |
| That's fine. | Va bene. | va **beh**-neh |
| Where is/are ...? | Dov'è/Dove sono ...? | dov-**eh**/doveh**soh**noh? |
| How long does it take to get to ...? | Quanto tempo ci vuole per andare a ...? | **kwan**-toh **tem**-poh chee voo-oh-leh pair an-**dar**-eh ah...? |
| How do I get to ...? | Come faccio per arrivare a ...? | koh-meh **fah**-choh ar-ri-**var**-eh ah...? |
| Do you speak English? | Parla inglese? | **par**-lah een-**gleh**-zeh? |
| I don't understand. | Non capisco. | non ka-**pee**-skoh |
| Could you speak more slowly, please? | Può parlare più lentamente, per favore? | pwoh par-lah-reh pee-**oo** len-ta-**men**-teh pair fah-**vor**-eh? |
| I'm sorry. | Mi dispiace. | mee dee-spee-**ah**-cheh |

## USEFUL WORDS

| | | |
|---|---|---|
| big | grande | **gran**-deh |
| small | piccolo | **pee**-koh-loh |
| hot | caldo | **kal**-doh |
| cold | freddo | **fred**-doh |
| good | buono | **bwoh**-noh |
| bad | cattivo | kat-**tee**-voh |
| enough | basta | **bas**-tah |
| well | bene | **beh**-neh |
| open | aperto | ah-**pair**-toh |
| closed | chiuso | kee-**oo**-zoh |
| left | a sinistra | ah see-**nee**-strah |
| right | a destra | ah **dess**-trah |
| straight on | sempre dritto | **sem**-preh **dree**-toh |
| near | vicino | vee-**chee**-noh |
| far | lontano | lon-**tah**-noh |
| up | su | **soo** |
| down | giù | **joo** |
| early | presto | **press**-toh |
| late | tardi | **tar**-dee |
| entrance | entrata | en-**trah**-tah |
| exit | uscita | oo-**shee**-ta |
| toilet | il gabinetto | eel gah-bee-**net**-toh |
| free, unoccupied | libero | **lee**-bair-oh |
| free, no charge | gratuito | grah-**too**-ee-toh |

## MAKING A TELEPHONE CALL

| | | |
|---|---|---|
| Could I charge my phone? | Posso ricaricare il mio telefono? | Po-ssoh ree-ca-ree-ca-reh eel mee-oh tai-lai-pho-noh? |
| What's your Wi-Fi password? | Posso avere la password dell' internet? | Po-ssoh ah-vai-reh lah password dell Internet? |
| I have no signal | Non ho campo | Noh-n oh cah-mpoh |
| Is there an app for public transport? | C'è una app per i trasporti pubblici? | Cheh oona App pair eeh tras-por-teeh poob-blee-chee? |
| Do you have an online shop? | Avete un negozio online? | Ah-vai-teh oon nai-go-zyoh online? |
| Can I leave a message? | Posso lasciare un messaggio? | **poss**-oh lash-**ah**-reh oon mess-**sah**-joh? |
| Hold on | Un attimo, per favore | oon **ah**-tee-moh, pair fah-**vor**-eh |
| Could you speak up a little please? | Può parlare più forte, per favore? | pwoh par-**lah**-reh pee-**oo** for-teh, pair fah-**vor**-eh? |

## SHOPPING

| | | |
|---|---|---|
| How much does this cost? | Quant'è, per favore? | kwan-**teh**, pair fah-**vor**-eh? |
| I would like ... | Vorrei ... | vor-**ray**... |
| Do you have ...? | Avete ...? | ah-**veh**-teh...? |
| I'm just looking. | Sto soltanto guardando. | stoh sol-**tan**-toh gwar-**dan**-doh |
| Do you take credit cards? | Accettate carte di credito? | ah-chet-**tah**-teh **kar**-teh dee **creh**-dee-toh? |
| What time do you open/close? | A che ora apre/ chiude? | ah keh **or**-ah **ah**-preh/kee-oo-deh? |
| this one | questo | **kweh**-stoh |
| that one | quello | **kwell**-oh |
| expensive | caro | **kar**-oh |
| cheap | a buon prezzo | ah bwon **pret**-soh |
| size, clothes | la taglia | lah **tah**-lee-ah |
| size, shoes | il numero | eel **noo**-mair-oh |
| white | bianco | bee-**ang**-koh |
| black | nero | **neh**-roh |
| red | rosso | **ross**-oh |
| yellow | giallo | **jal**-loh |
| green | verde | **vair**-deh |
| blue | blu | bloo |
| brown | marrone | mar-**roh**-neh |

## TYPES OF SHOP

| | | |
|---|---|---|
| antique dealer | l'antiquario | lan-tee-**kwah**-ree-oh |
| bakery | la panetteria | lah pah-net-tair-**ree**-ah |
| bank | la banca | lah **bang**-kah |
| bookshop | la libreria | lah lee-breh-**ree**-ah |
| butcher's | la macelleria | lah mah-chell-eh-**ree**-ah |
| cake shop | la pasticceria | lah pas-tee-chair-**ee**-ah |
| chemist's | la farmacia | lah far-mah-**chee**-ah |
| department store | il grande magazzino | eel **gran**-deh mag-gad-**zee**-noh |
| delicatessen | la salumeria | lah sah-loo-meh-**ree**-ah |
| fishmonger's | la pescheria | lah pess-keh-**ree**-ah |
| florist | il fioraio | eel fee-or-**eye**-oh |
| greengrocer | il fruttivendolo | eel froo-tee-**ven**-doh-loh |
| grocery | alimentari | ah-lee-men-**tah**-ree |
| hairdresser | il parrucchiere | eel par-oo-kee-**air**-eh |
| ice cream parlour | la gelateria | lah jel-lah-tair-**ree**-ah |
| market | il mercato | eel mair-**kah**-toh |
| news-stand | l'edicola | leh-**dee**-koh-lah |
| post office | l'ufficio postale | loo-**fee**-choh pos-**tah**-leh |
| shoe shop | il negozio di scarpe | eel neh-goh-tsioh dee **skar**-peh |
| supermarket | il supermercato | eel su-pair-mair-**kah**-toh |
| tobacconist | il tabaccaio | eel tah-bak-**eye**-oh |
| travel agency | l'agenzia di viaggi | lah-jen-**tsee**-ah dee vee-**ad**-jee |

## SIGHTSEEING

| | | |
|---|---|---|
| art gallery | la pinacoteca | lah peena-koh-**teh**-kah |
| bus stop | la fermata dell'autobus | lah fair-**mah**-tah dell **ow**-toh-booss |
| church | la chiesa | lah kee-**eh**-zah |
| | la basilica | lah bah-**seel**-i-kah |
| garden | il giardino | eel jar-**dee**-no |
| library | la biblioteca | lah beeb-lee-oh-**teh**-kah |
| museum | il museo | eel moo-**zeh**-oh |

| | | |
|---|---|---|
| railway station | la stazione | lah stah-tsee-**oh**-neh |
| tourist information | l'ufficio turistico | loo-**fee**-choh too-**ree**-stee-koh |
| closed for the public holiday | chiuso per la festa | kee-oo-zoh pair lah **fess**-tah |

## STAYING IN A HOTEL

| | | |
|---|---|---|
| Do you have any vacant rooms? | Avete camere libere? | ah-**veh**-teh **kah**-mair-eh **lee**-bair-eh? |
| double room | una camera doppia | oona **kah**-mair-ah **doh**-pee-ah |
| with double bed | con letto matrimoniale | kon let-toh mah-tree-moh-nee-**ah**-leh |
| twin room | una camera con due letti | oona **kah**-mair-ah kon doo-eh let-tee |
| single room | una camera singola | oona **kah**-mair-ah **sing**-goh-lah |
| room with a bath, shower | una camera con bagno, con doccia | oona **kah**-mair-ah kon ban-yoh, kon **dot**-chah |
| porter | il facchino | eel fah-**kee**-noh |
| key | la chiave | lah kee-**ah**-veh |
| I have a reservation. | Ho fatto una prenotazione. | oh **fat**-toh oona preh-noh-tah-tsee-**oh**-neh |

## EATING OUT

| | | |
|---|---|---|
| Have you got a table for …? | Avete un tavolo per … ? | ah-**veh**-teh oon **tah**-voh-loh pair …? |
| I'd like to reserve a table. | Vorrei riservare un tavolo. | vor-**ray** ree-sair-**vah**-reh oon **tah**-voh-loh |
| breakfast | colazione | koh-lah-tsee-**oh**-neh |
| lunch | pranzo | **pran**-tsoh |
| dinner | cena | **cheh**-nah |
| The bill, please. | Il conto, per favore. | eel **kon**-toh pair fah-**vor**-eh |
| I am a vegetarian. | Sono vegetariano/a. | **soh**-noh **veh**-jeh-tar-ee-**ah**-noh/nah |
| waitress | cameriera | kah-mair-ee-**air**-ah |
| waiter | cameriere | kah-mair-ee-**air**-eh |
| fixed price menu | il menù a prezzo fisso | eel meh-**noo** ah **pret**-seh-foh |
| dish of the day | piatto del giorno | pee-**ah**-toh dell **jor**-no |
| starter | antipasto | an-tee-**pass**-toh |
| first course | il primo | eel **pree**-moh |
| main course | il secondo | eel seh-**kon**-doh |
| vegetables | il contorno | eel kon-**tor**-noh |
| dessert | il dolce | eel **doll**-che |
| cover charge | il coperto | eel koh-**pair**-toh |
| wine list | la lista dei vini | lah **lee**-stah day **vee**-nee |
| rare | al sangue | al **sang**-gweh |
| medium | a puntino | a poon-**tee**-noh |
| well done | ben cotto | ben **kot**-toh |
| glass | il bicchiere | eel bee-kee-**air**-eh |
| bottle | la bottiglia | lah bot-**teel**-yah |
| knife | il coltello | eel kol-**tell**-oh |
| fork | la forchetta | lah for-**ket**-tah |
| spoon | il cucchiaio | eel koo-kee-**eye**-oh |

## MENU DECODER

| | | |
|---|---|---|
| apple | la mela | lah **meh**-lah |
| artichoke | il carciofo | eel kar-**choff**-oh |
| aubergine | la melanzana | lah meh-lan-**tsah**-nah |
| baked | al forno | al **for**-noh |
| beans | i fagioli | ee fah-**joh**-lee |
| beef | il manzo | eel **man**-tsoh |
| beer | la birra | lah **beer**-rah |
| boiled | lesso | **less**-oh |
| bread | il pane | eel **pah**-neh |
| broth | il brodo | eel **broh**-doh |
| butter | il burro | eel **boor**-oh |
| cake | la torta | lah **tor**-tah |
| cheese | il formaggio | eel for-**mad**-joh |
| chicken | il pollo | eel **poll**-oh |
| chips | patatine fritte | pah-tah-**teen**-eh **free**-teh |
| baby clams | le vongole | leh **von**-goh-leh |
| coffee | il caffè | eel kah-**feh** |
| courgettes | gli zucchini | lyee dzoo-**kee**-nee |
| dry | secco | **sek**-koh |
| duck | l'anatra | **lah**-nah-trah |
| egg | l'uovo | loo-**oh**-voh |
| fish | il pesce | eel **pesh**-eh |
| fresh fruit | frutta fresca | **froo**-tah **fress**-kah |
| garlic | l'aglio | **lahl**-yoh |
| grapes | l'uva | **loo**-vah |
| grilled | alla griglia | ah-lah **greel**-yah |
| ham | il prosciutto | eel pro-**shoo**-toh |
| cooked/cured | cotto/crudo | **kot**-toh/kroo-doh |
| ice cream | il gelato | eel jel-**lah**-toh |

| | | |
|---|---|---|
| lamb | l'abbacchio | lah-**back**-kee-oh |
| lobster | l'aragosta | lah-rah-**goss**-tah |
| meat | la carne | la **kar**-neh |
| milk | il latte | eel **laht**-teh |
| mineral water | l'acqua minerale | **lah**-kwah mee-nair-**ah**-leh gah-**zah**-tah/ |
| fizzy/still | gasata/naturale | nah-too-**rah**-leh |
| mushrooms | i funghi | ee **foon**-gee |
| oil | l'olio | **loll**-yoh |
| olive | l'oliva | loh-**lee**-vah |
| onion | la cipolla | lah chee-**poll**-ah |
| orange | l'arancia | lah-**ran**-chah |
| orange/lemon juice | succo d'arancia/ di limone | **soo**-kohdah-**ran**-chah/ dee lee-**moh**-neh |
| peach | la pesca | lah **pess**-kah |
| pepper | il pepe | eel **peh**-peh |
| pork | carne di maiale | **kar**-neh dee mah-**yah**-leh |
| potatoes | le patate | leh pah-**tah**-teh |
| prawns | i gamberi | ee **gam**-bair-ee |
| rice | il riso | eel **ree**-zoh |
| roast | arrosto | ar-**ross**-toh |
| roll | il panino | eel pah-**nee**-noh |
| salad | l'insalata | leen-sah-**lah**-tah |
| salt | il sale | eel **sah**-leh |
| sausage | la salsiccia | lah sal-**see**-chah |
| seafood | frutti di mare | **froo**-tee dee **mah**-reh |
| soup | la zuppa, la minestra | lah **tsoo**-pah, lah mee-**ness**-trah |
| steak | la bistecca | lah bee-**stek**-koh |
| strawberries | le fragole | leh **frah**-goh-leh |
| sugar | lo zucchero | loh **zoo**-kair-oh |
| tea | il tè | eel **teh** |
| herb tea | la tisana | lah tee-**zah**-nah |
| tomato | il pomodoro | eel poh-moh-**dor**-oh |
| tuna | il tonno | eel **ton**-noh |
| veal | il vitello | eel vee-**tell**-oh |
| vegetables | i legumi | ee leh-**goo**-mee |
| vinegar | l'aceto | lah-**cheh**-toh |
| water | l'acqua | **lah**-kwah |
| red wine | vino rosso | **vee**-noh **ross**-oh |
| white wine | vino bianco | **vee**-noh bee-**ang**-koh |

## NUMBERS

| | | |
|---|---|---|
| 1 | uno | **oo**-noh |
| 2 | due | **doo**-eh |
| 3 | tre | treh |
| 4 | quattro | **kwat**-roh |
| 5 | cinque | **ching**-kweh |
| 6 | sei | **say**-ee |
| 7 | sette | **set**-teh |
| 8 | otto | **ot**-toh |
| 9 | nove | **noh**-veh |
| 10 | dieci | dee-**eh**-chee |
| 11 | undici | **oon**-dee-chee |
| 12 | dodici | **doh**-dee-chee |
| 13 | tredici | **treh**-dee-chee |
| 14 | quattordici | kwat-**tor**-dee-chee |
| 15 | quindici | **kwin**-dee-chee |
| 16 | sedici | **say**-dee-chee |
| 17 | diciassette | dee-chah-**set**-teh |
| 18 | diciotto | dee-**chot**-toh |
| 19 | diciannove | dee-chah-**noh**-veh |
| 20 | venti | **ven**-tee |
| 30 | trenta | **tren**-tah |
| 40 | quaranta | kwah-**ran**-tah |
| 50 | cinquanta | ching-**kwan**-tah |
| 60 | sessanta | sess-**an**-tah |
| 70 | settanta | set-**tan**-tah |
| 80 | ottanta | ot-**tan**-tah |
| 90 | novanta | noh-**van**-tah |
| 100 | cento | **chen**-toh |
| 1,000 | mille | **mee**-leh |
| 2,000 | duemila | **doo**-eh mee-lah |
| 5,000 | cinquemila | **ching**-kweh **mee**-lah |
| 1,000,000 | un milione | oon meel-**yoh**-neh |

## TIME

| | | |
|---|---|---|
| one minute | un minuto | oon mee-**noo**-toh |
| one hour | un'ora | oon **or**-ah |
| half an hour | mezz'ora | medz-**or**-ah |
| a day | un giorno | oon **jor**-noh |
| a week | una settimana | oona set-tee-**mah**-nah |
| Monday | lunedì | loo-neh-**dee** |
| Tuesday | martedì | mar-teh-**dee** |
| Wednesday | mercoledì | mair-koh-leh-**dee** |
| Thursday | giovedì | joh-veh-**dee** |
| Friday | venerdì | ven-air-**dee** |
| Saturday | sabato | **sah**-bah-toh |
| Sunday | domenica | doh-**meh**-nee-kah |

# ACKNOWLEDGMENTS

DK would like to thank the following for their contribution to the previous edition:

Ros Belford, Olivia Ercoli, Roberta Mitchell, Natasha Foges, Hilary Bird

The publisher would like to thank the following for their kind permission to reproduce their photographs:

Key: a-above; b-below/bottom; c-centre; f-far; l-left; r-right; t-top

**123RF.com:** Roman Babakin 142bl; Viktor Gladkov 43c; gonewiththewind 71br, 277tr; Wies aw Jarek 152cr; jipen 80br; manjik 290t; Valerio Mei 325tr; Yana Menshchikova 184cla; Alessandro Russotto 176-7; sedmak 142crb.

**500px:** Bruce Ingwall 30t.

**Alamy Stock Photo:** AA World Travel Library 205cr, 218cl, 218clb, 219tr; Mauricio Abreu 232-3; Adam Eastland Art + Architecture 49cl, 324-5b; Adam Eastland Rome 305tc; AF archive 185tl; AM Stock 30bl; Arcaid Images 318cr, 318-9t; Vito Arcomano 32tr, 41crb, 148clb, 186cl, 187cr, 223bl, 227tl, 227tr, 236-7b, 238bl, 240bl, 274bl, 299cr; ART Collection 89clb, 287br; Azoor Photo 275crb; Paul Springett B 91t, 184-5b; Carlo Bollo 28cr; Bridgeman Images 287clb; Michael Brooks 39br; BYphoto 187crb; Marco Campagna 59cra; Douglas Carr 13t; Collection Christophel 40-1t; Chronicle 54bl, 55cla, 56bl, 108clb, 233cl, 275tr; Classic Image 54crb, 88bc, 109tr; Clearview 310bl; Razvan Cosac 268bl; Luis Dafos 33cra, 313br, 324cl; Ian G Dagnall 30crb, 101br; Gabriele Dessì 190b; Adam Eastland 126bl, 195b, 275bl, 275bc, 292bl; edpics 12clb, 28cl, 35br, 132-3; Reiner Elsen 305br; Equatore 317br; F1online digitale Bildagentur GmbH / Ritterbach 83t; Falkenstein Heinz-Dieter 216bl; Falkensteinfoto 286cb; Nick Fielding 186-7b; Findlay 39tr; FineArt 147tr; freeartist 8-9b; Vladislav Gajic 59tr; Givaga 10cla; GL Archive 56cr, 57bc, 124cb; Godong 147br; Granger Historical Picture Archive 57cra, 58bl; Susana Guzman 8cl; Dennis Hallinan 296tl; Gary Hebding Jr. 293t; HelloWorld Images 11t; Hemis 12t; Heritage Image Partnership Ltd 32-3t; Peter Horree 261, 291clb; IanDagnall Computing 68bl; imageBROKER 13cr, 43tr; insidefoto srl 59br; Ivoha 68cr; maurice joseph 67ftr; B.O' Kane 42tl, 55tl; Boris Karpinski 216-7;

John Kellerman 218cla; Keystone Pictures USA 59bc; Kosobu 234t; Art Kowalsky 199tr; Lanmas 107tl; Enzo Lisi 39clb; LOOK Die Bildagentur der Fotografen GmbH 37t; Dennis MacDonald 12-3b; MARKA 140br, 301br; Stefano Politi Markovina 26cr; Martin Norris Travel Photography 69crb, 250t; Martin Thomas Photography 222t; mauritius images GmbH 291fcrb, / ClickAlps 53c; Andrew Michael 297; Mikel Bilbao Gorostiaga- Travels 290br; Hercules Milas 26cl, 68t, 69tc, 95bl, 144-5t, 159tr, 187cra; ilpo musto 35cl; National Geographic Image Collection / Kenneth Ginn 329tr; Niday Picture Library 54t; Nikreates 108-9; Sérgio Nogueira 287crb; George Oze 37cr; Pacific Press 287cr; Andrea Palma 49br; Panther Media GmbH 35tl; Stefano Paterna 26bl; Pictorial Press Ltd 58crb; J. Pie 69bc; Danilo Poccia 170tl; The Print Collector 89bc; RalphWilliam 84-5t; M Ramìrez 146-7b; Stefano Ravera 148cra; Realy Easy Star 58cr, / Daniele Bellucci 20tl, 116bl, 180-1; John Rees 94bl; robertharding / Neale Clark 289tr; Felipe Rodriguez 260cl; ROPI 89crb; Clemente do Rosario 125bl; Ian Rutherford 19t, 136-7; andrea sabbadini 37br; Riccardo Sala 47cb; Science History Images 55clb; Scott Hortop Travel 116tc, 211br; jozef sedmak 87bl, 300t; Andrea Spinelli 52bl; Krystyna Szulecka 94br; Glyn Thomas 208-9t; Rabrizio Trolani 269cra; Universal Images Group North America LLC / DeAgostini 267b; Stefano Valeri 30cr, 241crb; Ivan Vdovin 192tl; Valery Voennyy 36cl; VPC Photo 233cra; Sebastian Wasek 131b; Jannis Werner 328bl; Zoonar GmbH 299cla.

**AWL Images:** Francesco Iacobelli 2-3; Maurizio Rellini 4, 18tl, 102-3, 124-5t.

**Bridgeman Images:**; Stefano Baldini / Galleria Nazionale d'Arte Moderna e Contempora, Rome, Lazio Giorgio de Chirico ©DACS, London 2018 *Spettacolo Misterioso* (1971) 33clb; Buyenlarge Archive / UIG 56-7t; De Agostini Picture Library /G. Nimatallah / *Giotto Boniface VIII announces Holy Year fresco* (1300) 216cla, / A. Dagli Orti / Gabinetto Comunale delle Stampe, Rome, Italy / Andrea Sacchi and Filippo *Gagliardi Saracen joust in Piazza Navona, February 25, 1634* 124clb, / G. Dagli Orti / *Painted terracotta Sarcophagus of the Spouses, from Cerveteri* 148bl; / L. de Masi / *Close-up of a piano designed by Bartolomeo Cristofori di Francesco*